INTRODUCTION

CHAPTER ONE

Giving Up the Struggle

Life presents problems because we fight it, we don't accept what-is in the present moment. We want to become something other than what we are. We want something other than what we now have.

—Ramesh Balsekar

I WAS WEARY. Profoundly weary. Never in my life had I experienced such depression. Never before had I felt so despairing.

In actuality, nothing really terrible was going on in my life. True, I'd just had another argument with my husband. But this was nothing new, nothing that couldn't be either ignored or fixed in some way, one more time. And yes, I was having some difficulties with one of my clients at work. But this, too, I knew I'd eventually be able to straighten out.

But that wasn't the point. As I sat slumped in a chair at my kitchen table, numbly staring out the window at the dusk that was gathering outside, I realized that I was feeling tired to the very depths of my being, simply because I was having to deal one more time with my upset emotions. I was tired because I was *always* having to deal with my reactivity, *always* having to work on myself, just to get along somewhat smoothly in my life. I was tired because things *should* have been different by now. After almost twenty-five years of diligently following a spiritual path, hundreds of hours of meditation, deep and sincere efforts at self-improvement, after the dozens and dozens of New-Age books I'd read and the myriad of workshops and spiritual-growth trainings I'd taken—I should have been at least *close* to experiencing the on-going happiness and peace for which I'd been striving, for so many years. I should have been at least *close* to feeling free. And I wasn't.

Except for a few brief and glorious experiences that had come and gone, I still wasn't experiencing the higher Truth of who I was. Most of the time I was still caught in believing myself to be my limited ego-self—my mind, my emotions, my body. And I was still being emotionally triggered by so many things, sometimes profoundly so.

In short, I was still trapped in suffering. "Freedom," "awakening," "enlightenment"—these were essentially just words to me, terms I suppose I understood intellectually. But I didn't *really* know what they meant. I certainly wasn't experiencing them.

At times, I felt as far away from the experience of spiritual freedom as I'd been at the very beginning of my spiritual searching so many years before. A lot of my suffering at this point, in fact, stemmed from a deep sense of doubt within me about all the spiritual "work" I'd done over the years. Had it really gotten me anywhere after all? Was I really any closer to freedom, to the realization of my true nature, than I'd been at the beginning?

It was true, I had to admit, that with all the inner growth work I'd done throughout the years, I had managed to create a somewhat fulfilling, creative, and abundant life for myself. Most of the time, I basically felt a lot better about myself and my life than I ever had before. In fact, on the outside, my life probably looked rather happy and rewarding. Certainly, compared to a lot of people I knew, my life was pretty good. To begin with, I had a very comfortable life-style. I was living in my dream house in the exquisitely beautiful mountains outside of Boulder, Colorado, with my husband, our dog, and our cat. On the purely physical level, I couldn't think of a more perfect setting or situation in which to live.

I also had many satisfying and intimate relationships—something very important to me. In particular, although my marriage demanded some work, I both deeply loved and felt loved by my husband. I was also blessed with a close relationship with my 19-year-old daughter, who lived nearby in town. And I had a number of close relationships with friends with whom I had much in common.

As far as work was concerned, I was pursuing a career as a psychotherapist and workshop leader that I found extremely fulfilling. I only needed to work part-time, and this was great. I spent the rest of my time expressing creatively through writing and fabric art, and also in hiking through the mountains, a favorite pastime of mine. And then there were my daily meditations and spiritual studies, and the spiritual gatherings I attended that were nurturing me, as well, in a profound way. In so many ways, it seemed as if I truly "had it made."

And yet, whenever I became really quiet inside, as I was this evening, I became painfully aware that the contentment I was feeling was actually rather superficial and incomplete. When I was really honest with myself, I had to admit that at the very core of my being I was still experiencing a sense of profound dissatisfaction and meaninglessness. True, on-going, inner peace continued to elude me. There was always, at the deepest level, a sense of inexplicable anxiety, loneliness, and emptiness. There was a black hole—one that could never really be filled by any thing or person or spiritual practice.

What was most painful, perhaps, was the utterly profound yearning that would arise at these times, a yearning for something … *more*. It was hard to express what this something *more* was—it was peace … love … freedom … joy … fulfillment—and yet so much more. The best word I could come up with for it finally was *Home*. With all the longing of a weary, homesick traveler, I simply wanted finally to go *Home*.

From time to time, I had had profound, exquisite glimpses of this *Home*—when I had deeply experienced a sense of peace, a wholeness, a oneness with all of creation, infused with an unutterable love and joy. But these had always eventually dissipated and disappeared, and I never knew how to bring them back.

And now, finally, from within the very depths of me, I felt myself crying out in anguish for the final and permanent experience of this *Home*—and for the end of my suffering. I was so very, very weary of this world and of my on-going struggle to fulfill that deep inner yearning for peace.

I sighed, deeply experiencing the dark and dreary emptiness inside me. At this point, as I sat there staring out at the night, I realized that the depression had become so severe, I couldn't even cry. All I could do was wonder how I was going to go on.

As it turned out, hunger pangs finally saved me. Unable to ignore them any longer, I managed to pull myself out of the chair so I could start making dinner. But for a number of weeks afterwards, I continued to live in this inner hell. To my despair, I was finding that none of the spiritual teachings I'd ever learned were helping to bring me out of the depression. It felt as if there were no place for me to go, nothing I could do. I was totally stuck within the on-going despairing emptiness of my life.

The Book

Then there came a day when I was in a bookstore, quietly perusing the books that were on display—and a book literally dropped off the shelf in front of me onto the floor. As I leaned over to pick it up, I saw it was called *Wake Up and Roar*. It was a series of *satsangs** given by the Indian man whose photo was on the cover: H.W.L. Poonja—"or more affectionately known as Papaji."

Upon reading this, I thought, *Oh give me a break—not another spiritual path, not another guru!* My cynical disillusionment with spiritual paths and teachers by this point was at its peak.

I was about to plop the book back on the shelf, when I suddenly heard a firm voice inside me say: *Stop! Pay attention. This is what you've been praying for.* Surprised, I looked at the book again. Very doubtful, I hesitated. I had read so many of these kinds of books in the past. But then I thought, *Oh what the hell!* And I turned to go buy the book.

To my utter surprise, when I finally sat down to read the book a few days later, I was immediately plunged into a profound state of bliss. This continued to occur throughout my entire reading of the book. It wasn't just his words, I realized, although I had to admit they really were different from anything I'd ever read before. It was as if something were coming right off the page, an energy that was somehow bypassing my mind and entering a very deep place inside me.

---

*Satsang: Literally meaning "in association with Truth," *satsang* is usually a gathering with an enlightened master, generally in which questions and answers about the Truth are exchanged.

Even after I'd finished the book, I continued to experience many spontaneous blissful glimpses of the Truth—glimpses that came more and more frequently, that lasted longer than ever before, and that were of profound depth. Sometimes, out of nowhere, a deep sense of peace would suddenly descend on me. At these times, I knew that everything in my life was truly perfect, just as it was. I knew that everything had a place and a purpose. There was no reason ever to be upset about anything again. And enormous gratitude would well up in me, filling my eyes with tears.

At other times, an incredible sense of joy would suddenly bubble up inside me, not caused by anything happening at that moment. It was a profound and simple joy, arising from the very core of my being. My body was so overcome at these times, I would have to start dancing or singing, just to move the energy pouring into me. What was really incredible was that I soon found that there were actually things I could do to invite these glimpses.

Then I discovered that there were other books of *satsangs* I could read, given by Papaji's master, Ramana Maharshi, who had lived at the beginning of the century. To my delight, I had similar experiences in reading these books. And soon I found myself attending *satsangs* being given by an American woman called Gangagi, who had recently been to India to see Papaji and had become enlightened. By this time, I could feel something was finally shifting inside. The despair had truly dissipated.

The Advaita Tradition

The *satsangs* given by these teachers were not like any spiritual gatherings I had attended in the past. I found that they were part of a tradition known as *Advaita* (pronounced Ad-vī-ta), also known in the West as the "direct path" to enlightenment or "non-dualism." Many different teachers basically teach this.

Essentially, the teachings tell us that all that exists is Consciousness—pure, permanent, unchanging Consciousness. This is what each of us is—the one Consciousness. All form—indeed the entire universe—exists within us, as Consciousness.

The extraordinary news the teaching brings us is that we can directly experience this reality within an instant. We can discover right here, right now, that all we have been searching for—love, joy, fulfillment, peace, freedom—is entirely present, just waiting to be discovered in this moment.

Rather than struggling with the notion that we must become, create, or find something at some point in the future, we simply need to realize that what we are seeking is already present, always, eternally. It is already present because it is who we ARE. It is so close and so simple that we miss it. There is truly nowhere to go, nothing to gain, nothing to create. In fact, there is essentially nothing to do but drop all mental concepts about what this Self is and what we think we need to do to become aware of It. We simply need to BE and discover who we are, naturally.

As such, *Advaita* is a direct path to the realization of Truth. It essentially involves no beliefs, rituals, or doctrines. Indeed, it involves no spiritual practice whatsoever, except to "seek the seeker"— to turn back within oneself to see who it is that is seeking. This process is known as "self-inquiry"; one simply asks the question, "Who am I?"

As I was to find, the experience that ensues can be both startling and profoundly joyful. What is discovered is that nothing actually is there—except pure Consciousness, the very essence of life itself. It is seen that, in reality, no individual entity exists separate from everything else. There is only vast spaciousness, filled with freedom, joy, and a deep abiding peace.

For a number of months, the discovery of these teachings filled me with an ineffable joy. I experienced a quiet serenity and a sense of hope I hadn't felt for a long time. The depression was far behind me.

The Yearning

Probably because I was now having more and more of the exquisite glimpses of the Reality I so craved, I soon began to experience profound grief each time a glimpse eventually faded. I began raging at the fact that it just wouldn't "hold."

The yearning that arose was like none I'd ever felt before. The desire for permanent freedom began screaming inside me. It was insatiable, a raging fire. At times, I thought my body would explode. I was burning up with my desire, ravaged from the inside.

My reaction to the yearning was to resist it. I hated it; I railed against it. I wanted it gone. I wanted the peace back. But I couldn't just wish the yearning away. Soon it became clear that trying to resist it was only strengthening it. In despair, I returned to my other habitual method of dealing with an unpleasant feeling: I began trying to fix it. I began feeding it positive thinking, visualizations, and affirmations. This utterly failed. Apparently, I not could affirm or visualize myself into a peaceful state of mind in the face of this yearning.

Nor could I distract myself with other things, such as books, TV, sex, or hobbies. I couldn't even find a way to talk about it to anyone. It was so strange, somehow, that I felt incapable of finding the words for what I was feeling. I was spending more and more time alone. Barely eating or sleeping, I felt exasperated and worn out. My yearning desire for permanent freedom and peace was eating me alive.

The Surrender

Then one night, I finally found I could do nothing with the yearning but simply give in to it. Too tired to do anything else, I just let go of the whole struggle to hold it back and decided to let it have me. At that point, it didn't matter if falling into the fire of this agonizing yearning killed me; I simply didn't care anymore. Finally, with total abandon, I experienced myself just letting go—and falling down into the fire of desire inside me.

To my great surprise, nothing dreadful happened. In fact, this act of surrender was actually like a wet rag thrown on the fire raging inside me. The fire hissed, fizzled, and then slowly died. There was finally a quiet calm inside.

I walked around for days after this in sort of a washed-out state, feeling like the survivor of a war. To my relief, I finally saw no more burning desire within. No more incessant thoughts about attaining freedom. In actuality, there was really no more caring. I'd given it all up. Forget freedom. Forget bliss. I didn't care any more. I'd had enough. It was time to get on with my life again. And with this, there was a kind of peaceful emptiness.

CHAPTER TWO

The Shift

The waking life is just a long dream which keeps our attention away from what we really are.

—Ramana Maharshi

ONE WINTER EVENING A FEW WEEKS LATER, as I sat reading in my favorite armchair by the fire, I suddenly felt something shift inside me. Something subtle and quiet—yet dramatic. It was as if I had suddenly died.

My body still seemed to be pumping blood and breathing air; in fact, it felt quite alive. But I knew at that moment that something very fundamental about me had simply ended, completed itself, died. My life as I'd known it was irrevocably over.

I sat there astonished. There had been no warning, no sign that this event was going to happen. No strange feelings of life draining out of me, no feeling of completion of events in my life. It was as if I had been walking along the path of my life, engaging in all the usual situations and relationships—and then suddenly, the path came to an end. There was nowhere else to go. Throughout all the previous years of meditation and spiritual study, including the *satsangs*, nothing I'd ever learned or experienced had prepared me for this kind of strange and disorienting event.

I sat for a long time, feeling a sensation of emptiness. I noticed no motivation whatsoever to do anything anymore—including getting up out of the chair I was sitting in. There was no *reason* to do anything. I was simply finished with my life.

I wasn't feeling depressed or fearful about what I was experiencing. In fact, I wasn't feeling any discernible feelings at all. Yet I wasn't numb inside; I was simply devoid of emotion—and of thought, as well, for that matter. What seemed to remain was simple, pure awareness—as if I were witnessing this sudden death in someone else.

For almost a half hour, I looked out the large window of my mountain home, staring into the night. The stars and the moon seemed unnaturally bright to me, alive. The tall pine trees swaying in the wind were vividly outlined with a supernatural light, and they too were very much alive. As they moved softly in the wind, they seemed to be calling in hushed but jubilant voices to me: "Welcome! Welcome Home!" As clear awareness, I rushed out to them, deeply experiencing their embrace of homecoming.

Then my attention was pulled inside the house again, and I looked around me. The fire crackling in the fireplace seemed the same as it had before—and yet it wasn't. Like the trees and the stars and moon, it too was alive in a new way. In fact, everything I looked at—the books in the bookshelf, the fern on the coffee table, my bedroom slippers on the floor—all appeared to be dynamically alive, relating to me in a whole new way. Essentially, there was no difference, no separation, between any of us. We were all of the same essence.

In one way, experiencing this oneness with all of creation was not new to me. This same exquisite experience had been in the awakening glimpses I'd had before. And yet this was different. It was hard to say what was different, but I knew something profound had shifted permanently this time. Something had died and would not be back.

As I sat there, I now experienced myself to be falling into a deep well of Silence—a boundless spaciousness—a profound emptiness that was at the same time an incredible fullness. Peace hummed through my being. Joy welled up inside me, and soon I was experiencing wave upon wave of love that began exploding within me until I was sobbing, unable to contain it all. I realized that I had finally come *Home*....

And then I was aware of what it was that had changed, of what was different from all the other experiences I'd had in the past: my identity had shifted. I was no longer someone having the experience of spaciousness, silence, peace—I *was* the spaciousness, the silence, the peace. My identity as a separate being living a life in the world had fallen away, had somehow unhitched itself.

I couldn't say *where* I was now. I no longer felt myself to be inside my body, but it wasn't like I was outside of it either. I was nowhere—and everywhere. Somehow in another dimension altogether. I had no form, and yet I was in and around all forms. I was that which held all form. I was the life force itself, the creator and the creation. I was all that exists.

I continued to sit there by the dying fire for a long time, not moving. In a way, I was stunned, realizing that I had just witnessed my own death. In another way, it was as if I had suddenly awakened from a long, unpleasant dream that had seemed very real. Having awakened, I was now aware of what was actually real and had been all along. With this awareness was tremendous joy—and an enormous sense of relief.

Finally, after what must have been several hours, I got up to get ready for bed. As I got out of the chair, I found the experience of moving my body to be extremely strange. No longer inside of it, I found myself simply watching the body move, listening to it talk, seeing feelings and thoughts pass through it. I was totally detached from it. And yet I was not dissociated from it. I was, in fact, extremely aware of everything going on inside the body and mind; they simply were no longer ME.

The next morning was the beginning of a long series of profound and exhilarating experiences that continued to deepen the reality I'd fallen into that evening. Almost every day, I'd find myself journeying into new and fascinating "territory" within this reality, receiving new insights, revelations, and full-body experiences of bliss. The whole world was an alive and wondrous place for me to wander around, and I was constantly in awe. I saw myself everywhere, in everyone and everything. There was no place I was not. And beauty often overwhelmed me, as I'd stand looking at a flower or a rock—or even a neon sign—and I'd begin weeping for the sheer joy of seeing such beauty.

It was interesting that, along with these extraordinary experiences, I was also watching my whole life beginning to change in a radical way. With my identity as an individual person unhooked, and with the consequent detachment toward everything happening in my life (both inwardly and outwardly), I suppose situations in my life couldn't help but alter.

In one way, it probably looked as if I were experiencing a lot of loss. Certainly many things and relationships that had been an important part of my life till then fell away. Among other things, within a month, I left my marriage, my dream house, my dog, and my comfortable life-style. But I cannot say that I was experiencing loss about any of this or grief in any way. My experience was that things and situations were simply altering. I, myself, was not being changed in any way. I was simply Consciousness—observing, untouched by it all. In fact, what was becoming most apparent to me was the profound peace I experienced at all times. Even through all the change and loss that were happening, never once did the peace disappear. It was always present, if not as foreground, then as background.

Perhaps the most astounding realization, however, was that fear was now absent inside me. There were fears of the body that would occasionally arise. For example, when a car almost hit me one time, my body flinched and contracted. But clearly this was just the body's natural and automatic response; it wasn't *I* who was experiencing the fear.

This was incredible to me. In my past, fear had been a prevalent emotion for me. In fact, most of my response toward life had been based in fear—fear of people, things, situations, poverty, violence. Now all that was gone. It was replaced by a miraculous sense of trust in life itself, a knowing that I would be okay, no matter what might happen to my body or my life. I knew I would be just fine— untouched by any of it. Indeed, what seemed to be more and more apparent, as time went on, was that all suffering had ceased. No one was here anymore to experience it.

At times during this period I would wonder, "Is this enlightenment? Is this what all those teachers labeled *awakening* or *freedom*?" I wasn't sure. In some ways, it was what I had imagined it would be like, but in others, it was not. What was important was that it no longer mattered. I was no longer experiencing the old, unfulfilled yearning; I was no longer suffering. Knowing myself to be every-thing, I no longer felt a need for anything. Without a sense of an individual self, I existed in a sweet oneness with everything. I was complete and full and at peace.

The Return

This experience of "no one home" lasted approximately six months—six exquisitely beautiful months that were suffused with an ethereal magic. I was floating through life on a cloud of bliss, empty and joyful, intensely alive.

And then, at some point, a subtle shift occurred. I can't say exactly when. But one day, a sense of my old body/mind identifica-tion came wafting through my awareness. It was a translucent ghost of its former self, but still, it was present, hovering just on the outskirts of my awareness. I was stunned. After six months of its absence, to find this sense of being a separate individual back again was extremely disorienting.

And I was chagrined—deeply so. What was this? Why was it happening? What had I done wrong?

After watching a sense of grief wash through me, I suddenly remembered a statement by Krishnamurti I'd once read. It was something like, "To wake up takes just a moment. To eliminate the little 'me' takes time." So here I was—still awake, still experiencing myself as pure awareness, still feeling peace and a sense of detach-ment toward life at all times—and yet a sense of identity with the ego-personality self was now beginning to visit me more and more. Such a strange and confusing state of affairs!

I have since met a teacher who explains very well what I was experiencing at that time. Adyashanti, a young man with a Zen background who instructs using *Advaita*-like teachings, speaks about how when awakening first occurs, the ego-self suddenly disappears. This situation remains for a period of time (anywhere from a few moments to a number of months), and the ecstasy of the ego's disappearance is experienced. Then a sense of ego returns, though less powerful than before. This is the beginning of a process in which we are awake, and yet we are letting go of the identity with the ego over and over and over again. Each attachment to ego comes up, one at a time, and it is up to us simply to keep letting it go until, at some point, the ego once again evaporates.

Hearing this meant a great deal to me, because it outlined so well my experiences these last nine years since my original "death" experience. Just as he said, after the return of the ghost-like ego-self, I had to let go, over and over again, of the sense of identity with it—the sense of being my mind, my body, and my emotions.

During these nine years, I have watched as the little "me" has gradually become again but a faint whisper in my awareness. At this point, except for occasional momentary "blips" on the screen of awareness, my life has essentially returned to the experience of those first six months, where clear and empty Consciousness is all that is present. Thoughts and emotions and reactions to situations still arise within this Consciousness, but nothing sticks. And the peace, which never once abandoned me, continues to deepen as time goes on. What is different now is a sense of stability. I'm no longer floating. I'm free—yet grounded.

The Process of Letting Go

At some point during the last nine years, I realized that the process of continually letting go of identity with the ego-self was a specific path I was following—one focusing on the teaching of surrender that is so prevalent in the *Advaita* tradition. I realized, in fact, that I had been following this path ever since I first became aware of the *Advaita* teachings through Papaji, and that it was this path that undoubtedly led me to my shift in identity.

Then, as I became more aware of what was happening, I began introducing certain counseling clients and groups I was working with to the process of letting go, as I myself was experiencing it. Much to my delight, many people related to what I was sharing with them and benefitted greatly from it. Some had had glimpses of awakening before; others had not. But all reported to me a greater and greater sense of freedom and a deeper knowing of their true spiritual nature.

With this book, I wish to reach others who may benefit from this path of letting go I have taken.

In retrospect, I can identify four main steps to this path. "Steps" may not be the best word to use because, although the aspects involved can be experienced one after another, and later ones depend to a degree on earlier ones—they can also all be done simultaneously. However they are viewed, for clarity's sake I will present them in a specific sequence.

The first step involves getting to know and directly experience the Self—our true nature. For many people it takes just an instant to experience the Self, by inquiring "Who am I?" and then directly discovering what is there. This practice, especially if done consistently throughout the day, can eventually create a powerful familiarity with and trust of the Self.

For others, it may be necessary first to cultivate an inner environment which "invites" glimpses of the Self into their lives. This can involve, among other things, meditating, yoga, contemplation, or other spiritual practices that calm the mind. In some cases, it may involve therapy or other self-discovery techniques. The clearer the mind is of chattering, the better. I will also describe the experience of the Self as I know it, to point you in the right direction to have this experience yourself, if you have not had it before.

It is important to recognize glimpses of the Self when they do come. Sometimes they are exquisitely beautiful, awe-inspiring, and life-changing (these, of course, are hard to miss), but sometimes they are much more subtle and fleeting and are likely to be dismissed. It is essential to pay attention to *all* of them, to allow them to deepen, and to open to them so they may appear more often and stay for longer periods of time. Then, as the Self becomes more and more familiar to us, it will become easier and easier to trust and surrender our life to it.

The second step involves a process of detaching from our ego-personality self and the eventual disidentification with it. I will describe this ego-self at greater length in Chapter Three, but briefly, as I use the term, it includes our whole sense of an individual self: our body and our personality (our mind, emotions, desires, and the roles we play).

Detaching from all this is an involved process because we have identified with the ego-self for eons of time, and it takes a while to realize that all our suffering has stemmed from this. So, as I have said, although the initial awakening to the Self can happen in an instant of time with the very first true glimpse, the disidentification with the ego-self usually takes some time and patience.

The third step is the process of surrendering to the Self and allowing it to live our life for us. This generally happens in small increments. It usually depends on a growing familiarity with the Self and on some progress in disidentification with the ego, but it can be started right away.

The fourth step—experiencing a shift in identity to that of the true Self—is perhaps not really a step at all. It seems to happen naturally, as all three of the other steps are taken. Perhaps more importantly, the shift in identity is actually the purpose of doing the steps to begin with. Although the gains of greater happiness, trust, and peace in our life are wonderful enough to pursue, the true point of this path of letting go is to eventually wake up to the glorious reality of who we are—to realize the unbelievable truth that *we* are that which we have been yearning for our entire life. It is to realize that who we are is the very essence of love, joy, and enduring peace. We are pure Consciousness, the life force itself, that which permeates all of creation.

The following chapters outline in detail these four steps toward realizing this Reality.

EXPERIENCING
YOUR TRUE SELF

CHAPTER THREE

Becoming Aware of the Self

How can the divine Oneness be seen?
In beautiful forms, breathtaking wonders, awe-inspiring miracles?
The Tao is not obliged to present itself this way.

It is always present and always available.
When speech is exhausted and mind dissolved, it presents itself.
When sincerity is unconditional, it unveils itself.

If you are willing to be lived by it
You will see it everywhere, even in the most ordinary things.

—Hua Hu Ching

GETTING TO KNOW THE SELF on a direct experiential level is essential for true spiritual awakening. Understanding what it is on the intellectual level can certainly be a start, but real understanding of it is beyond the mind. As much as the mind might try to grasp this understanding, it is ultimately incapable of doing so. It is therefore necessary to somehow seek beyond the mind to truly open yourself for a direct and intimate meeting with the Self.

Having this kind of direct experience is not, however, as hard as it may seem—no matter how caught in your mind you may believe yourself to be. In fact, you have probably already had experiences of Self, perhaps countless times in your life, and simply haven't recognized them. They may have been momentary glimpses that you either dismissed at the time or you've since forgotten about. The important thing is to recognize them—even in their subtlest form—

so that you can learn how to allow them to become more profound experiences for you.

You may be very clear about certain experiences of Self you've had and long to have more of them. Or you may feel that you have not had them and want to know more about what they are. I will therefore attempt, first of all, to describe the Self to you, based on experiences I have had and on those of others I've heard or read about. Then, in the following chapters, I will describe ways I have discovered to help deepen and prolong these experiences, and I will suggest certain things you can do to cultivate your "inner environment" in order to welcome more of them into your life.

Actually, the Self cannot be described in words. This most profound and mysterious Truth of who we are is something that must be experienced directly. Words can only reflect what it is. But my hope is that you will use my words as pointers, and seek past them to glimpse the unutterably exquisite experience to which they point. I have no doubt that this experience is one you will find intimately familiar to you at the core of your being; you simply may not have been aware of it for a long, long time.

What Is the Self?

Your true Self is so natural, so familiar, so close, that it is easy to miss. It is closer to you than your breath, closer than your thoughts. It is that most subtle essence that animates your body, gives it life. It is the awareness inside you that has never changed, no matter how much older your body has gotten or how mature your personality has become—it was the same when you were age 5, age 25, age 45. It has never been born; it will not die. It is changeless, permanent beingness.

Your true Self is pure Awareness, pure Consciousness. When all thoughts have left, it is what remains. It is always present, as your real and natural state of being. Everything else in life, from the most gross level of matter to the most subtle level of energy, exists within it. It is that which permeates all of existence—it is the very life force itself. It is the source of all existence.

Your true Self is the Stillness deep inside you—clear, pristine, untouched. It is the deep, serene Silence. It is the presence of fathomless Love, profound joy, boundless freedom. It has no form, no boundaries—you can fall endlessly into its blissful depths.

The Self is the true YOU.

Glimpses

People have experiences of the Self in countless ways. These experiences are often referred to as "glimpses." I see glimpses essentially as gifts from the Self, times when the Self graciously reveals itself to us. At their most subtle, glimpses bring joy and peace into our lives; at their deepest, a sense of rapture and ecstasy that can alter our lives in the most profound way.

The rapturous and ecstatic glimpses are the easiest to describe. They are the most obvious and also naturally the kind that people long to have. If you are not familiar with these or would like to know more about them, I will attempt to describe from my own experience the qualities they often seem to have.

As I mentioned earlier, the best description of a profound glimpse of Self is the experience of waking up from a long, unpleasant dream that has seemed very real. Upon awakening, you realize you've just been dreaming, and the reality into which you have awakened is what is actually real. An enormous sense of relief comes with this realization, and a profound joy. You are remembering, after a very long time of being unconscious, who you truly are and what life is really about.

There is an exquisite feeling of timelessness, a sense of stepping out of ordinary consciousness into a broader view of life, a seeing of the big picture. With this comes a peace and serenity that is profound beyond words. All worries and concerns about life are amazingly absent. A deep sense of well-being pervades your entire being. An exhilaration lifts your heart.

Paul Brunton describes at length his experiences of profound glimpses of Self, as well as those of others, in his book, *Inspiration and the Overself*. He describes the experience as one of "tremulous happiness … inarticulate breathless stillness." We are intensely happy for no apparent reason. The "burden of past sins and errors falls away … we are cleansed, purified, made whole…." We feel protected, secure, and provided for; there is a feeling of support from some vast mysterious source. All "evil and madness in the world are like a quickly receding nightmare."

In my own experiences, I have become aware of how different facets of the Self are often accentuated in different glimpses. I sometimes refer to these as "flavors" of the Self. The following are some of the most common flavors I've experienced:

1. **Love**: An experience of indescribable love for everyone and everything. The love can feel so intense and full, I feel I may explode with it. Often tears or laughter erupt from me, because my body cannot contain it.

2. **Peace:** An experience of profound peace and stillness. This can be accompanied by a thought-free state that is positively blissful. My mind is completely still.

3. **Freedom**: A sense of pure freedom. There is a knowing that I am not bound by anything outwardly or inwardly. Intense joy often attends this knowing, and a sense of breaking free into a new consciousness.

4. **Sense of Well-Being**: A sense of well-being—even in the midst of crisis. There is a knowing deep inside that everything is okay; it always has been and always will be. Despite what my mind may be telling me, I know that I am completely being taken care of; there is nothing I need worry about.

5. **Vastness**: An experience of vastness, an exhilarating feeling of spaciousness. I know that who I am has no boundaries and no form; indeed, I extend into everyone and everything—and way beyond, throughout space and time.

6. **Omniscience**: A sense of omniscience, a knowing that all there is to be known is known by me. A natural sense of connectedness to all of creation is present, and a feeling of intense power.

7. **Emptiness**: A feeling of vast and profound emptiness—which at the same time is an utter sense of fullness. There is an experience of absolute nothingness, and yet everything is present and available to me. I lack for nothing.

8. **Oneness**: A sense of oneness and unity, a knowing that I'm part of everything in creation. I am more than connected to everything—there is no separation at all. It's all the same essence.

9. **Knowing**: A knowing that who I am is the Life Force itself, infusing all of creation; I am the Source of all beingness. I am everywhere, always.

If you have had profound glimpses of the Self, you probably recognize some of these experiences. You may have had glimpses that were filled with somewhat different flavors—or perhaps a combination of several of them.

As I've said, these profound, ecstatic kinds of glimpses cannot be missed. They are usually well-remembered, treasured, mulled over time and time again—and longed for again in the future. Unfortunately, they tend to happen rarely in people's lives, if at all. Yet all it takes is one of these glimpses to awaken us to our true nature—and to let us know to what the rest of our lives will be dedicated.

The Glimpses We Tend to Miss

There are, however, glimpses that visit us all during the course of our ordinary, mundane lives that most people dismiss or entirely miss, because the experiences seem so faint or fleeting. And it is such a loss to let these go by, because ways exist, I've discovered, to allow these faint glimpses to deepen into more profound ones. And there are ways to help prolong them, as well.

First of all, of course, you need to recognize these more fleeting glimpses when they do appear. Many people, for example, experience a glimpse of Reality out in nature. In the out-of-doors, our minds tend to be a lot more at rest, and we are more open to the pure and silent way in which the Self manifests itself in this environment. The trees, the sky, the mountains, the lakes, streams and oceans—along with all the animal and plant life living in them—seem to have such a clear and unobstructed way of reminding us of simply *being*. Within this environment, most of us find it easy to feel more at peace with ourselves.

But there may be moments when a sudden deepening of this peace occurs; a stillness pervades our being. Perhaps we experience a shift in perception about our life for a moment; our cares and worries about our future recede. In view of the timeless reality in which all of Nature resides, our petty concerns about life seem dim and unimportant. The experience deepens for a moment—or perhaps for a number of moments—but then it begins fading, as thoughts tumble into our mind again, and we follow them into a more ordinary reality.

Some people experience similar moments when they are particularly moved by a piece of music or a work of art. Perhaps you have experienced this, when you suddenly feel a lifting of the heart, an expanding of your awareness ... or a flooding of love. Your breath is taken away. Or perhaps this has happened when you've watched a beautiful sunrise or sunset. The vastness of the universe pervades your being; your spirit rises. You are awestruck. Again, this feeling can last a moment or may persist for a while. But eventually it fades— usually when ordinary thoughts, feelings, or body sensations once again claim your attention.

Still other experiences of the Self can come at those times when disaster of some sort has struck. Ironically, at the very time when you would expect to be overwhelmed by emotions of fear, anguish, and heartbreak—a quiet, still peace will slowly enter into your body and mind. An unaccounted for sense of well-being begins to pervade your consciousness, a knowing that despite the tragedy that is obviously taking place, everything really is okay.

As in the other examples, this feeling begins to recede, either slowly or abruptly, when thoughts again invade the awareness. It is as if you've been visited by an angel for a spell and then left again on your own. Many people might simply attribute the experience to a strange side-effect of shock. And in one way, it is. Shock often stops all thought for a period of time; the mind goes numb. In this rare absence of thought, Self has the opportunity to make itself known to us.

Other experiences of Self you may have had due to an empty mind are those moments in your everyday life when your mind just naturally becomes still. You may be staring out the window, daydreaming for awhile, when a simple, clear stillness becomes present inside you. There are no thoughts for a change—just a clarity of awareness. A subtle feeling may be drawing you inward to a deeper state.

If you have felt it to be an appropriate time and place to do it, perhaps you have allowed your awareness to drift inward to see what might take place. You may have even closed your eyes. If so, perhaps you have experienced a feeling of peace, a sense of well-being, a profound stillness. Or maybe a lightness or brightness has greeted you, as you dropped more deeply inside yourself.

If you haven't followed the urge to be drawn more deeply inside and instead have been pulled back into ordinary thought patterns, emotions, or bodily sensations, the moment of possible deepening has probably faded and then been forgotten. The call of the Self has been missed.

All of these kinds of moments I've been describing are usually brief—often fleeting. But it is important not to dismiss them—no matter how faint or subtle they may be—because these are times when you are standing at the doorway of what could become a profound and rapturous glimpse, if you only knew what to do (or not do) at that moment. In the following chapter, I will describe what can be done to help transform these subtle visitations of the Self into ones of greater joy, peace, love, and fulfillment.

CHAPTER FOUR

Deepening and Prolonging the Glimpses

When the sacred moment comes, let him not hesitate to let himself go, to adore the Overself ecstatically, and to let his heart be ravished.
—Paul Brunton

W HAT I STRONGLY URGE YOU TO DO when you first become aware of a glimpse—no matter how faint or fleeting it may be—is to pay immediate attention to it. If you can, stop everything you are doing. Become still and meet this visitation of the Self with instant acceptance, welcome, and love. Your warm receptivity to the glimpse will greatly enhance the clarity and intensity of it.

Then gradually, gently open to the experience. Allow it slowly to deepen in whatever way it wishes. Remain quietly receptive. As Paul Brunton encourages: Act as if a butterfly has landed on you. Be as relaxed as possible, while delicately focusing your attention on it.

Then move slowly into surrender to it. Allow it simply to have you—all of you—with complete abandonment. Hold nothing back. This is your Beloved come to call. Lovingly give yourself to its ardent embrace. Fall deeply into its tender care. Be willing to die in its arms, if this is what's called for. Allow yourself to be swallowed by it, until there is no more you.

At the same time, take care not to be clutching. Make no attempts to possess the experience. It cannot be captured or controlled. It will do with you as it will for as long as it wishes. All you can do is openly trust and embrace it while it is there.

Do your best to linger in this place of openness and abandonment as long as you can. At some point—probably much to your dismay—thoughts, emotions, and bodily sensations will reappear and try to claim you. Stay alert to these. Even thoughts about what is happening to you at the moment will unwittingly bring the mind back into play and dismiss the glimpse. Therefore, do not follow them, but do not try to get rid of them either. Simply let them be, without giving them any energy. The object is to focus as fully and intently (yet gently) as you can on the experience of the glimpse, allowing it to take you where it will as long as possible.

When you finally feel it receding, do not fret. Simply continue to be still. Allow the fragrance of the experience to linger as long as possible. Do not try to get up or move too soon afterwards, or you will begin to immediately lose some of the afterglow. Be careful not to try to speak right away. Stay centered within. You might find it useful to write down the details of your experience, however; often it will begin to dim, as the ordinary concerns of your world finally flood back into your awareness. In other words, do everything you can to prolong the afterglow.

I have had success with this approach a great number of times. I began realizing at one point how many "doorways" into Self I had come to in my life—where I'd stood for a moment and glanced in, and then passed on by, believing there was nothing more I could experience than that fleeting glance or sensation. I therefore decided to experiment with these brief glimpses, and attempted to allow, if I could, a deepening of the glimpses when they came.

The first time I tried this I was waiting for an elevator in a large building in downtown Boulder. I was on my way to an appointment for car insurance (about as mundane a task as there is!). Not much was going on for me that day; I was probably daydreaming, not thinking about much at all. Suddenly I became aware of a subtle sense of detachment that had stolen into my awareness. My perception had shifted just slightly; I was somehow observing myself from the outside, standing at the elevator.

This, I realized, was a rather common experience for me. Nothing breathtaking, just a subtle shift in my awareness. But instead of letting it pass this time, I made the decision to fall more deeply into the experience, if I could. I became aware at that point that my elevator had arrived. People around me were all getting on it. But, ignoring my mind's directive to stop being silly and just get on the elevator, I instead stood still, acting as if it were the wrong elevator for me. The door eventually closed, leaving me standing there.

I immediately focused on the sense of detachment, the sense of witnessing myself, and I opened myself to falling more deeply into that experience. Within a moment, the subtle sense of observing myself became vivid—alive and very real. And with this sensation came an incredible surge of expansiveness. I knew myself to be not only outside my body (as well as inside it)—I was everywhere, in everything. Inexpressible joy burst through my entire being.

All this took place within a matter of moments—perhaps ten seconds. I stood there, rapt, probably smiling idiotically. I became aware of people beginning to gather near me for the elevator's next arrival. But, falling ever more deeply into a sense of rapture, I again ignored the now very dim voice of my mind pleading with me to start acting "normal," and I continued to surrender to the fullness of my bliss.

I have no idea what people were thinking, watching me in that state. But at a certain point, even my mind no longer cared. I was out of time, floating around in my own universe of joy.

At some point (probably only three or four minutes later—although it felt like hours), the elevator arrived perhaps for the fourth time. This time when the doors opened, I did get on. I was aware, as we all ascended into the air, of a glow radiating from me. People I didn't know were smiling broadly at me.

My visit with the insurance agent became a brilliantly warm and personal sharing. I felt unbelievable love for this woman I had never before met. We spoke for almost an hour after my appointment was finished, before I finally left. For many hours afterward, the glow remained. I was so ecstatic that I had taken those few moments to respond to the call of the Self—even in such an unlikely place as an insurance building—and vowed to do it again as often as I could.

I took a similar opportunity some time later, on an evening as I was taking my dog for a walk. I remember it was a warm and peaceful night. Although I could hear sounds coming from houses that I was passing, an unusually quiet feeling seemed to be in the air. I was beginning the leg of the walk back toward my home and the mountains, when I suddenly became aware of a delicate sensation passing throughout my body. It was very pleasant—even sexual in nature—but quite subtle.

My inclination, after noting this feeling, was just to keep walking and follow the thoughts I was having about what I'd be doing the next day. But instead, I decided to stop walking and just stand still so I could pay closer attention to this feeling. Immediately as I did this, it became more intense. A delicious warmth began flooding my body, centering finally in the area of my heart. As I stood, focusing inward, my heart suddenly seemed to burst open with such a profound joy, I thought I would explode. My whole body was trembling.

I can only describe this feeling as an intense and ardent desire for the Beloved—a yearning so powerful that I burst into tears and threw open my arms. The longing tore at me, rending my heart. I thought I would die, as I finally gave myself to this desire completely, flinging myself into its flames.

Just when I thought I could endure no more, an intense and powerful flood of love washed through me. It rippled through every cell of my body. It ruptured and laid waste the walls of my mind. With rapturous joy … I realized the Beloved had arrived.

Enveloping me in a brilliant glow, it overtook me with the most tender and fulfilling love I had ever known. I wept and wept, feeling eons of abandonment and rejection melting away. All separation had vanished. There was only the Oneness. Pure and cleansed, I once again was whole.

I don't know how long I stood there, absorbed in this bliss. I was faintly aware of my dog coming back to me at one point, inquisitively sniffing my hand—probably wondering why I had stopped. A while later, a couple out for an evening stroll passed quietly by me. I just stood still, embraced and absorbed by the pure and radiant energy that was devouring me.

Again, unbelievably, this experience could have passed me by. I could have taken some note of the unusual feeling in my body and

then continued walking and following the thoughts I'd been thinking before. Instead, I had decided to see if this sensation might
possibly be a calling card of the Self. What joy to have made this
choice!

This type of experience may not be available with every faint or
fleeting feeling you experience. Certainly not all the experiences I
have had in following such feelings have been rapturous ones. And
indeed, sometimes I have stopped and focused on a sensation that
didn't produce much at all. But, most times, I have been able to
experience some deepening of the experience and have often prolonged the experience. And, considering what might possibly happen if I do pay attention to the sensation, I figure, why take a chance?
Who knows how far the Self may take us, once we make it known
that we are truly open to its embraces—at any time, any place?

CHAPTER FIVE

Once the Glimpse Has Passed

You want something like around-the-clock ecstasy. Ecstasies come and go—necessarily, for the human brain cannot stand the tension for a long time. A prolonged ecstasy will burn out your brain, unless it is extremely pure and subtle.

—Nisargadatta Maharaj

THERE ARE SEVERAL OBSERVATIONS I'd like to make at this point, based on my own personal experience and on those of others I've known, regarding the period of time following a powerful glimpse. The first is that, although certainly not inevitable, it is common for people to experience a period of depression. Often I've heard people bemoaning the fact that they have somehow "lost" the incredible glimpse they had, and they're experiencing an enormous sense of loss and depression about this. Some even feel they somehow must have done something "wrong" to have lost it.

Part of this stems from simply not being familiar with the nature of glimpses and from having inaccurate assumptions and expectations about them. Quite often during the glimpse, Truth seems so very obvious to us; our clarity is profound. It seems unbelievable to think we could ever lose this clarity. There is a feeling that, having now entered into this new awakened state, we will never again return to "ordinary consciousness."

Unfortunately, almost without exception, this illusion eventually bursts, as the mind does again begin to "return," and everyday concerns start slipping back into our awareness. Unbelievably, the crystal clear knowing of Reality and the profound feelings of joy and peace begin to fade.

I know the excruciating suffering that can accompany this experience. My first profound glimpse, almost twenty years ago, lasted for a number of weeks. I felt I had transcended my ego consciousness and had become a higher form of myself living in a whole new reality, and it seemed as if this would continue forever. But because I had no reference points at the time as to what had happened to me, nor any support or guidance for it, I was nonplussed and filled with grief when I eventually felt the experience beginning to fade and my old ego consciousness returning.

This common reaction happens because people are not aware that the eventual fading of a glimpse is natural and to be expected. These rapturous highs, filled with clarity, understanding, and bliss, are *states of mind.* And the truth about states of mind is that they come—and they go. That is the nature of the mind. They are not permanent. The important thing to realize, however, is that although the states of mind do not last, the Truth that is revealed in the glimpses is permanent, and that does remain.

Something else that can follow a powerful glimpse into Reality (especially if it is your first) is an unhappy dissatisfaction about your life. Some people actually experience their whole life turned upside down by the glimpse, and they can't seem to "right" it in any of the old ways. They become irritable and disgruntled at everything and everyone around them. The feeling is that something inside them that has been numbed for years has suddenly thawed—a deep yearning that is now demanding to be fulfilled. They can no longer go about their life in the old numbed way, trying to satisfy superficial, mediocre desires. Their priorities have abruptly rearranged themselves.

Again, this is to be expected—especially for people who generally have not been basing their lives up to that point on strong spiritual values. Their lives will undoubtedly go through major upsets and changes after a powerful glimpse—necessarily so. Life can never be the same again.

But what is important to remember—even while experiencing disappointment, depression, and upset about the turmoil in your life (if these things are happening)—is the gift of realization that has been given to you in your experience. What a rare and precious gift! And gratitude for this gift will go a long way to help assuage the upsetting feelings.

Realize that with this glimpse you have been granted the clarity to see what at some point may be your on-going and permanent experience. You have been kissed by your True Self; you have been given a foretaste of Paradise and are now being beckoned Home. You can now understand the purpose of life, what it is we're all on the earth for: to fully and permanently wake up to the Truth of who we are. Truly, there is no greater gift we can be given.

Once this realization has been given to you, it is up to you to begin living your everyday life more in accordance with what you have realized. You now have the opportunity to set different priorities, make important changes in your life, if necessary, and live with greater integrity because of what you know to be true. You really have no other choice. But it is an effortless choice, if you can simply stop resisting the changes and allow them to take place naturally.

But what is perhaps most important following the passing of a glimpse is to be alert to what it is that has not left you, even though all the blissful sensations have receded. Something very precious always remains—the whole point, in fact, to these glimpses of Self. And that is *realization of Truth.*

Gangaji speaks very clearly about this point in *satsang* and proved to be very helpful to me about it. She encourages everyone who has had a true glimpse of the Self (especially if they are bemoaning their fate for having "lost" it) to simply check and see what has not left. What knowing still remains, even after the high has totally dissipated? What is it that can never be taken away? I have found that the knowing of Self, the realization of who I really am, has indeed never left me—ever since my first true glimpse twenty years ago. And this realization is the true treasure—not the glorious high. The rapturous glimpse was simply the exquisitely beautiful wrapping in which the treasure of realization was brought to me.

CHAPTER SIX

Attracting Glimpses into Your Life

If we want to hear the voice of the Overself, we have to create a quiet all around us and within us, and we have to listen and go on listening with patience.

—Paul Brunton

ONCE YOU HAVE BEGUN HAVING GLIMPSES of the Self, you will likely find yourself preoccupied (even obsessed) with how to have more of them. This is a tricky area, because it's important to realize that we have no actual control over *causing* them to happen. Somehow, Grace bestows them on us—sometimes at the most unlikely and surprising times.

The Self Is Everywhere

However, I've come to discover ways in which we can "cultivate" our inner environment so as to open ourselves for more and more of these experiences. The first thing to do, I've found, is to look for them everywhere, expecting them to happen at any time. Self truly is everywhere, in everything—it is ALL that exists. The opportunities to see and experience it are therefore countless, available in every moment. So the point is to focus your attention on potential glimpses in every way you can, as often as possible throughout your everyday life. Actively invite these visitations into your life through a prayerful openness of attention.

Every Glimpse Is Unique

Another suggestion is to remember that every glimpse of the Self is unique. Be careful not to expect the same experience to happen twice. Every glimpse, although possessing certain similar qualities, happens in a fresh new way each time. This is where many people get tripped up. Once they've had an incredible glimpse, they want a repeat performance; they want the same feelings, the same sensations, the same insights. This can greatly hinder the next glimpse from coming in, in its own unique and new way.

I have found that it is okay to mull over past glimpses (and continue to get as much "juice" out of them as I can); sometimes the re-experiencing will even precipitate a new glimpse. However, an openness to all the endless new and fresh ways glimpses decide to come in is essential, or we may unwittingly keep them from happening.

Creating a Welcoming Environment

I have also found certain things we can do to invite the visit of a glimpse. As I mentioned earlier, going out in Nature is one of these. Listening to music or visiting an art gallery or museum are others. You can also read inspiring books, or go to spiritual gatherings with enlightened teachers. Many people claim that simply being in the presence of someone who is enlightened greatly increases the opportunity for profound experiences of the Self.

Spending time with others who are on a similar quest is also very helpful. Talking about glimpses and other spiritual experiences can be uplifting and can also greatly enhance one's own experiences. On the back side of this, try to avoid spending time with people whose company brings you down in some way. Also, you might want to be careful about what movies you choose to see, which television programs you watch, and which books you choose to read. In other words, be responsible for creating your own inner environment that will be as conducive as possible to visitations from the Self. Do beware, however, of becoming self-righteous or arrogant about what you feel is spiritually "clean." What feels right and appropriate for you to create an energetically-clean environment may not be best for someone else.

"Who Am I?"

One of the most effective tools I know for inviting glimpses is the one I mentioned in Chapter One: asking yourself, "Who am I?"—and then going inside and directly looking to see who is actually there. The object in doing this is not to come up with an intellectual answer to this question but to wait quietly for an experiential response. For me, the awesome discovery each time is that no one is there; indeed, nothing of any substance is there, except Consciousness—pure Awareness that never changes, even as thoughts, emotions, and bodily sensations come and go. This discovery usually comes as a sudden current of awareness or knowing that my body, mind, and emotions all experience—and yet is beyond all of them.

There are variations on this technique. If you are suffering about a particular issue, you can ask, "Who is suffering?" Again at this point, investigate directly—look within. See what is actually present. Other variations might be, "Who is thinking?" or "Who is feeling anger (joy, love, fear, etc.)?" All these questions lead back to the one having the experience, rather than to some object of the mind, and that is what is so unusual and powerful about it.

Meditation

Most spiritual teachings tell us of the importance of some kind of meditation on a daily basis. If you have been meditating daily for a number of years as I have, you may also feel that the years of meditating have helped your mind remain relatively clear and calm most of the time. I would guess you have probably had a number of glimpses of the Self as well.

You also may have discovered, as I have, that after years of taking special time every day to meditate, it doesn't really feel necessary to do so anymore. I have found that most of my waking hours now have a meditative quality to them, no matter what I am doing. It's somehow as if I am constantly meditating wherever I am. Perhaps the years of meditating have finally penetrated my on-going everyday consciousness.

However, if you still find it difficult to calm your mind and relax, and you have not yet experienced glimpses of the Self as deeply as you would like, adopting a daily meditation practice may be very useful. Meditation habituates the mind to moving consistently inward toward clarity and relaxation—even during mundane or demanding tasks.

Many people I've worked with have had difficulty with developing a daily meditation practice. I believe this is due to several things. One is that developing such a practice takes time, discipline, and patience. Yet many people feel they should be successful at it immediately, simply because they want to be. It's not that easy. Generally, the mind, the emotions, and the body are not habituated to being still for any length of time while we are awake. This habit has to be cultivated.

It is therefore important to practice daily meditation beginning with short periods of time and then gradually increasing the time. Even ten minutes a day is helpful at first—any amount of time that is spent entirely and fully on cultivating an inner environment conducive to experiencing the Self. Little by little, the time can be increased, as is comfortable.

For most people, finding a particular time of the day in which to meditate is also very helpful, as well as finding a particular place in their home for it. You begin creating a certain energy in that place that will draw you in after awhile. Making sure you will be comfortable (not too hot or cold, too full or hungry, etc.) will further ensure success in your practice.

Another difficulty people sometimes run into in beginning a meditation practice is that they believe that the only way to meditate is to sit still and try to quiet the mind. There may be a type of meditation like this; if so, I'm not familiar with it. At any rate, it seems to be a very difficult method to attempt right off the bat. The mind simply rebels and tends to bring in as many thoughts as it can. Frustration and a sense of failure are sure to result.

I've encouraged people instead to try many different things initially—anything that will gently encourage their mind to relax and begin focusing inwardly. Listening to visualization tapes can be very helpful for this. Listening to certain pieces of relaxing music can also work at first—or moving to meditative music. Different forms of yoga can be extremely beneficial. Some people find it helpful to start out by journaling or by allowing their "higher self" to write a letter to them. All of these activities can serve as a way to eventually enter into more serious and demanding forms of meditation.

Something that greatly assisted me in my early days of meditating was doing it in a group setting. The combined focus and energy can be very helpful to everyone in the group. A class in meditation can be a great way to get this group support, as well as learn a specific form of meditation.

Do keep in mind, however, that no matter how much a teacher may try to convince you that his or her type of meditation is the best (or only) way to meditate—there are many, many different forms of meditation. After trying a few, you can then decide which will work best for you. Be aware also that, at some point, a certain form of meditation that once worked for you may be less effective after awhile. It may be time to begin trying new forms. Sometimes we can "outgrow" a particular spiritual practice (or teacher) and need to look for what is "next" on our spiritual path.

At any rate, developing a daily spiritual practice of some kind—at least at first—is generally important in a quest for attracting glimpses of the Self. The aim is to learn how to still the mind as much as possible. As Nisargadatta states in his book, *I Am That*: "When the mind is still, Reality rushes in." It's as if the Self is just standing there, waiting patiently for us to put aside the thoughts—even just for a moment—so it can then rush in to greet us.

Psychotherapy

For some people, simply meditating or doing other spiritual practices every day doesn't seem to be enough to create a clear environment for glimpses of the Self to happen. Somehow, their minds are too restless; negative emotions continue to obsess them;

powerful desires keep pulling them out in the world; or their identification with the body is very deeply embedded in their consciousness.

If this is true for you—especially if you do not wish to do endlessly long years of spiritual practice—my experience is that entering into some sort of therapy for awhile can speed up the process of "purifying the vessel." (I include in this recommendation any and all of the many forms of what is called "therapy" today; there is a whole variety from which to choose.) Therapy can also be helpful for just brief periods of time, when there is a particular issue that keeps getting in the way of your ability to meditate or deeply experience the Self.

A woman by the name of Linda once came to me for this reason. I'd known her for awhile, and I therefore knew she had had numerous profound glimpses of Self in the past. Most of the time when I had been with her, I'd experienced her as a very joyful and awake person.

But this day she revealed to me that she had not had a deep experience of Self for quite some time—ever since she'd become involved in a romantic relationship with a particular man. She stated that every time she attempted to move into the Silence within her, obsessive thoughts about him would come into her mind, giving her no rest. She felt hopelessly distracted by this and mourned deeply for the Silence she felt she could no longer contact.

We discussed how everyone has these kinds of "egoic tendencies" in certain areas of their life—even the most awake people have them—and how sometimes it can be helpful to do some therapeutic self-discovery work around these issues. We therefore decided to explore her relationship difficulties to see if anything could break free for her in this painful area.

Within just a few sessions, she realized the reason for the obsessing she was doing and was able to begin to let go of it. She later reported that she had a powerful glimpse of Self during meditation—along with some very clear insights about herself in relationship to other people in general.

I wish to note, however, that during the sessions we had, I consistently reminded her not to get caught into believing that something was "wrong" with her that needed to be fixed. I reminded her that all we were doing was attempting to dissipate some of the "clouds" that had been obscuring her view of who she really was— the Self. As far as I was concerned, that was the only reason for doing therapy: to help clear the way for deeper experiences of Self to take place.

Summary

As you can see, this first step on the path of letting go—having direct experiences of your true Self—is essential. We must begin to directly experience our true Self and become familiar with it, before we can trust and eventually surrender our lives to it. To have this direct experience, it is first of all helpful to have an idea of what this Self actually is. Then we need to be open to glimpses of it: recognize the glimpses when they appear, even in their most subtle form; learn how to deepen and prolong them; and then do what we can to attract them into our daily lives as often as possible.

The second step on the path, which I will describe in the next section, involves a process of detaching from your ego-self—and the eventual disidentification with it. This process is easier to undertake if you've had at least one true glimpse of the Self, because a glimpse gives you the direct knowledge of another more real identity; you experience for yourself that who you are is not the limited form of the ego-self.

However, having such a glimpse is not at all mandatory for starting the process of detaching from the ego. Much can be learned and experienced by simply understanding more clearly what the ego-self is and how we get caught into believing that that is who we are. In fact, it may even be possible that this kind of initial understanding about the ego-self can help prepare the way for a first glimpse of Self. There are certainly no set rules about any of this.

DETACHING FROM
THE EGO-SELF

CHAPTER SEVEN

Understanding the Ego

The ego is a monkey catapulting through the jungle:
Totally fascinated by the realm of the senses,
    it swings from one desire to the next,
    one conflict to the next,
    one self-centered idea to the next.
If you threaten it, it actually fears for its life.

Let this monkey go.
Let the senses go.
Let conflicts go.
Let ideas go.
Let the fiction of life and death go.
Just remain in the center, watching.

And then forget that you are there.

—Hua Hu Ching

*T*HE SECOND STEP on the path of letting go—the gradual process of detaching from the ego-self—is an on-going process. This is the step Krishnamurti was referring to in saying that it takes time for the "little me" to disappear. In my experience, it also takes much patience. But the energy spent in this process is infinitely worth it. You can experience incredible freedom and peace, even as you begin this process, just in knowing more and more fully that this limited and imperfect identity you've believed yourself to be is not who you truly are.

45

What Exactly Is the Ego-Self?

I wish to make clear what I am referring to when I use the term "ego-self," because it is used in a number of different ways these days. In particular, people often use the term to refer to that part of themselves they consider "bad" or unacceptable—their negative emotions and thoughts, their arrogance, lust, greed, and ignorance—or whatever else they consider "unspiritual." I consider these negative qualities to be just one part of the ego—a part that is disliked by another part.

When I use the term "ego-self," I refer to the entire personal, separate, individual sense of identity. This includes the body and all its sensations; the mind and all its thoughts, beliefs, judgments, and desires; and the emotions (even the positive ones)—along with the memories of all of these. It also includes all roles a person plays in his or her life. In other words, it is the entire personal "me," living in its story of life.

Another way the ego can be described is as *conditioned consciousness*. It is clear Consciousness that has been conditioned or distorted by our particular upbringing and by the culture to which we've been exposed. Some believe that it has also been influenced by *karma*, the results of actions carried over from past lifetimes.

The important thing is that your ego is conditioned consciousness—molded, constricted, and distorted by circumstances, experiences, and beliefs that you have encountered in your life. If you identify yourself as this conditioned consciousness (as most people do), you are necessarily creating a highly unstable, constantly changing, and insecure experience for yourself.

The Cause of Suffering

Perhaps the most important thing to understand about the ego is that **our identification with it is the sole cause of our suffering**. The ego-self, as Arthur Osborne puts it, "is in constant turmoil, plagued by hope and fear, anxiety, regret, attachment and bereavement—foredoomed by death." The Self, in contrast, exists in unchanging peace and freedom. It has no birth or death, no beginning or end. It is beyond all experiences of insecurity or struggle.

Truly knowing yourself to be the Self rather than the ego therefore eliminates all suffering. The ego can continue to do all its little numbers, based on its belief that it is a separate little being, subject to the whims of the universe and fate (or God), but if you know that that is not who you are, it does not trouble you. You can simply watch it with detachment and compassion, as it struggles with its little strategies, attempting to create security in the world. You remain untouched by any of it.

The Ego's Game Plan

Perhaps the most tragic strategy the ego-self employs is its game plan to try and ensure lasting happiness in your life. What it doesn't understand is that, as valiantly as it may try to accomplish this, it is totally unequipped to do so. This is because it does not understand that the cause of your suffering is your belief that you are it, rather than your true Self.

It instead keeps trying to convince you (usually quite successfully) that its own game plan for happiness will work. Its plan is quite simple: *Follow your desires.* First become aware of what they are, and then do everything you can to fulfill them. Run after and cling to things that bring you pleasure, and run from and fight those things that bring you pain.

Sound familiar? It should, because this is precisely what just about everyone in the world is doing: seeking happiness through attempting to fulfill desires. Unfortunately, most people don't realize that this game plan simply doesn't work. If you're honest, you'll realize that no matter how many desires you've fulfilled in your life, none of them has ever brought you true, lasting happiness. It's always been temporary. There are always more desires to fulfill; they are, in fact, endless.

I will go into this unsuccessful game plan in more detail in a later chapter, but for now, just be aware of this illusion under which your ego-self is operating. Your ego simply doesn't know how to bring you true happiness. And you can be sure that, as it begins realizing that you're seeing the truth about this, it may well become nervous and afraid.

But fear not; there are ways to educate your ego-self and gently coax it toward letting go of its hold and its age-old ideas. It can eventually come to see the errors of its own plan and realize how utterly weary it's become, trying for so long to bring happiness to you in this way. It may actually even come to see the wisdom in "retiring" from its job as your master and finally learn to be your servant (its true job) instead.

Detachment Is Not Dissociation or Denial

I would like to caution you at this point about certain misunderstandings that can arise when one begins the process of detaching from the ego-self. The first is that you might tend to confuse the concept of detachment with dissociation or denial. In particular, you might think that to detach from your emotions would mean entering into a dissociated state in which you wouldn't be in touch with them. Or if you were to detach from your body, this would mean denial of your body. Believing this to be so, you might understandably resist the idea of detachment.

So let me make it clear: This is not at all to what I'm referring when I use the word "detachment." What I'm speaking of is creating a distance in your awareness from your emotions, body, and mind, to become more of a witness to them. It's about becoming an observer of yourself, one who is not so embroiled in the drama or so attached to the outcome of events and circumstances.

As such, far from putting you out of touch with your thoughts, emotions, and bodily sensations (as in the experiences of dissociation and denial), detachment can actually help you be *more* aware of them. You are training yourself to carefully observe what is happening within you. Ironically, the process of detachment can actually assist you to participate more fully, with greater interest and caring, in the activities of all these aspects of your life—precisely because you are not so attached and lost in the miasma of feelings and sensations that are going on.

For me, this happened the most dramatically in my relationship to my body. Before I began the process of detaching from it and realizing that it truly was not who I was, I had generally been someone who paid little attention to my body. For a number of different reasons, I gave little value to my physical form. I enjoyed many of the pleasures it offered me, but like an ungrateful child, when it became ill or hurt, I would feel angry or annoyed. My body often seemed to be something that got in the way of what I wanted to do. I rarely pampered it or thought too much about taking good care of it.

Because of this attitude, not surprisingly, my body did not thrive. Since I generally ignored early warning signals of illness, I often ended up sick, and I eventually created some chronic diseases. I was often irritated at these diseases, but then, as time went on, I also began feeling guilty and inadequate about letting them happen. Unfortunately, however, my upset and guilt did nothing to create a better attitude in me about taking care of my body. I was so caught up in my conditioned feelings about it, that I could do very little to turn things around.

Once I began the process of detaching from my body, however, all this began to change. As I stepped back from my body, I began to truly see that this was not who I was; it wasn't the true "I" that was getting sick, that was imperfect, that was aging. And with this realization, for the first time in my life, I was able to have some compassion for this poor body I had so sorely neglected.

Like never before, I began taking care of my body: feeding it better, taking it to health practitioners when necessary, giving it enough rest—and, perhaps most importantly, loving it. I could not have done this had I remained believing that this body was who I was. I probably would have continued neglecting it, while staying caught in all the emotions involved in the drama I'd created around my neglect.

So it's important to understand the difference between detachment and dissociation or denial. As I've stated, the process of detaching from the ego-self, unlike dissociation or denial, actually creates a greater awareness of the ego (and its thoughts, emotions, and bodily sensations). It also helps develop a greater caring and effectiveness in your life, while it brings in a deeper sense of ease and relaxation. Most importantly, the process of detachment can assist you toward ultimately experiencing your true identity with the Self. By creating a distance from your ego-self, you begin to see its inherent illusory nature, and you naturally begin to experience that which is your true nature.

Spiritual Polarization

The second misunderstanding that can occur as we begin the process of detaching from the ego is what is known as "spiritual polarization." This happens when we begin to make the true Self "good" and the ego-self "bad"—and then attempt a program of "getting rid" of this terrible thing that's kept us from lasting happiness. This approach is based on a false understanding of the truth—and furthermore it simply doesn't work. This kind of polarization simply indicates that one part of the ego is trying to get rid of another part that it doesn't like.

The ego-self is not inherently bad. It just is what it is. The problem is that we have generally given it too much power; we have let it be in charge and have imagined it to be who we really are. So the answer is not to attempt to get rid of it. It is simply to see it clearly for what it is, see its inherent illusory nature. It is to realize that, by itself—without Consciousness—the ego-self would not exist.

In other words, there is no need to oppose the ego-self with the Self. The ego is something that arises from within Self; it is created by Self. The Self is its source. The ego is just one of many forms that the Self appears as. If you understand this, you'll see that the ego really cannot give you trouble on its own. The problem only comes when you believe that who you are is this very limited, imperfect, and impermanent form.

Letting Go of the Self-Improvement Urge

The third caution I offer, as you begin the work of detaching from the ego, is to remember that this is a process of *letting go* of the ego-self—not a program to fix or change it in some way. "Self-improvement" activities can be okay; as I mentioned earlier, many different kinds of therapy can at times be helpful. (In fact, in certain cases, it can be a good idea, if you have persistent, negative subconscious patterns that continue to drive you in your life.) It's just that it's important to keep the idea of "self-improvement" in perspective: to remember that that which appears to need fixing is not who you truly are.

For those of you who have been engaged in "improving" yourself for a long time and feel you have gotten in touch with your basic personality patterns and cleared out a lot of the "stuff" that has gotten in your way—I would suggest that you might want to give it a rest at this point. Abandon the ingrained "self-improvement urge," at least for awhile, and realize that improving yourself finally proves endless; the ego cannot be perfected.

Try instead to simply relax and let go. Let yourself be, just the way you are. Focus on gently surrendering your attachment to the ego, on giving up your identity with your thoughts, emotions, and bodily sensations. Understand that the cause of your suffering has been a case of misidentification: believing yourself to be the ego-self. Begin waking up from this trance and discover your true identity.

Understand that all suffering is caused by identification with the ego. Ironically, the reverse is also true: Suffering can serve to keep us hooked into this very misidentification. It's the old proverbial vicious cycle. In the following chapters, I will discuss how this cycle works in the various aspects of life. Then I will describe ways I've discovered that can help you to step out of that cycle and find your way past both the identification with the ego and the suffering it causes.

CHAPTER EIGHT

Detaching from the Roles We Play

Leave all definition behind. Immediately upon birth, you were already possessed by your parents. Then some priest came to initiate you into his fold or sect, and you belonged to that religion.... Then you became a student, then a wife, then a mother of children. Some day you will fall sick and the doctor will say, "You are my patient." Death. And then even the mourners will claim, "This is my corpse." What a joke!

—Papaji

THE FIRST TYPE OF MISIDENTIFICATION I will focus on is with the roles we play in life. I start here because this misidentification and the suffering it causes are perhaps the most obvious and therefore the easiest to see and let go of.

Roles are unavoidable. From the very beginning, each one of us was born as someone's child and perhaps as someone's sibling or grandchild. We were likely some doctor's or midwife's patient, as well. Then we became somebody's friend, and eventually somebody's student, etc., etc., throughout life. Roles are simply an integral part of life as we know it.

There is nothing inherently wrong with roles and playing them. Where the difficulty can arise is in how we become attached to these roles and in how much we identify with them. This is where we can create a great deal of unnecessary suffering for ourselves.

Rules and Expectations in Roles

First, what needs to be understood is that with every role, "rules" and expectations seem to naturally go along with it: our own and those of other people around us. For example, if you are playing the role of someone's wife, your husband may have a number of varied expectations of you—both spoken and unspoken. Some of these expectations may be so important and believed in so strongly that he inwardly sees them as "rules" that someone in that role "should" play.

He may expect you, for instance, to be responsible for all the housework, even though you also work a full-time job. Or he may expect you to act as the primary parent to your children. He may expect you to be loyal, supportive, and responsive to his needs. Or he may expect you to make certain decisions for the two of you. These kinds of expectations, of course, can go on and on. Many of them are assumed and unexpressed between spouses, and this so often causes difficulties in a relationship.

On the other hand, what can cause just as much distress inside you are your own expectations and rules about yourself in your role as a wife. Your husband may, in fact, have very few expectations or demands on you as his wife, but, for whatever reason, you may have many expectations of yourself. If you take this role very seriously and use it as your primary identity, for instance, you may have very stringent (and ultimately unachievable) expectations of yourself— like believing you should always be supportive of him, always have the housework done, always pay the bills on time, never feel attracted to another man, or whatever. This is what "wife" means to you.

It is clearly important to be aware of the expectations you are living with as you play a role (both your own and those of others involved), to try and avoid unrealistic or conflicting notions about what you "should" be doing. However, the important thing to see here is not so much the expectations that exist about the roles you play—but the fact that if you are attached to the roles you're playing, if you identify with them, then you are likely to suffer every time you don't live up to the rules and expectations that go along with them. Your sense of worthiness, even your whole sense of "self," can be greatly disturbed. In fact, the degree to which you hold a role important and identify with it is precisely the degree to which you make yourself vulnerable to suffering in the role.

I once had a friend named Diane who took her role as the mother of her five-year-old son Randy very seriously. It was clear that she felt herself first and foremost to be a "mother" in life; more than anything, this was her identity. In some ways, of course, this was wonderful. Randy had a mother who deeply cared about him, and the two of them had a very close and satisfying relationship.

On the other hand, I could also see that her seriousness in her role involved a great deal of attachment and therefore could lead to much suffering for her. Sure enough, this began happening almost as soon as Randy entered school. Because of hyperactive tendencies, he was soon identified as a "problem child." Many notes from the teacher, the counselor, and the principal began to arrive home about Randy's learning problems and misbehavior. Because he also seemed incapable of making friends, he soon began resisting going to school every morning. Diane was devastated.

Of course, this kind of situation can be distressing for any parent. But Diane, I knew, was particularly vulnerable to this distress because she was so heavily (and solely) identified as Randy's mother. Even the smallest problem with him at school threw her into deep anxiety and depression. Each time she received a new note or complaint, her entire sense of self and worthiness were profoundly threatened. She constantly asked what she was doing wrong, wondering how she had failed as a mother. Being told that hyperactivity was a biochemical problem seemed to have no affect on her. Her attachment to being the "perfect mother" was so blinding, she could not absorb this information.

In one way, Diane probably wasn't that unusual. I think we all at times become this attached to certain roles in our lives. They seem important and necessary for us to play, and we naturally become very involved and identified with them. And since we can't always play the roles perfectly, we end up suffering.

So how can we solve this dilemma? How can we play the roles that are necessary in life without causing this type of suffering? The answer, of course, is to remember that these are roles we're playing and not who we really are. This idea is probably not new for you. Perhaps you've even found help in dealing with problems in a certain role by using this understanding. But if you are still suffering within that role, even just occasionally, perhaps your understanding is simply intellectual and not a direct experience of knowing it.

The point is to truly *realize* that you're not the role, through fully experiencing your true identity beyond the role. It's to learn how to play the role without fear or anxiety, so that your sense of self and worthiness remain intact, no matter how well you play it. It's to experience that your performance of the role has no power to threaten the core of your identity, the essence of who you are. The point, in effect, is to learn how you can be *free* while playing a role, undisturbed by it and everything that goes along with it.

What Attachment to Roles Can Create

So how can this be accomplished? How can this freedom truly be experienced? First, it is helpful, I've found, to get in touch with what actually happens for you while in the process of playing a role. Often we numb ourselves to some degree to on-going pain that we feel is unavoidable in life. So to help you get better in touch with your experiences within roles you play, I list below a few things you can do.

Exercise: *Detaching from Roles*

1. First of all, make a list of all the roles you play in life. This will help you to see just how many countless roles you play throughout your everyday life. To remind you of them all, the following are some important areas in which people assume roles in their lives:
   • Relationship Roles (e.g., mother, son, sister, friend)
   • Work Roles (e.g., profession or job, other roles within the workplace, such as chairperson, volunteer coordinator, foreman, birthday party coordinator)
   • Hobby Roles (e.g., gardener, singer, weaver, athlete)

- Roles Based on Philosophies You Believe In (e.g., Feminist, Unitarian, Democrat, New Ager, Atheist)
- Roles Stemming from What You Do or Have Done (e.g., alcoholic, college grad, over-eater, rape victim, bowling champion)

2. Star the roles that seem most important to you, the ones to which you are most identified and attached. Then choose the most important of all these.

3. Now list the following about the role you've chosen:
   - All the activities involved
   - All the responsibilities involved
   - All the expectations you feel others have of you in this role (In order to be considered "good" in this role, what is expected of you?)
   - All your feelings and thoughts and judgments of yourself in this role: How well do you do in it? How often do you fall short of what you consider "adequate" or "good?" How do you respond when you do fall short? What kinds of judgment or pressure do you put on yourself for not being perfect in the role?

4. At this point, take the time to really get in touch with these feelings.
   - Become aware of the emotional response you have to other people's opinions, expectations, and judgments about you in this role. Be aware of your own internal judgments and your response to these.
   - Get in touch with any anxiety you have (or sometimes have) about "failing" in this role; feel your self-doubt. Become aware of the image you feel you need to maintain.
   - Now become aware of all the energy you put into this role and in trying to be perfect in it; feel the burden of this expenditure of energy.
   - Be aware now of the pride you experience when you do feel you've done well in the role. There's no need to give up this good feeling, but do become aware of the anxiety that can also arise, along with the good feeling. For instance, do you feel you now have to maintain the success you've achieved? Do

you put pressure on yourself to keep getting better? What if someone else you know in the same role gets better than you at it? See clearly how even success in a role can bring its own set of anxieties.

- Now think for a moment of the pleasure you get from playing the role. Again, become aware of the potential suffering that can ensue, even amidst the pleasure you may experience from the role. For example, what happens when the pleasure ends? How do you respond? If this role helps to create a sense of self for you and a sense of worthiness, then do these leave when the pleasure leaves or when you feel yourself failing in the role? Feel the inherent insecurity and instability of all this. See what a pain being attached to a role can be!

The good news is that I have found that this kind of suffering is not inevitable when playing roles. There is always a way out.

Detaching from Your Roles

The way out, very simply, is to begin detaching your identity from the roles you play in your life. I'd like to make it clear that what I am talking about is not just a mental exercise, when you intellectually understand that you are not the roles you play. What I'm referring to is something that involves a whole shift in your experience of identity.

The first step in achieving this shift is perhaps fairly obvious: to realize that you are not the role you are playing, but the human being who is playing the role. You are, in fact, a person who plays many roles in life. And each time, after a role has been played, you can drop the costume and script that went along with that role and resume just being the person you are behind all the roles you play. You can feel free to be your "natural self."

This was brought home quite poignantly to a young man who came to see me for therapy a few years ago. John had been an associate attorney in a large law firm for about a year at that time. Like most men in our culture, he took his profession quite seriously, and his sense of self-worth was deeply hooked into his performance in this role.

Unfortunately, he was having a lot of difficulty at his job. He struggled constantly with feelings of not being as good at his work as other associate attorneys in the firm. He felt he wasn't being given any of the most coveted assignments and also that he was being judged unfairly by one of the partners in the firm. Because his work was so important to his sense of identity, he was suffering greatly on an on-going basis.

After listening to his long tale of woe about this situation, I asked him, "So what else do you do in your life?" He seemed a bit taken aback by this question. I suppose he was expecting me to begin delving into the drama at work he'd just spent so long telling me about. He paused a few moments after my question, but then he answered, "Well, not much. I sail sometimes on the weekends with friends. And I play racketball. Sometimes I go to concerts or plays with people."

"And when you're doing these things with friends, are you playing the attorney?"

"Well, no. I'm just having fun, relaxing."

"And what else do you do with your time outside of work?"

"Well, I spend time on some weekends with my 3-year-old daughter, Sarah." His eyes softened as he said this, and he smiled.

"And do you play attorney when you're around her?"

He laughed and said, "No. I play father—and friend. We have a lot of fun together." He became somewhat quiet.

"And how about when you're alone? What kinds of things do you do?"

"I don't know. I guess I read or watch TV. Sometimes I just sit and look out the window. I like watching the birds."

"And I don't imagine you're playing attorney at those times."

"No," he said quietly. "I'm just me … I'm just a human being—like everyone else." He began smiling. "I'm just a human being," he repeated. "Playing attorney—as you so quaintly put it—is just something I do for a job. It's not who I am." A sense of relief and then a deep peace settled into his face, as what he'd said registered within him.

This was such a simple realization for John and yet so powerful. He told me later that from that point on, his whole experience at work shifted dramatically. Just coming to the realization that behind his role of attorney he had an identity as a human being brought in an unprecedented sense of calm for him at work. His sense of worth in his role as attorney rose, and somehow, "coincidentally," the partners began giving him more desirable cases on which to work. As obvious an insight as it had been, he had received it on such a deep experiential level that an important and actual shift happened in his life.

Most therapeutic and self-help strategies tend to leave the matter here, figuring that this is the best that can be done. (And, at the time, it was where I left it. Both John and I seemed satisfied that if he could accomplish just this much, if he could feel relatively free as he played the roles in his life—it was the most that could be expected.) And certainly, this kind of insight is a step above being caught in the belief that your identity rests in a role.

But if you think about it, you may realize that this approach doesn't really solve the problem, because there is still a catch involved: Even if you now believe yourself to be a human being behind all the roles you play, there's still potential suffering in this—because, usually, to feel good about yourself, you need to feel like a "good" human being. Probably much of the time you do feel you are this; you're generally kind, loving, and considerate of others—or whatever your belief system dictates you need to be in order to be considered "good." But what about the times you're not? What about the times your lust or greed or selfishness or arrogance slip in? What happens then? What happens in your gut?

If you're like a lot of people, probably a deep, automatic, subtle (or maybe not so subtle) sense of suffering occurs. It's generally not comfortable to feel "bad" or "unspiritual" in some way. And so you're still trapped. You are still subject to suffering, even while knowing yourself to be a human being behind the roles you play, because there are expectations (your own and those of others) about being a certain way as a human being, in order to be a "worthwhile" and "good" one. And as we all know, it's impossible to live up to these expectations all the time.

The usual advice offered us at this point is to simply let go of these kinds of expectations. We're told it's okay to make mistakes; we're only human. We can't be perfect. Or we simply need to learn how to forgive ourselves. All this can be helpful, up to a point. But does it ever really do it? For me, this kind of self-talk has never totally worked. The urge toward perfection is too insistent, too ingrained. And since perfection on this level is inherently unachievable, the suffering remains.

Going the Step Beyond

What is necessary, I have found, is to go a step beyond trying to fix and change expectations and judgments—to a place where **there simply are no rules, expectations, or beliefs** to begin with. It's to find a place where we do not fall subject to disappointment, regret, unworthiness, anger, or any of the other experiences that seem to go with believing yourself to be a human being.

This can happen when you truly realize that who you are in reality is not anything so limited as a human being. "Human being" is just one more role you are playing; it's one more costume and script you've taken on. It is not who you truly are.

Exercise: *Becoming the Observer*

A powerful way you can begin to directly experience what you are beyond the role of human beingness is to step back in your awareness from yourself and begin observing yourself in your life. As you begin to play a role, sit back and watch yourself as you go through all the activities in the role.

Then tune into a more subtle level: Begin watching the expectations you have of yourself in the role and also your response to the expectations of others. Watch the judgments that appear, the anxiety. There is no need to react to any of these feelings; just observe them. When feelings of unworthiness about the role arise, observe those. When feelings of pleasure or success arise, observe those. Observe it all.

In other words, become the audience as well as the actor or actress in this soap opera you call your life. Watch the whole thing: everything going on outside on the stage and everything inside the hero or heroine. Then see yourself changing into another role. Observe the new set of feelings and experiences that come with this new role. Watch the entire drama that goes on in the life of this human being up there on the stage.

If you do this exercise for awhile, you will soon begin to feel the relief and freedom that naturally come with being simply the observer of a play. Then, at some point, you can take it further: Try stepping back one more step and observe the observer. And ask yourself, who is it that is observing the observer?

A number of years back I tried this technique as an experiment. I had just made what I felt was a very serious mistake as a therapist with a client who had just begun therapy with me a short time before. Sandy had come to me originally with profound wounding around trust and abandonment issues. I was aware of this and had been attempting to keep this in mind in all my interactions with her, both in and out of session.

But one day, I had a lot of my own personal issues on my mind concerning my marriage, and thoughtlessly, I scheduled another appointment for the time when Sandy was due to come in. To make matters worse, I forgot to call Sandy or the other person ahead of time, when I first discovered this, in order to reschedule one of them. Then, unbelievably, I was also unavoidably late to the appointment. When I arrived at my office, they were both sitting in my waiting room feeling anxious and confused.

A bad situation to start with, it got even worse as I somehow managed to treat Sandy in a way that came across as uncaring. I knew I was making a mess of things, but I somehow couldn't help it. I was still in the process of dealing with my own very difficult emotions on that day, and it was all I could do at times to keep on breathing. So I'm sure it was clear to Sandy that her feelings were not uppermost in my mind, and understandably, she felt rejected, abandoned, and hurt by me as she left my office.

I subsequently went into total upset about all this, feeling guilt and anger at myself—and then shame about myself as a therapist. Being fairly new at the profession, I was taking my role very seriously and had quite deeply attached my sense of worth and self-esteem to how well I performed in the role. Although I attempted to call her and apologize, I realized I had messed up too badly with her; she had been too fragile to handle the way I'd treated her and had decided to find another therapist.

Although I told myself that all therapists make mistakes, that I couldn't have known the depth of her fragility, and that I'd done the best I could under the circumstances—none of this helped. My stomach wrenched in the agony of having not only failed a client but of actually doing her more damage than good. I was feeling that through my irresponsibility and my self-centeredness, I had failed as a therapist and also as a decent human being.

I sat at home that evening, going through the scenario in my head over and over again, trying somehow to fix it. It was to no avail. Finally, in great pain, I decided to sit back and simply become the observer of this drama that was going on in my head. Somewhere I'd heard about this technique, and although it seemed somewhat simplistic, there appeared to be nothing else I could do at this point. I could not dislodge the knot in my stomach. I took a deep breath and inwardly created some distance from the poor woman who was agonizing over her failure. I saw her up on a stage, writhing about in emotional pain.

I smiled as I realized that the name of this drama I was watching was called "The Great Therapeutic Fuck-Up." I watched, becoming more and more still and detached, as this woman (who was such a good actress!) continued to convulse in inner turmoil. Such guilt and shame she was feeling! My heart went out to her with compassion—and yet *I* was somehow no longer suffering. I knew this to be simply a play; it wasn't real. *I* was the one who was real, sitting here in the audience watching her. I knew at some point the play would be over (she'd either resolve her turmoil or not), and I'd simply get up and go home. As I sat there becoming more and more detached about this little drama, I became extremely relaxed and calm for the first time that day.

Then suddenly I became aware that I was now in back of the one in the audience who was watching the woman on stage. Startled, I asked myself: What's this? Who am I now? And I realized that I was no one in particular—no-body. Simply pure Awareness—something without thoughts, without emotions. I was just there as this Awareness, watching. An incredible serenity swept through me, as this realization deepened and deepened. The woman agonizing on the stage finally became very small, insignificant, altogether unreal, as I sank more and more profoundly into the serenity. The suffering about the situation was utterly gone.

But the real test came the next day, once the blissful experience had faded. Upon awakening, and on a number of occasions thereafter, I questioned how I felt about my therapeutic error with the client. To my great astonishment, I felt a clear absence of guilt and shame. Of course, what I'd done wasn't something I felt good about, but I no longer felt bad. There was just a clear knowing that I'd learned some important lessons, nothing more. I was just going to go on with my life.

I realized that the observer exercise I'd experimented with had given me great rewards indeed. More and more deeply, from that point on, I knew that I was not a therapist; this was simply a role I was playing. And I further knew on a deep experiential level that I wasn't even a human being playing the role—or even someone watching the role. I was pure and simple Consciousness that was totally untouched by my drama as a therapist. Such relief and joy!

I have since shared the technique with a number of people. I've seen that it can work in any number of situations. And from my experience, if you can sincerely and persistently do this process throughout the day, you will begin to directly experience what it is that is simply watching it all—the true essence of who you are: pure Awareness. It is that which never changes, that which is never touched by anything that is going on, that which never suffers. And as this Awareness, you simply observe the drama dispassionately— and yet utterly compassionately at the same time. This is an experience of your true nature: free, loving, and at peace.

* * * * *

So it's clear that roles in themselves are not inherently problem-atic. They can even be a lot of fun to play. We can be very present and involved in these roles, and at the same time, we can sit and watch the show and really enjoy ourselves. We just have to stay alert to the fact that we are not the roles we are playing. Nor are we the human being who is playing the roles; this is just another role. What we are is pure Consciousness, taking on all these roles.

To truly experience this, an important step is to learn how to become the witness of our own lives. In this process, experiencing the true Self seems to happen naturally. An effortless surrender of our identity with all the roles occurs—along with the suffering that goes with them. And it's easier than we might believe.

CHAPTER NINE

Detaching from the Body

Remove the concept that you are your body. Remove it by truly, deeply, earnestly, alertly, and in surrender, asking, "Who am I really?"

—Gangagi

D ETACHING OUR IDENTITY FROM OUR BODY is probably even harder than detaching it from the roles we play in life. In fact, in my experience, just bringing up the subject of detaching from the body can actually cause nervousness or resistance in some people. For those who have a strong identification with the body, this idea can be threatening. For others, the body is important because they have experienced it as a vehicle toward greater spiritual awareness (for example, through Hatha Yoga), and they are therefore wary when encountering the term "detaching" in regard to it, believing this to mean a denial of it.

I'd therefore like to clarify again what I mean when I speak about "detaching" from the body, or when I state that "you are not the body" or that the body is "unreal." First of all, I am not referring to dissociating from the body or denying it in any way. As many of us who have experienced these states will attest, dissociation and denial offer very limited relief from suffering, if any at all.

As I use the term, "detaching" from the body does not refer to detaching one's awareness from the body or to seeing the body as "bad" or in any way ignoring it. Indeed, true detachment can actually enhance your awareness of the body, as well as your love for it; as I've discussed earlier, it can even help you to take better care of it. More importantly, what detaching from the body does is help you to detach from the *suffering* that the identification with the body can cause.

Secondly, I'd like to clarify what I mean when I state that the body is not who you are or that the body is unreal. This is not denying the body's existence on the third-dimensional, dualistic level, where it undeniably does exist. When I speak in these terms, I am referring to that which is experienced from the perspective of the Self. If you have had a true glimpse of the Self, you will know what I mean: From the perspective of directly experiencing all that exists as Consciousness, the body (indeed, all form) has a sense of illusion about it, a feeling of unreality.

Even without this direct experience of Self, it can be understood that the body is not who we are, in that it is only one very small, limited part of us. The true essence of who we are includes *everything*—all bodies, all that exists in creation. And, because the identification with our own particular body is so strong for most of us, I generally speak in extreme terms of it not being who we are in order to make it easier to get past this limited, habitual identification with it.

With this preamble, in hopes of easing any resistance to the notion of detaching from the body, let's now take a look at what this process actually entails.

Attaining a state of detachment from the body is usually difficult because most of us have deeply-embedded conditioning that this form is who we are. From an early age, we've been taught that we were born, we get bigger, we get old, and then we die. As a result, when asked how we are, we often answer how our body is: "I'm sick," "I have a cold," "I've lost weight," rather than "My body is sick," "My body has a cold," or "My body has lost weight."

Many religions, perhaps inadvertently, also teach that we are bodies. They tell us that we *have* a soul—not that we *are* a soul (and that we have a body). So people believing this go around feeling that they, as their body, have to somehow be careful and "take care of" their soul. This is all part of the paradigm under which most of the world is struggling, based on the illusion that each one of us is the particular, separate, individual form we each call "me."

As becomes only too apparent, this belief that we are the body creates much suffering. This is because inherently—like all form—the body is imperfect, is subject to disease and aging, and eventually dies. And if we believe that this is who we are, then this is what we believe is happening to *us*. Our sense of well-being and our feelings of self-worth are all attached to how our body happens to look, what it is capable of doing, how healthy it happens to be, and what others may think about it.

Certainly this identification causes more suffering to some than to others. Some people were fortunate enough to have been born with relatively healthy, strong, and attractive bodies. But even the most fortunate have to face, from time to time, an illness in the body, injuries to it, and its eventual aging and death. So, although there are degrees of suffering involved in the identification with the body, there is always suffering of some kind, simply because the body is vulnerable to all the same laws of the universe that all other forms are: injury and disease, aging and death.

Ways in Which We Suffer Due to Body Identification

There are three specific ways I have found in which identification with the body commonly causes people suffering: a) when our bodies experience either illness or injury; b) when we don't happen to like the way our body (or parts of it) look; and c) when thoughts or feelings about dying arise.

In my experience, people tend to numb themselves as best they can to suffering imposed on them by their belief that they are their bodies. Feeling somehow that this suffering is inevitable and that nothing can be done about it, they do what they can to push it into their unconscious mind. But it is nonetheless there, always nibbling away at their awareness in some way or another, and often affecting many of their actions and attitudes in life.

There are times, for numerous reasons, when people can no longer avoid suffering around their physical bodies, and they seek relief from this suffering through medical, religious, therapeutic, or self-help approaches. These approaches tend to include either changing the body itself in some way, changing the beliefs about the body, or accepting the body the way it is. All these approaches can provide some relief to people in their suffering. However, I have found they all also ultimately have limited results.

Altering the Body Itself

The first approach, for example—altering the body itself—can have certain favorable results. Certainly, when someone with an illness finds a cure for it, there can be considerable relief. People who alter how their body looks can also feel better about themselves, if their body is successfully changed to how they think they want it. They often seem happier, at least for a time, after they've dieted and exercised to lose weight or after they've had plastic surgery.

But this relief is often sorely limited. So often, people who significantly alter their body tend to continue judging what they look like, no matter what; they are never quite satisfied with what has changed. They can never quite reach the perfection they want and are always seeing what more can be done. It can be a painful process to watch.

I once knew a woman like this who had nine different plastic surgery procedures done to her poor body. I personally did not find her body all that unattractive to begin with, but she certainly did. And, over and over again, after each surgery, she would come home feeling pleased with herself. With each procedure, she felt she was coming closer to "perfection." But she could never reach the perfect state. Even after nine procedures, she still felt a sense of dissatisfaction with how she looked.

She finally had to cease the operations because doctors told her she was seriously threatening her health. Unfortunately, she never saw the meaninglessness of what she'd been doing. She was left believing that had she been able to continue altering her body's appearance, she would have finally achieved true happiness.

This isn't to say that people should never seek to change their physical body in any way. Of course not—dieting, exercising, and even plastic surgery can often produce a sense of well-being and increased self-esteem. The point is that if we hope these kinds of changes will end our suffering around how we feel about our body, we will be sorely disappointed. This is because physically changing the body does not strike at the root of the suffering; it only touches the symptom.

Changing Beliefs

The second approach, changing one's beliefs, has become more and more popular in therapeutic and self-help arenas and has offered relief to many people. For example, if someone is unhappy about how their body looks, they might be helped to develop new beliefs about what makes a body "attractive," so that their body might eventually look more attractive to them. Or they might be encouraged to develop more accurate beliefs about what their body actually does look like, thereby realizing they've been misjudging how they look.

If a person is suffering from ill health, this belief-changing approach might encourage them to develop new beliefs about how to create a healthy body. Metaphysical literature abounds with these methods, teaching basically that we create our physical health through our mental beliefs.

In fact, much of this literature is addressed to people with "terminal" diseases who are faced with the possibility of immanent death. These people are assured that, with the correct beliefs, it is actually possible to overcome a terminal disease.

Although perhaps more effective for many problems than the first approach (changing the body itself), this approach too has its limitations. I personally followed it for a number of years and guided many other people on this course as well. I found that if practiced religiously, this method could help turn a negative outlook on life (or on the body) into a more positive one, which could bring significant relief to the person.

It could even create better health for people—and, in rare instances, even appear to help them avert a predicted death for a while. (I use the term "appear" because, of course, there can never be hard "proof" about any of this.) But the important contribution of these belief-changing teachings, I believe, is not keeping the body alive, but the positive and therefore happier attitude a person can adopt while the body is handling a serious disease.

I have also found that, however powerful this belief-changing method can be for relieving suffering, it is ultimately quite limited in its success rate for most people. This may be partially due to the fact that people who attempt to make these changes often start too late in life. Their beliefs (many of them unconscious, to boot) are simply too deeply ingrained. The work involved can therefore be gargantuan and endless.

But the low success rate that I've seen over the years may be also due to the fact that all we are doing with this approach is replacing one belief for another. Unfortunately, beliefs are only that—something we *believe* in—not something we *know*. They are not a true, direct understanding of Truth. So long as we simply believe something to be so, we will never experience the continuous serenity or the lack of fear we long for in life. This is because beliefs, no matter how close to the Truth they may be, are constantly challenged by other beliefs we have, by beliefs other people have, and by our experiences in life that seem to contradict them. Simply replacing them with other beliefs is therefore ultimately ineffective in bringing lasting relief from suffering. Only true knowing can give us this.

Accepting the Body as It Is

The third common approach to relieve suffering around issues with the body—learning to accept the body just as it is—is perhaps the most effective for some people, especially if they are facing a serious illness or the approach of death. But this is only so if acceptance is taught as a wise and realistic approach to life, rather than a passive, depressive resignation to fate.

Unfortunately, I have encountered this resignation only too often in people who have been deeply inculcated with a certain religious belief that states that we humans are on this planet to suffer—it's what life is about. We must accept our fate and have faith that some day, if we have been "good," we will experience an afterlife in which there will be no more suffering. Not only is this type of teaching frightfully depressing, it doesn't remove the suffering; all it does is attempt to explain it.

A very depressed woman, Barbara, came to see me for therapy a few years back, telling me that whenever she would just barely begin to achieve some semblance of happiness in her life, an automatic sense of fear and doubt would immediately take over. In exploring this with her, we discovered that, as an ex-Catholic, she was dealing with a deeply rooted belief that the nature of life was suffering. In fact, in her belief system, suffering was actually a good thing; the more you suffered, the better a person you were and the more likely to go to Heaven after death. Her fear was that if she were to stop suffering, she would somehow cease to be a good person and might ruin her chances for Heaven.

I think we all probably know "recovering" Catholics who suffer from this unfortunate delusion. (Of course, Catholicism doesn't have a patent on this belief system about suffering. Other religions can lay claim to it as well.)

Clearly, a passive, resigned acceptance of suffering does not give us relief from it. Even the most realistic and uplifting, simple acceptance of what is can ultimately be ineffective as well. If we still believe ourselves to be the body, then unavoidable suffering can still occur, simply because the body is imperfect and impermanent. I think few people can truly be at peace with the body's inherent imperfection and impermanence if they believe that this is who they are. They somehow need to experience, beyond belief, beyond doubt, that they are that which is untouched by any illness or by death. This need seems to be natural; I believe it arises from the deep intuitive knowing we all have that in truth we ARE that which is beyond the touch of mortality.

So how can this intuitive knowing be reached? And how can the seemingly inevitable suffering due to identification with the body truly be resolved? As you've probably surmised by now, the answer is in somehow detaching from identification with the body. If we truly know that who we are is something beyond the body—something that is totally untouched by how the body looks, feels, acts, or survives—only then can suffering about the body truly cease.

In the next three chapters we will look more closely at the basic ways in which we seem to cause suffering for ourselves due to our identification with the body, and then specifically at how we can begin dissolving this identification.

CHAPTER TEN

Dealing with Health Issues

If you believe "I am sick," then there is suffering and the attempt to escape suffering. Stop all attempts to escape and ask yourself, "Who is sick?"

—Gangagi

SO HOW DO WE CAUSE OURSELVES SUFFERING when it comes to health issues in our life? If you have ever had the misfortune of experiencing either a serious disease or injury, you have undoubtedly suffered from some form of fear, anger, or depression—on top of the immense physical pain that can also occur. It's only natural—especially if you, like many people, have your identity deeply attached to your body.

In some ways, I believe, this reaction of anger and fear to serious illness and injury to the body is caused by certain values that seem profoundly embedded in our culture. As the dozens of magazines on health and fitness published today attest, our culture seems to worship the healthy body. Modern medicine, perhaps the most highly-revered "God" in our Western society, promotes this worship. Its main goal appears to be keeping bodies alive and as healthy as it can for as long as possible—as if this alone assures the quality of life that everyone wants.

There also seems to be an extraordinary emphasis in our culture on strength and fitness. Of course, making this important in life can be helpful; it feels good to have a strong and fit body. It enables us to enjoy life in many ways. But so often, the preoccupation with fitness seems overdone. In fact, I believe the extreme emphasis on both health and fitness can at times do much damage.

The worst problem I see is that it ignores (and actually denies) the fact that bodies naturally do get sick from time to time; they are not designed to be perfect. They're part of the material world, subject to illness, injury, and eventual death. No one can successfully avoid this fact. And yet, living amidst the tremendous emphasis in our culture on health and fitness, it's hard not to feel pressure to keep our body constantly healthy and fit at all costs. If we don't manage this, it is often assumed that something is flawed or deficient about us.

To make matters worse, New Age literature on healing has unfortunately added even more pressure on people. Although, as I mentioned earlier, this literature can be helpful in some important ways, its emphasis on our responsibility in "creating" diseases in our body has managed to produce in certain people what I call the "New-Age Neurosis." Hearing that their negative thoughts and beliefs create their illnesses, these people have responded by dumping guilt and shame on themselves whenever their body becomes ill or is injured. Adding insult to injury, not only are they in pain, they also feel they've done something wrong to create this. Such craziness!

In certain ways, it does seem as if we can create both illness and healing in our bodies; there does seem to be truth to the assertion that the mind has some control over the body. But what is usually forgotten in this common interpretation of the "mind-body connection" is that it works the other way around as well: The body also appears to have some control over what is happening in the mind. This is supported by the number of mental and emotional illnesses that seem to disappear almost magically when people start taking antidepressants, hormones, lithium, or thyroid medication, all of which alter the body's chemistry.

Something else seems to be missing in much of the New Age literature concerning healing the body through the mind. It is the fact that many, many people, who ardently and assiduously apply the principles involved, simply do not succeed in healing their bodies. This fact is usually ignored or explained away, much to the detriment of people who end up feeling they have "failed" in healing their bodies, and that somehow they just aren't "spiritual" enough to the make the principles work.

It seems clear to me that something else is definitely at play here. It can be argued that the people who fail to heal their bodies just haven't used the metaphysical principles well or long enough. I don't believe this is always the case, by a long shot. I believe a force is at work that overrides anything the mind may set out to do. Some people might refer to this force as *karma*, which is said to be automatically set in motion by actions one has committed previously (either in this or in another life) and must be somehow balanced.

Another explanation that is sometimes offered is that the person who has been unsuccessful in healing their body through metaphysical principles is suffering from the illness or injury because this is what Spirit (or God or whatever) has deemed to be best to help bring spiritual awakening into their consciousness. This idea may also have some merit. People who have undergone serious injuries and illness do often seem to make considerable positive changes in their lives. At times, remarkable spiritual awakening experiences do occur.

Whatever the reasons may be for the illnesses or injuries people experience, and whatever the reasons may be for why they can't recover from them at a given time no matter what they do physically or mentally—the fact remains that bodies get sick and become injured. It's a natural phenomenon. And it's important to see the suffering we can experience by ignoring this fact and allowing the pressure our society seems to put on us about the inherent superiority of healthy, fit bodies.

Getting Free from the Identification with the Body

Even more important, however, is to understand what lies beneath the extreme emphasis on health and fitness: a belief system based on fear—fear that an ill or injured body means an ill or injured identity, a deficient or flawed self. What suffering this can cause! Therefore, what is important is to focus on how we can let go of this belief system, so that we are free simply to be and feel good about ourselves—no matter what state of health or fitness our body happens to be in.

Before discussing how to do this, however, I'd like to make clear what I mean when I speak of "suffering" in terms of the physical body. I am NOT referring to physical pain. Physical pain seems to be a fact of life, part of being with a physical body. At times, there seems little way to get around it (although even this pain, as I will describe later, can become much more manageable if the psychological suffering is not added to it). What I mean by "suffering" is the psychological suffering—both emotional and mental—that we commonly add to the physical pain. This is something we can eliminate from our lives. We can discover, in fact, that it is utterly unnecessary.

So, with this distinction between physical pain and psychological suffering made, let's turn now to how this suffering can be alleviated. It is, of course, through learning how to detach from your identification with the body.

Surrendering to the Pain

Much research has been done on pain and how people can increase and decrease it in their bodies. The results of this research show quite consistently that the more people resist and fight the pain, the worse it becomes. And conversely, of course, the more they accept and relax into it, the weaker the pain becomes.

I can personally attest to this. Over a number of years, I experienced bouts of intensely painful colitis with which no health practitioner or doctor had ever been totally successful in helping me. For years, especially after I learned that my father was dying of colon cancer, I would enter into severe fear and anger whenever I would begin to experience intestinal pain. As I entered more and more deeply into my fearful and angry thoughts about what might happen to me, the pain would continue to deepen. The worst was when I'd begin projecting into the future about it. What if I never got over it? What if I ended up in the hospital with it? Sometimes I'd go into guilt, regret, or shame about it: How did I cause it? If only I'd done something about it earlier....

One afternoon, as I lay on my bed in great pain, thinking these thoughts, I finally began seeing the craziness I was creating in my mind—all stemming from fear and from resistance to simply what was. I decided that rather than fighting the pain, for a change I would just accept it. Much to my relief, the pain immediately began to lessen.

Some time later, when I was experiencing another bout of the same pain, I decided to try to go even further with the act of acceptance. Rather than simply allowing the pain to be and refraining from thinking about the possible dire scenarios concerning my condition, I decided to actually *surrender* to the pain—just give myself to it completely.

What an incredible experience this was! Not only did the pain lessen and my body experience a much needed sense of relaxation—but an unexpected peace and bliss began washing through me as well. As I lay in bed, still very aware of the pain in my abdomen, I was soon floating in a cloud of gentle and detached awareness, serenely watching it. I was actually luxuriating in a total state of surrender, while the pain continued. I was no longer suffering because of the pain; it was simply something vaguely present within my awareness that I could focus on if I chose—or not. This experience lasted for almost an hour, at which point I finally fell asleep, totally at peace with the fact that I was once again undergoing the dreaded intestinal pain I had suffered from for so many years.

Since that experience, I have actually learned to *embrace* and *welcome* the pain when it appears. Such a difference this makes now when pain or illness occur! The discovery I have made is that my resistance to pain not only increases the pain itself—it also keeps me attached to my sense of identity with the body. And acceptance of my pain and illness, surrendering to it and actually welcoming it, on the other hand, help me to effortlessly detach from this identification.

Having Compassion for Your Body

Another method that has assisted me in detaching my identification from my body when I've found myself ill or suffering from a bodily injury is to develop a strong compassion for my body in its pain. I become aware that this poor entity, my body, is struggling valiantly to heal itself from some terrible insult that's been thrust on it. What it most needs from me at these times (besides help from appropriate health practitioners when that is called for) is love, support, and compassion.

Although understanding this intellectually in the past, I still often found it hard to actually experience compassion for my body when it was in pain. My fear and my anger at the inconvenience it was causing me were just too powerful. But then I discovered something that enormously facilitated my moving into compassion. This involved taking the time to mentally step outside my body and see it objectively.

I was once suffering terribly from a severe headache I'd had for several days. No matter what I did or what I took to clear the headache, it kept getting worse; it would not let go. I found myself getting more and more irritated at it—and then fearful that maybe something might really be wrong with me.

After a spell of frustrated tears about it, I finally let go for a moment and gave up in despair. Suddenly, I found myself standing outside myself in my awareness, looking at my body. My poor head! I could see it was throbbing in utter agony. My response to it at this point was one I might have in seeing a puppy in pain. My heart immediately reached out to it and enfolded it in love. I felt so bad at how I'd been treating my head, adding all my negative emotions to the pain it was already feeling. I sat there in my mind's eye, holding and stroking my head, just pouring love into it.

Giving my head this soft, gentle healing energy instead of anger and fear, of course, helped it finally to relax and eventually let go of the headache. It was obvious to me afterwards that my callous treatment of my headache had only made it worse. Compassion for it as a living being in pain made all the difference.

But what really struck me was how the experience of detaching myself from my body had made this realization so clear. It had served to remind me that I wasn't my headache or even my head. Who I truly was, was untouched by the headache. It was as if the headache were actually happening to someone else. It had nothing to do with me and so could not affect my sense of self or my well-being. I was therefore free to give true comfort and healing energy to it.

Dealing with Severe or Chronic Illness and Pain

I realize that the techniques I have described here—surrendering to the pain and having compassion for your body—may seem helpful for minor illnesses or pain, but, you may be asking, what about when you are confronted with severe pain or an on-going illness? In these cases, truly detaching your identification from the body can seem insurmountable. Pain does seem to anchor us into the body. But I do believe detaching is possible, and, in the end, severe or chronic pain can actually be seen as our ally in this process.

I have a good friend who has been suffering from chronic fatigue syndrome for over eight years. If you have ever known anyone with this disease, you know just how debilitating it can be. It not only causes great on-going distress in the body, it also interferes with a person's entire life. Often someone with the disease cannot even work. And, of course, any social life or pleasurable activities they once enjoyed eventually disappear from their lives. They have no energy to do anything much but sleep or lie exhausted in bed. I heard about one person who actually decided after five years of this kind of life that it wasn't worth living—and she killed herself.

My friend Karen certainly had come close to doing just that on a number of occasions. Although she has just barely been able to keep a psychotherapy practice going throughout most of the years she's had the disease, it is about all she can do. Frequently, much to the irritation of her clients, she has to cancel appointments—sometimes at the last moment.

Throughout the years, Karen has sought help from every source she hears about. Help from the medical profession gave out quickly. She then turned to every source of alternative healing she could find. At times, it looked hopeful; she would find some relief and feel that she had finally found something that would help her to heal. But always, after a time, it would become apparent that the healing was only temporary—or illusory. She wasn't really getting any better.

For the first six years or so of this dreadful experience, Karen's attitude toward her illness was filled with anger, frustration, fear, and depression. It was also filled with great self-doubt and despair.

What terrible thing had she done to "deserve" this? Why had God abandoned her? The many years she'd spent on a spiritual path seemed to offer her nothing that could give her any real solace.

Then there came a time when she was rather seriously considering suicide; she was feeling the most depressed and desperate she'd ever felt. As often happens at such times, a "miracle" occurred: she came across the spiritual teachings of the direct path through the Papaji book, *Wake up and Roar*—the one I myself first read. With great joy, she latched onto something in this book that she now sees as the life raft that has kept her here on the planet—the teachings about surrender.

Finally giving up fighting and resisting what the disease had done to her life, she simply decided to surrender to it—to just give up her entire struggle, even her desire to get well, her desire for anything to be at all different from the way it was. And she moved into complete and absolute surrender to what her life had become.

What ended up happening to Karen moves me so deeply, it brings tears to my eyes every time I think about her. I have never witnessed such a transformation in anyone else. It didn't happen overnight, and it wasn't without intermittent struggle. But it did not take long, either. This decision to surrender her will to the force that was in charge of her life (a force she now calls "Self") has created an entirely different woman.

Her symptoms continue. Her life is just about as restricted as it's ever been. BUT, Karen is happy. In fact, she's often radiantly happy—totally serene and accepting of her life. She finds joy in the smallest pleasures. She laughs a lot. She no longer takes her life so seriously. Through the simple act of surrender, she has come to know beyond a doubt that she is not her body; she is pure Being, serene and joyful Awareness that is untouched by illness or anything happening in the life of her body.

And she has endless love and compassion for others in pain. I know she has always been an excellent therapist, but what a gift she must now be giving her clients—this radiant joy and purity of Presence. She has simply given her life into the hands of the Beloved, totally trusting that whatever is happening to her is in her best interests. She has no doubt about this. And I have never known her to be so happy and at peace with herself in her entire life.

Karen, to me, is a living testimonial to the power of surrender in one's life. Her body may never recover from chronic fatigue—or it may. What is important is that it no longer really matters to her. All that she lives for now is the joyful bliss that she consistently experiences in the process of surrendering her will to that of her Self. That is enough—and is certainly more than most people on this planet are ever blessed to receive.

So it seems that even chronic and severe illness need not stand in the way of detaching from our identity with the body and from the suffering that this misidentification appears to produce. Surrender, which naturally reveals love, compassion, and joy, truly seems to be the key.

CHAPTER ELEVEN

When You Don't Like Your Body Image

The body gets old and one day it dies. But who you are is not touched by any of this. You are eternal.

—Papaji

A SECOND AREA where body-identification can bring great distress is when we don't happen to like our body the way it is. You may be fortunate enough to like the way your body looks and not experience much of this kind of suffering. But most people seem to have some reservations—or a lot—about their body's appearance and suffer a great deal because of this.

It is particularly difficult that our culture not only worships the healthy and fit body, but also the beautiful and youthful one. There seems to be enormous pressure in the West to have as beautiful and youthful a body as possible. From what I've experienced and seen, this makes life difficult even for those who have what are considered "beautiful" bodies, because even these people must eventually experience the process of aging.

In fact, it is sometimes even harder for people who had a beautiful body in their youth to undergo the inevitable process of aging. Often, having deeply invested their sense of identity and their feeling of self-worth in their body, when the aging process becomes apparent, they are particularly vulnerable to deep suffering. We are all familiar with the stereotype of the pathetic aging starlet who feels her life is over now that her body is no longer considered beautiful.

As much recent literature describes, the process of aging in the American culture is even more difficult than it is in many others across the world. Here, there is no automatic respect given to someone of advanced age, as there often is in other cultures. At best, a sort of patronizing pity is bestowed upon elderly individuals in our society; at worst, a dismissal, an ignoring, or even an abusive attitude. Underlying all this, an attitude seems to exist that the aging body is something undesirable and repulsive. Women with aging bodies, in particular, seem to be the butt of many jokes revealing this attitude.

These attitudes and the inevitable suffering they cause would not be so prevalent—or indeed, might not even exist—if so many people did not identify themselves as their bodies. Their sense of self-worth and identity would not be dependent on what their bodies happened to look like. But as it is, most people, especially in our culture, do see themselves as bodies, and so this suffering continues.

You may be someone who believes you are not the body. You know your identity to be your mind or your personality—or even your "spirit" inside the body. As will become clear in later chapters, even identifying yourself with what you feel is inside your body has its own form of suffering. Even aside from this, if you are still suffering from time to time due to how your body happens to look, this probably indicates that your "knowing" that you are not the body is still intellectual. Knowing something with your mind is an important start, but for the suffering to completely cease, a true and direct understanding must take place.

Releasing Judgments about Your Body Image

One of the things that keeps us hooked into believing ourselves to be our bodies is our judgments about them. Negativity about anything always serves to keep us in bondage to that about which we are negative. So a first step toward freedom from body-identity is to do what you can to release whatever negative judgments you may have about your body. The following is a technique I've used with clients to help them do this.

Exercise: *Releasing Negative Judgments About Your Body*

1. Write down all the judgments you have about your body. In-clude all negative thoughts and feelings you have and also the negative messages you can remember that were given to you in childhood about bodies in general and your own in particular.
2. On a large piece of paper, draw a picture of your body (prefer-ably undressed). With words written directly on the drawing, write down the negative thoughts, feelings, and judgments about the different parts of the body. Include all aches, pains, and injuries your body is currently handling. Also write what your body is saying about itself.
3. Sit and look at your drawing, allowing this representation of your negative attitudes toward your body to sink in. Feel the pain that your judgments cause you. Feel your body's sorrow in response to them. Become aware of something obvious but usually forgotten: Your body is doing the very best it can. All it knows is how to be the way it naturally is. Heaping blame and shame onto it for how it looks or feels accomplishes nothing but suffering. Realize the pointlessness of your judgments of your body.

    At this point, I offer a caution: As you become aware of the suffering you have been causing yourself through your judg-ments, be careful now not to progress into guilt and shame about these judgments. (This is another aspect of the "New-Age Neu-rosis:" feeling guilty about feeling guilty or ashamed of feeling ashamed.) Simply mentally note the feelings and insights and let them be.
4. If there is a way, at this point, to safely light a fire and put your drawing into it, do this. Rituals of this sort can be very helpful for releasing feelings, thoughts, and judgments. Watch the drawing disappear into the flames and feel all your judgments, negative thoughts, feelings, and memories release into the fire along with

it. (If building a fire is not safe, tearing the drawing up into tiny pieces and throwing them into the trash can work.)

5. Now close your eyes and become aware of how your body is feeling. If there are parts of your body that are not relaxed, gently focus your attention there and coax them into relaxation. Tune into your love for your body. Become aware of all it has done for you, all that it has survived—often without your help. Feel gratitude about this.

6. Finally, write a love letter to your body. Include your gratitude to it for keeping going at all costs during your life. Tell your body all the things you do like and love about it. Give it positive love messages. Thank it for all the pleasures it has given you. Let it know that you are going to try to allow it to be simply the way it is and be more accepting of it.

After you have written this letter, sit with it and allow what you have said and your commitments to sink in. Allow a sense of trust about your body to enter you, accepting that perhaps you have the body that is perfect for you at this time.

The next step, then, is to become truly aware that this body is not who you are. It is simply a vehicle that you as pure Consciousness are using to experience the material world. That is all. There is no reason to attach any other significance to it. There is no reason to feel either ashamed or proud of how it looks or functions, no reason to feel anything about the process of aging that is taking place. This is just a natural process of all form. It means nothing about YOU.

Detaching from Your Body

Completing an exercise such as I have outlined above can be very helpful in releasing the suffering caused through judgments and negative feelings and thoughts about your body. It may even be a necessary first step in releasing the suffering, since, as I've mentioned, negativity toward something tends to keep us attached to it.

However, I have found over and over again that these kinds of exercises are often not enough. The conditioning that we are our bodies is usually too powerful and ingrained, so a further step must be taken. This involves doing whatever you can to truly experience a sense of detachment from your identification with your body. The following two exercises have been very useful to me in doing this.

The first is an exercise that I have actually had a lot of fun with. It involves detaching from your physical form in your awareness and watching yourself in everything you do.

Exercise: *Standing Outside Your Body*

In your mind, stand or sit right next to your body during all of its activities and observe it. Become aware of everything this fascinating thing—your body—is doing. Watch your hands (such amazing instruments!) in all their various activities. Watch your legs, your feet, your stomach—all the different parts of the body you can see. Then, in your mind's eye, watch your head and your face. Become aware of what a complex, fascinating vehicle and tool your body actually is.

Now become aware simultaneously about what is going on inside of this body on the physical level. Blood runs through every part of it, all on its own. Food digests on its own. The lungs breathe on their own. So much is happening inside this form; it's totally mind-boggling! Absorb the mystery of all this. Your body is wondrous, indeed.

Once all this has been experienced, begin to be aware of what is going on in the mind inside this body. Watch the thoughts and feelings as they pass through. Also observe the body's reactions to these thoughts and feelings. Be aware of all the passing sensations that are occurring within this marvelous machine.

This can be done at almost any time, during any activity or non-activity, although it is obviously easier at some times more than others. Most fun for me are the times when my body is engaged in interesting activities, such as eating or moving in some way, but it can be equally interesting when I am performing mundane, every-day rituals, such as showering or driving a car. I am sometimes struck with such wonder: How does the body know how to do all this?

During this process of observing everything the body is involved in from the outside, from time to time also reflect on who *you* are—the consciousness watching all this. Although you will have the sensation of being outside your body, you will still have the awareness of being inside your body as well. This can help you to realize that who you are has no specific location; you are both inside and outside your body. In fact, if you really check, you'll find that you have no boundaries at all. There is no outline where you end and the air begins.

I found that after doing this exercise for awhile, a greater and greater appreciation began forming in me for my body. Seeing it so objectively really assisted me in releasing both judgments about my body and my identity with it. It became this wondrous little form I was simply playing with, as I explored the world of phenomenality. Such a feeling of release and freedom this brings!

Exercise: *All Bodies Are an Expression of the One Self*

Another focus you can have as you step outside your body is to look around at all the other bodies around you. Take in the infinite variety of them. Experience the marvel of how Self can appear in so many different shapes and forms. See the unique beauty of each one. Observe them as if you were someone from another universe. Then look back at your own body and see that this is just one of many forms—one with its own unique attributes. Suspend all judgment about any of the attributes—just observe them.

Now realize that every one of these bodies is an aspect of YOU. As Self, who you are includes *all* bodies. You are also the space within which they appear. You are all that exists; everything is YOU. You are the Source of all these forms.

I once knew a man who was anxiously intent on keeping his body in shape, mainly through jogging. Jonathan felt he needed to jog in order to keep a body image with which he was happy. He was in his mid-forties and beginning to put on weight, and this was unacceptable to him. So, almost religiously, he made it a priority to take time to jog every day.

One day I happened to pass him on the street as he was coming to the end of his jogging for the day. I was amazed at the elation on his face. His whole being seemed to emanate an ecstatic joy. I was happy to see him stopping to greet me, because I was curious about what was going on with him. I knew that jogging can produce a kind of high for people, but what I saw on his face seemed quite beyond an endorphin high.

After he caught his breath, he told me what he had just experienced. He said that jogging had started out that day pretty much as it usually did: He ran along the same streets and pathways, seeing much the same scenery as he always did. He maintained his usual inner sense about his breathing, his pulse, and his leg muscles.

Suddenly, he said, out of the blue, he felt a strange sensation. He surprisingly found his awareness outside of his body. He explained that this was not like astral travel in which you find yourself completely separated from your physical body; he was simply outside his body in his awareness. He was aware of his body from the outside of it, not just the inside. He could see his legs moving, one after the other. He could see one shoe and then the other. His arms were also alternating, moving forward and backward. He could also somehow see his breath. All this, understandably, considerably changed his experience of running. He was not only the runner; he was also the observer of the runner.

Then, he explained, something else began occurring. He found himself looking around at all the other bodies he was passing. Some of them were running also, some were walking; others were standing or sitting. Although every body had similar characteristics—arms, legs, head, etc.—they were all so different. He found himself marveling at the variety of these things we call "bodies."

At some point, he indicated, he "dropped into a whole different dimension." No longer was he seeing all of the bodies as different from each other—they all became obviously one and the same thing. All bodies, including his own, were made of the same ineffable essence. And, the truly amazing thing, he said, was that he realized that this essence was who he, in reality, was. There was nothing else that existed. There was only the One. Indescribable joy rushed through him as this realization dawned.

He told me he floated along in this ecstasy for the full half-hour that was left of his run. He continued to be aware of his body as it moved, but it was like watching it from a distance. He was no longer confined to feeling his awareness inside his body. He could be present in that experience if he wanted to—at times, of course, it could be totally pleasurable—but he was no longer limited to that one experience. He could be inside all bodies at once—or outside of them—or nowhere in particular. It didn't matter. He was free to simply be awareness.

He told me some time later that his experience of jogging after that—and indeed, of doing almost anything—had totally altered. He had come to know on a profound, experiential level that he was not his body. I believe he continued to jog as much as before—but his anxiety about his body image had greatly diminished. "So my body's getting a little flabby," he said. "So what. That's what bodies do." He'd come to accept the inevitable aging of this human form, because he'd experienced on a direct level that this was not who he really was.

CHAPTER TWELVE

Facing the Fear of Death

To be a living being is not the ultimate state: there is something beyond, much more wonderful, which is neither being nor non-being, neither living nor non-living. It is a state of pure awareness, beyond the limitations of space and time. Once the illusion that the body-mind is oneself is abandoned, death loses its terror; it becomes a part of living.

—Nisargadatta

*P*ERHAPS THE MOST DIFFICULT EXPERIENCE that identifying with the body can produce for people is the fear of death. You may be one of the rare and fortunate people who has no real fear of death. You may truly know that it will not be YOU who dies when your body dies. But most people do not know this as a certainty and therefore have at least some fear of death, if not a great deal.

People strive to alleviate this fear in a number of different ways. Many turn to religion for guidance. Most religions attempt to address the fear of death by telling us that we have a soul that lives on after the death of the body. This information is probably helpful for some people. But unfortunately, even those who very badly want to believe this can still suffer from uncertainty. This belief requires faith that a soul and an afterlife exist, and some people just are not convinced of this. They want proof; they want to know beyond a doubt. As I've noted before, faith and belief are not true knowing.

Furthermore, many religions add an important adjunct to this teaching that counteracts much of the solace it could bring. They tell us that our soul will only go to heaven if we're "good;" otherwise, it might go to purgatory or even hell. I have found this to be a horrendous teaching. Perhaps originally designed to keep people's behavior in conformance with society's moral laws, it has produced, I believe, more suffering for people than good. Fear about going to hell is now added to their already present fear about death.

Many people who grow up being taught about heaven and hell eventually drop this belief intellectually and believe they are therefore free of it—only to find at some point later in life that, underneath their intellectual overlay of disbelief in such things, the fear about death and hell is still in their subconscious minds, sometimes quite active and alive.

Some people I know have attempted to alleviate their fear of death by reading books about "near-death" experiences. The accounts in these books can be very convincing—as well as uplifting and moving—and they can provide people with some comfort about their own death or death of loved ones. But, in the end, these are still just secondhand accounts and cannot be substituted for true knowing about what happens at death.

Still another method I believe certain people use in an attempt to deal with fears around death is watching the plethora of movies that portray death over and over again in various forms. Even after so much outcry from parents and other concerned adults about the violence in movies these days, violent movies continue to be produced by the hundreds. So many of them contain totally uncalled for details of mutilated and dead bodies.

Sometimes I can't help but wonder why the people involved in creating such movies are drawn to producing these dreadful portrayals of death. (Or why people turn out in droves to watch them.) My guess is that, among other reasons, they are all attempting to deal with their fear about death stemming from their strongly ingrained identification with the body. Perhaps they hope that if they can see something they fear over and over again, they can begin to numb the fears they have about it. Unfortunately, numbing these fears does not eradicate them.

I once heard about a rather innovative attempt a man was making at dealing with his fears about death. He was trying to convince his mind that fearing death was illogical. He asked, "If I'm dead, truly dead (which he conceived of as having no awareness of any kind), how can I suffer? I won't even know I'm dead!" This kind of mental trick can almost work; the mind rejects the lack of logic. Unfortunately, the fear about death will remain, because logic does not reach the profound (perhaps even cellular) level in people from which the fear arises.

Perhaps the most common way that people in the American culture tend to deal with their fear of death is through denial—denial that death even exists. It is rather amazing at times to see the extent of this practice. Although in recent years hospice movements and death-and-dying educational programs have become more prevalent and have been producing greater awareness of this denial of death in our culture, death is still, by and large, something that is not spoken about. It is neatly hidden away in back wards of hospitals and retirement homes. It is carefully pushed out of sight so that people can avoid experiencing it in their everyday lives. In fact, people who do dwell on death at all or who want to talk about it are often considered "unstable" or unduly "morbid."

No matter how much denial is practiced about the reality of death in life, or how many other methods we might seek out to help us deal with our fears about it, sooner or later we all have to face it. We have to face the fact that our form was born, it's going to die, and, as a matter of fact, it started dying as soon as it was born. This is the nature of matter.

The good news is that we all have the opportunity to face death *before* it actually happens, if we choose. And, if we are so blessed, we may even discover what it is that does NOT die when the death of the physical body occurs. If we are smart enough to take this opportunity when it presents itself, we can go through the rest of our lives never fearing death again.

Certain individuals learn to do this through the process of having important loved ones die. They are forced to face the fact of death, whether they want to or not. And many experience that their loved ones really have not left them at all, even though their forms may have. This can produce a profound acceptance and serenity about death.

Others are given the opportunity to investigate and discover the reality of what happens at death by nearly escaping death through illness or injury. Often they are compelled to face it head-on and can eventually come to peace with its inevitability. If they are fortunate, they may even have vivid glimpses of what lies beyond death.

Most people are not blessed with these opportunities and continue through life making attempts, in one way or another, to quell their fear of death.

Resolving the Fear

As we've seen with other fears about the body, the only truly successful way to deal with them is through becoming aware of who we are beyond the body. In dealing with the fear of death, it is the same: The point is to get to know, on a direct experiential level, that that which dies at death is not YOU. It's having the experience that who you are is eternal, that you have never been born and therefore can never die. It's realizing that you are that which exists beyond these polarities.

The exercise in the previous chapter involving stepping outside the body can be helpful in creating this direct understanding of the eternal nature of one's Self. But for many, this is not enough. The fear of death for them is simply too profound and powerful. For these people, something more is necessary.

Exercise: *Plunging into the Core of Fear*

One way to experience the reality of who you are beyond death is through an inner journeying process, which can have dramatic and surprising results. The process involves directly facing a fear at the moment it arises. Rather than attempting to push the fear down, or distract yourself with thoughts or activity, you instead find the courage to immediately focus on the fear itself and plunge directly into the core of it. You investigate what is actually there. It can be an amazing discovery.

It can be a fairly quick exercise, or it can take some time, depending on the depth or complexity of the fear. I have done it myself on numerous occasions with various fears and have assisted others in doing it as well. If done with courage and sincerity, I have found, it can actually release the fear entirely.

I once assisted a woman with the process, someone who had come to me with enormous fear about her own death. Jane was terrified when I first suggested the process to her. "You mean, just jump in there, into the middle of the black hole?" That idea had never occurred to her; she had come, hoping I could give her some sort of convincing philosophy about life after death. I told her I didn't think my philosophy could solve her fears. She needed to explore and directly investigate death herself. She hesitated for a few minutes, but then decided she might as well give it a try.

At first, as I tried guiding her down into the "black hole" of fear she sensed inside her, she managed to dance all around the outside of it. Accustomed to dealing with her fears through her mind, she began talking once more about her thoughts and feelings about her fear of death, rather than diving into it directly. This, of course, was her mind's ploy to procrastinate. Persistently, I kept encouraging her to leave her mind behind, to stop following any thought whatsoever, and simply "jump" inside of the fear.

At last she made the plunge. Barely breathing, she reported, "It's so dark in here. Pitch black. I'm so alone—I'm really scared. Ooh, there are bodies in here, dead bodies … yukky stuff, body parts lying around … it's awful!"

I could feel her understandable revulsion to what she was seeing and her immediate desire to leave and come back from that frightening place, but I said, "That sounds really awful. … I know it must be hard to want to stay in there. But see if you can just keep going. Who you are is much bigger, much more powerful than all that stuff you're seeing. Just keep dropping, deeper and deeper into—go right to the core of it."

I heard her gasp, and then immediately she nervously began analyzing her fear. Unconvinced by what I'd told her, she had somehow managed to scramble to the top of the hole and was once again engaging her mind. And once again, gently, I coaxed her to let go of her mind and dive into the hole. After some deliberation, she finally did.

This time she told me it was just "blank"—nothing there. All gray. And that she was suddenly feeling very depressed. I reflected what she had said and encouraged her to drop even more deeply down inside of the depression. Soon she was reporting a sense of despair. "There's just nothing here, nothing at all. I'm all alone. This is like my life—just dead grayness. I hate it. It's awful." I could feel her attempting to find her way out of this miserable despair and encouraged her to instead continue dropping down into it. "Go to the very core of the despair and see what you find there."

A few moments later, she exclaimed, "Wow, I see a wild woman screaming. She's enraged—totally enraged! God, is she wild—she's just raving. (pause) Hey, it's me! This wild woman is me! She's all my anger, all my rage about..." Before she could get caught up into the story of her rage, I reflected that she had found rage at the core of her despair, and then encouraged her to keep dropping even further into the core of the rage.

She finally seemed to be involved deeply in the process at this point. Her mind and its fumbling attempts to prevent her from facing her fear had been left behind. She now began reporting different things: "I'm really falling now—like down this long, dark, narrow chute. But I'm seeing these little windows—gorgeous scenery and neat little scenes with people. I see my dog and my mother. ... Oh! I can stop myself from falling by just holding onto the window sills...."

If we had been doing another kind of process, one that simply explores the various (and often delightful) recesses of the mind, I would have encouraged her at this point to take a better look at these little scenes she was passing and see where they would take her. But I knew this would probably be a diversion—simply a new way the mind had found to distract her. So I instead coaxed her to keep dropping further down the chute. She finally followed my instructions, although reluctantly. She had finally found some relief from the despair and rage she had been experiencing and wanted to stop there. But I sensed there was so much more to discover.

Sure enough, within a few moments, after bypassing the delectable scenes through the windows she was passing, she found herself suddenly at the bottom of the chute. "I've landed! I'm not falling anymore...."

"So what's happening now?"

"Oh," she moaned, as a sweet delight washed across her features. "There's this incredible light coming toward me." I let her experience this for a few moments, then asked again, "What's happening now?" I saw a tear appear in her eye and then run down her cheek. "Such beauty, such incredible beauty ... someone's here with me ... they're doing something to me ... I don't know what, but it feels so good. (pause) There are these beings here, like angels. I think I'm being anointed or something...."

A radiance began shining from her face. I decided to allow her to linger there for perhaps another minute or two to see what would happen. Tears began running down her face. I could only guess at what she was now experiencing; she was unable to explain anything further. But I still sensed that she had not reached as far as she could go in this experience, and I once again encouraged her to go even more deeply than this, and see what might appear.

Again she let out a startled gasp. "Oh my God," she cried, as tears now flooded her eyes. "I'm expanding.... I'm getting so big, so vast...." I could see on her face a remarkable glow beginning to form. And I could feel the warmth flowing from her. "I'm so vast, I'm everywhere ... everywhere!" she whispered in awe. "I no longer have a body or anything—I'm just clear space. I'm nothing. I'm nothing at all.... I'm totally free! Oh my God ... oh my God...."

She could no longer speak, and I no longer wanted to interrupt this glimpse she was having into eternity and into the source of her true identity. We sat in silence for almost twenty minutes before she finally opened her eyes. She was radiant and profoundly serene. She finally spoke from deep within the Silence in her. She said very simply, "I know who I am ... I know who I am...."

I smiled and nodded. Then she exclaimed, "God, there's really nothing to be afraid of, is there?" She laughed a delightfully spontaneous and free laugh.

I laughed, too, overjoyed. "Strange what you can find in the core of your darkest fear, isn't it?" She nodded, then shook her head unbelievingly. Who would have imagined? Who would have thought this kind of bliss could be waiting for her in the very core of her fear of death? She knew then that this tremendous fear she'd found haunting her for so long was simply her Self calling her Home.

I saw Jane again two weeks later. "I had a dream!" she exclaimed excitedly, as she sat down. "The same dream that I've had so many times since I was a kid. Except that this time it ended differently."

"Tell me about it," I said with great interest.

"Well, it started out like it always did: I'm in my house alone at night. I'm just sitting reading or watching TV or something, when I suddenly become aware that there's someone—or something—out on my front porch, trying to get in. It's always really scary. I'm sitting there not knowing whether my door is locked or not, but I'm too scared and frozen in my chair to get up and check. I just sit there, not being able to breathe, as I hear this thing turning the knob. Usually I wake up at this point, and it's really awful. I'm always too afraid to go back to sleep.

"But this time, it was weird. In my dream, as I was sitting there, I was scared, but then I got up and went to the door. For some reason, I was able to do this, this time. My heart was beating and I was really frightened, but I stood there, without moving. Then the door started opening slowly. Then more and more. Soon it was all the way open— and I saw that there was nothing there! Nothing at all.

"But the weirdest thing was I looked outside and realized it was daytime. The sun was really shining, and I knew it had been night time just a few minutes before. And then, the strangest thing of all— I looked across the street and saw the ocean! And I thought, 'Gee I didn't know I was living so close to the ocean!' I felt so happy. I started to walk out to the beach there, and then I woke up!"

She was beaming by the time she finished telling me the dream. Then she said, "We don't have to process the dream to figure it out— I already have. That thing that I was so scared of was death—and it turned out to be nothing. And the sunshine and the ocean—all the joy I've been feeling since I was here last. It's just amazing, you know? I've really been realizing, I'm just not scared about death anymore. I can't believe it!"

Exercise: *Body Expansion*

Another exercise to assist you in detaching from your identification with the body, and therefore let go of fear about death, is a form of meditation adapted from one I originally experienced with a teacher named Francis Lucille. With this meditation, people generally experience themselves as vast, uninterrupted spaciousness—rather than something enclosed in a body. It would probably be best to have someone else guide you through the steps, so that you can completely relax into your experience.

1. Begin by sitting comfortably and closing your eyes. Take a few deep breaths and let them out, and then start breathing naturally. Begin watching your breath as it flows in and out.
2. Become aware of how your body is feeling. Focus first on your head, then move down to your throat and neck, then your shoulders and arms, etc., all the way down to your toes. As your awareness moves into each part of your body, gently bring relaxation into that area.
3. Now become aware of the chair, or whatever you are sitting on. Feel your body sinking down into it. Sense how friendly it is, how receptive it is to your body.
4. Next feel the air around you. Feel it on your face, your arms, your legs. Be aware of how your body fits into this air, this space all around you.
5. Now focus on the space that feels like the "center" of your body. Feel it beginning to expand, and the cells of your body there beginning to float apart from one another. Then become aware of the atoms in these cells; feel them floating apart, as well. Sense the air completely filling the spaces in between them. All the atoms of your body are floating more and more freely now, as the spaces between them get larger and larger. Feel this sensation extending into your chest. The cells and atoms that make up your

heart and lungs are beginning to float gently apart, as air flows freely into the spaces in between them. Your body is becoming larger and larger, as your cells allow more and more space to surround them.

6. Feel the contours of your body now beginning to blur, disappearing into the very air around you. There is now little distinction between your body and the space around you. You are becoming pure energy extending into space. Now realize that even the energy is disappearing into the clear, vast space. You have become the space itself.

7. Take a long inhale and then a long exhale. Be aware of how this breathing happens inside of the vast space you now know as YOU.

8. Know that you are Awareness itself, pure and simple Awareness. Your body, when it appears, appears inside of YOU. You are the space around and through it. Indeed, the whole universe exists inside of you.

9. Sit experiencing all this for as long as you wish. When you finally open your eyes, look down at your hands and see that they are inside of YOU. Then your feet and legs. This form you know as your body is something inside of you, not the other way around. Yet you flow all though it, as well. There is nowhere that you are not.

In my experience, doing this exercise can assist you in directly experiencing the illusion of your body and the reality of your true identity as the primal essence that lies beyond the realm of form. Once you've done it several times as a meditation, you can then begin to do it with your eyes open, while engaged in many different activities. You may find your sense of doing these activities greatly altering, as you begin to know yourself to be that which has no form. It becomes a curious adventure to observe your body doing things without your personal involvement.

These exercises may or may not work for you in relieving your fears around death. You may have to find what will work for you. The key to remember is that simply approaching your fear intellectually or philosophically probably will not work. You need to directly face your fear head-on and to find a way to experience who you are beyond the body. Otherwise, the deeply ingrained body-identification will remain—along with the suffering that goes with it.

It's important to remember that learning to detach your identity from your body is a process that takes some time. Of course, experiencing profound glimpses of the Self assists tremendously in this process. But so does a constant and sincere effort to detach your awareness from the limited form of your body.

The experience that your identity is not confined to your body can become tremendously joyful and exciting. You can still enjoy your body and the pleasures it gives you—but you need not be caught in the fears and suffering that identifying with it can bring. You can just become the curious investigator, exploring this delightfully wondrous planet, as you drive around in the vehicle you've been given to use for the short while that you're visiting here.

CHAPTER THIRTEEN

Detaching from Your Emotions

The emotions that emanate from realizing true love are true emotions, not sentimental emotions revolving around an imaginary you and your needs.

—Gangaji

HAVING EXPLORED HOW WE KEEP OURSELVES TRAPPED in suffering due to identifying with both the roles we play in life and with the body, let us now turn to the emotions. What is it we do with emotions that keeps us entangled in the knot of suffering they can bring?

Once again, it will become apparent that our suffering is caused by our attachment to our emotions, and by our belief that our emotions are who we are. What follows is that the way out of this suffering is to detach our identity from them.

As always, by "detachment," I am not talking about not feeling emotions or denying them. And I'm certainly not talking about getting rid of them (if this could even be done). There is nothing at all wrong with emotions. There is no reason to not feel them. Indeed, emotions bring color and juice into our life in a way nothing else can. What I am speaking of is detaching our sense of identity from them— truly realizing that emotions, with all their unreliable, ever-changing impermanence, are not who we are.

The process of detaching from emotions can generally seem harder for women than it is for men. Many women are, in fact, quite entrenched in their emotional identity; emotions for them are very real and of utmost importance. It's hard to tell if this is so because women have generally been socialized to become emotional beings, or whether they are inherently more emotional than men. Probably a bit of both. Either way, it seems that women are generally more in touch with their emotions and tend to base their sense of identity on them more than men do.

Paradoxically, I believe this is probably to their advantage in getting free from emotional suffering, because we must first be aware of what emotions are. I have known many men who have tried to bypass the process of getting in touch with their feelings and move directly into the "spiritual realms." Only too often, it is brought home to them, finally, that avoiding or repressing emotions does not make them go away. Being out of touch with our emotions can, in fact, increase their power over us and complicate our lives by having them pop out in distorted and inappropriate ways.

To men's credit, however, I must say that I've noticed more and more men now turning to the wisdom of attuning to their emotions. Perhaps men's groups—that deal with emotions in a way with which men tend to be comfortable—are responsible, at least in part, for this welcome change. This growing awareness among men, I believe, has greatly assisted the communication between the sexes. More than ever before, emotional exchanges tend to be much better understood by both men and women.

The Worship of Emotions

It seems that the same forces that have produced a greater awareness about emotions in our culture have also now managed to create a cult out of them. For some people, emotions have become a god. This is especially true of people who have been involved in intensive therapy or self-help programs, where a major tenet has been: Most problems are caused by repressed emotions, and it is therefore necessary, beyond all else, to get in touch with them and experience them fully. People are especially encouraged to deeply experience the "wounding" they have undergone in their lives. In fact, re-experiencing and analyzing their wounding, in all its gory aspects, ends up becoming their most important goal.

Much to the discomfort of their families and friends, people who espouse such an approach also prod their loved ones to adopt the same philosophy. I have heard women, in particular, complain at length about the men in their lives who have not "acknowledged their own emotional wounding." There is certainly some truth to the notion that if we are not in touch with our feelings, they will get in our way in our quest for freedom. However, the examination of emotions can be overdone and in its own way become a barrier to true freedom.

I have found that the cult of emotion-worshipping can suck people in for many, many years. I realized this a couple of years ago, when I received a phone call from an old friend, June, to whom I hadn't spoken in over fifteen years. We had spent most of our time together then sharing about the emotional dramas in which we were each currently involved. It was something we did with most of our friends; it was what life and friendship were all about. We were all intimately involved in each other's stories—wanting to hear the latest episodes, giving our advice about the situations, and offering our support to each other in our suffering.

Talking with June brought this all back to me. I remembered the warmth and love we felt for each other during those days, and the depth of emotional sharing we had experienced. It also brought the realization that I was no longer relating to people in that way very often. I had come to see that dramas of suffering could get rather boring after awhile, especially if the same story kept happening over and over again. In effect, emotional suffering no longer had its old appeal to me.

I soon realized that June had not made this transition. After our initial catch-up exchanges about what we were doing and where we were now living, she launched immediately into the emotional drama that was currently unfolding in her life. I was incredulous, as I sat listening to her on the phone. It was as if no time at all had passed. All the same drama of suffering she had been experiencing fifteen years before was still going on; the prime players around her had simply changed faces and names. What was really startling to me was that she appeared to be still reveling in her role as the martyred-victim heroine and still analyzing and attempting to deeply experience and understand it.

I was especially amazed, because I knew June was not only a very bright woman, but also very spiritually aware. I couldn't quite believe that she was still putting so much energy into her emotional suffering and analyzing all the intricate reasons for it. I realized that she had truly become a victim of the emotional cult so prevalent in our subculture, and that I had had the good fortune to escape its seductive clutches sometime in the last fifteen years.

Focusing on Negative Emotions

It is difficult to escape from the cult of emotions in our Western culture, in part because of the thriving smorgasbord of therapies and self-help programs designed to assist people caught in emotional suffering. Although certainly serving an important need, I have found that many of them end up doing more harm than good. Some of them not only glorify the emotions in general, they glorify negative emotions, in particular—and end up creating wounded-victim heroes and heroines like my friend, June.

In the earlier years of my practice as a therapist, I was guilty of leading certain clients down this unfortunate path. Aware that my clients were suffering from repressed emotions, I began using an approach known as "insight therapy," which involved guiding them into the internal pathways that would reveal their repressed emotions to them. Quite often, this would initially produce immense relief and joy; finally allowing negative emotions to come to the surface can be greatly rewarding.

But a problem would always arise when we began "recycling" her emotions. Believing that talking about these negative emotions would eventually get rid of them, my clients and I would process and reprocess, analyze and reanalyze them—where they came from, who was responsible for them, etc., ad nauseum. Far from bringing relief, this process after awhile increased the suffering. The client became the emotionally wounded victim, whose whole identity was caught up in this role.

It took me awhile to realize that becoming aware of negative emotions was only the beginning of the road. Insight into how to release or heal the emotions did not automatically occur in most cases. Even when I saw this, and I suggested ways a client could release and heal these emotions, I found that many of them were resistant to doing this. They were getting too much out of the role of the wounded victim. Their sense of self-esteem was being fed by the feeling of specialness created by the understanding of how incredibly wounded they were.

I remember only too well a client by the name of Melanie—a very sincere woman, suffering terribly from depression and low self-esteem. In our initial sessions together, as I led her through the labyrinthine corridors of her past, exploring her childhood wounding and all the negative emotions she'd managed to repress, she would be somewhat worn out by the end of our session—but she'd also be elated. Exploring all these issues was both fascinating and relieving for her.

However, as we plowed on in this work for months, and as we covered the same ground over and over again, her elation understandably turned once again into depression. Nothing new was happening; the old problems she had dragged on.

I finally realized that insight therapy alone wasn't working for her. It wasn't producing, as it was intended to, automatic knowledge of how to change her life. So I brought in something new: behavioral therapy and cognitive therapy, therapies based on making changes through new behaviors and new beliefs. The novelty of these approaches lifted her spirits for awhile, and it seemed as if perhaps some positive changes might be happening. But ultimately, it became clear that these approaches weren't going to help, either. We were still covering all the same ground; we were still focusing on her wounding and what to do about it.

I then started bringing in more experiential, transpersonal processes: past-life regression, Gestalt, dreamwork, inner child work, visualization, chakra-balancing, depossession—you name it. As I introduced these new forms of therapy, I began reframing the work we were doing, referring to it as "transformational work." We were now focusing seriously on "healing" her wounding.

Again, initially, these new processes brought hope for awhile. But ultimately, since we were still focused on her wounding, her old depression appeared again, this time laced with profound feelings of failure. After all her hard work, she still wasn't "healed" of her depression. She was soon feeling anger—and much of it was directed at me. So we dealt with that for a while. Although she was able to work through the anger and feel good about me again, we were still back to where we had started. She was still feeling depressed and a lack of self-worth. The only difference was that she was now very informed as to why she was feeling this way—and she was also very established in the role of the victim.

It wasn't that Melanie didn't want to change. She did, quite desperately so. She took all we processed very seriously. She'd dutifully come in each week having done all the homework I'd prescribed. In many ways she was the "ideal" therapy client. It was just that we had focused for so long on what was "wrong" with her, that she had become stuck in the victim role, and neither one of us at that point knew how to help her out of it.

I knew I wasn't the only therapist producing these self-glorified victims; many clients came to me from other therapists already well-established in this role. I was to find that it took quite a bit of time and energy to lead someone out of this kind of distorted identity if they were already deeply entrenched in it.

Focusing on Positive Emotions

One path I eventually took with such clients was helping them focus on positive emotions, instead of negative ones. Although limited in its own way, this approach can at least begin to turn the glorified victim into a more happy and empowered human being. Numerous therapies, self-help approaches, and metaphysical and positive-thinking teachings help transform negative emotions into positive ones. People can, often for the first time in their lives, begin to enjoy life and feel empowered to create their own happiness.

For a number of years, I used this focus on positive emotions as my basic approach with clients. I taught them about affirmations and visualization, how to communicate with their spirit guides and angels, how to manifest what they wanted, and how generally to keep focused on everything positive going on their lives. Although much more successful in helping people toward happiness and empowerment, this approach, I was to find, also had its limitations.

I discovered that trying to experience more positive emotions in our lives just isn't the answer to ending emotional suffering. Eventually we realize that we simply can't focus on positive emotions all the time, no matter how disciplined we are. Negative ones keep appearing, no matter how hard we try to keep them away. And we can't hold onto positive emotions when they do appear, either; they come and they go.

In fact, even while we are experiencing positive emotions, there is always the awareness (although often subconscious) that they will eventually be gone, so it's hard to truly be happy even at these times. I've even known people who actually fear feeling good at all, because they know the good feeling will eventually leave, and they'd therefore rather not feel the positive emotion to begin with.

Another problem is that if we focus exclusively on positive emotions, making them "right" and negative emotions "wrong," we are likely to begin repressing the negative ones that do arise and then we have to deal with the unfortunate consequences of this action. Repressing emotions doesn't make them go away; it just gives them more power. So we're back to square one in this whole process of striving for emotional happiness.

It's clear that, although moving from the "hell realms" of emotion more into the "heaven realms" can produce great relief and is certainly a step up from dwelling in negativity, this approach does not produce true and lasting happiness either. A further step must be taken.

CHAPTER FOURTEEN

Experiencing
Emotional Freedom

When pain is met as it is, as simply pain, it can even be experienced as beautiful. It doesn't need to be anything different. When it is rejected, and something "not painful" is reached for, pain is experienced as suffering.

—Gangaji

*I*F YOU ARE AT A POINT IN YOUR LIFE where you are truly tired of being buffeted about by emotions and are not satisfied with being just somewhat happy some of the time, you are probably finally ready to move out of the knot of emotional suffering altogether and take the next step toward freedom. This next step is not an easy one, nor necessarily a quick one. But, I believe, it is an essential one—and can ultimately produce the emotional freedom you're looking for.

The next step is to learn how to *let go of your attachment to ALL emotions—both negative and positive.* Only this can release you from identifying with your emotions, and therefore only this will bring you freedom from emotional suffering. This step can be a challenging one if you have spent much of your life highly valuing your emotions and using them as a source self-worth. But, with practice and sincerity, it can be done.

I wish to emphasize, as always, that letting go of your attachment to emotions does not mean letting go of the experience of them, or denying them. It entails, instead, allowing feelings to simply be—without judgment, without attachment. It means not dwelling on them, not indulging them, not analyzing them; it also means not running from them, not fighting them, not avoiding them. No clinging and no resisting. It means just letting them be.

The following is a description of eight steps that can be helpful in taking this road toward emotional detachment.

1. **See Emotions for What They Are.** The first step is to become aware of what emotions actually are: simply energy—free-flowing energy. They flow into your awareness and they flow out. They are truly nothing to be valued or even much thought about. What you can discover is that the emotions you experience aren't even inherently "your" emotions. They belong to nobody. They're just a specific kind of energy that happens to be floating through your awareness at that time. There's therefore no reason to grab onto them and make them your important possessions (or allow them to become lodged as stuck energy somewhere in your body). You can just let them float on through without sticking to you in any way.

2. **Begin Observing the Emotions.** As you learn simply to allow emotions to float through your awareness without attaching to them, the next step is to begin observing them in a relaxed and neutral way. As they appear, just note them, acknowledge their presence, and observe what they feel like. Of course, you will also be feeling the emotions as you do this; experiencing them does not necessarily stop. But you can observe and feel them at the same time.

It's helpful at first to practice this observation process. You can start by closing your eyes and relaxing. Take a few deep breaths. Then become aware of emotions as they appear in your awareness. They come in differently for different people; they may appear as visual images, colors, sensations somewhere in your body, or in some other way. Be careful not to get caught up in analyzing them or in giving them any other kind of energy. Simply watch them in a relaxed and detached way, without interfering with them. Allow them to do whatever they want or go where they want. Most importantly, *do not follow any thoughts about them.* Don't go off into the familiar scenarios from the past or possible futures based on the feelings. Simply stay relaxed, watching the feelings themselves.

For example, let's say you have your eyes closed and are watching what is floating through your mind. Thoughts and images begin passing through. Perhaps there is the thought about how your girlfriend left you the week before, and then there's the image of her, angry with you, as she's going out the door. Do your best to do nothing with this thought and image. Just watch them as they float by.

You may become aware next of loneliness making its appearance. As you begin to watch this emotion, perhaps you realize it is a gray, amorphous mass that seems to settle in the pit of your stomach. Your tendency at this point might be automatically to think, "I feel so lonely," and then slide off into more images, thoughts, and feelings about this emotion. Don't do this; instead stay completely still, simply observing the emotion. Watch it as it settles into the pit of your stomach; note any tightness it may be causing there.

Become aware of what has just happened: a form of energy that you have identified as "loneliness" has just entered into the force field of your body (which is actually just another form of energy) and has settled into a place where it has probably habitually settled in all the past times it's ever visited this body. You are the **observer** of this phenomenon; you are not the loneliness nor the body in which the loneliness has settled. Gently and quietly keep focused on this fact.

Perhaps, as you do this, more images now flood your awareness—memories of when other girlfriends have left you and all that you suffered after those episodes. Don't follow these thoughts; don't even touch them. Give them no energy whatsoever. Simply observe them, as they do their little dance in your awareness, trying to get your attention.

Now maybe anger will make an appearance—anger at your girlfriend, or at all the girlfriends who have ever left you. Be attentive, don't allow this new emotion to drag you off to familiar doom-and-gloom scenarios. Stay focused on watching the anger as it enters into your awareness. What does it look like? Does it have a color? A form? Does it settle somewhere inside your body? Note the response your body has to this new energy. If the anger just passes on through, be careful not to go look for it; this is a sure way to drag it back in again.

You'll find that this process takes some concentration and practice at first. The habit of attaching to an emotion as it floats through our consciousness and then going for the ride it wants to take us on is usually so ingrained in us that it can happen in a split second before we know what is happening. If this does happen, and you find yourself trailing off after the emotion, simply let go of your grasp on it and once again sit back and begin watching it.

It takes a while to develop a new response to emotions, but after awhile, it won't even be necessary to stop and close your eyes to observe every emotion. It will become a natural way to respond to them throughout your daily life. You'll be happy to see that simply observing a mass of energy floating through your awareness is really much less exhausting than being dragged around by it!

3. **Accept All Emotions Equally.** As you simply observe emotions as they float through your awareness, and refrain from grabbing onto them, you will likely next become aware of an automatic tendency to want to cling to the positive emotions as they appear and to resist the negative ones. This is to be expected; naturally, you want to hold on to what feels good and pleasant and get rid of what feels bad or unpleasant.

This is all part of the ego's plan for achieving happiness—grasping at what's pleasant and resisting what's unpleasant—and it is ultimately unsuccessful. We can't get rid of negative feelings, while holding onto positive feelings, quite simply, because positive and negative emotions come together in the same package. We can't discard some emotions without losing the others; we can't cling to some emotions without keeping the others. Thus, this urge to either resist or cling to emotions must somehow be let go of. We simply need to accept all of them equally, without judgment or preference.

One way to begin doing this is to stop discriminating between what you deem to be "positive" and "negative" emotions, and attempt to see them all as simply emotions, period. This can be difficult if you have any notions about certain emotions being either "spiritual" or "unspiritual." If you do, you will likely try to avoid feeling any emotions you see as "unspiritual," and this, of course, leads to denying these emotions—which does nothing to get rid of them. More importantly, the whole notion of spiritual and unspiritual emotions is fallacious to begin with. Emotions themselves have nothing to do with spirituality; in one way, they can all be seen as "spiritual"; in another, none of them.

Whether you give emotions spiritual qualities or not, discriminating between positive and negative emotions in any way can hinder your becoming free of the suffering they can bring. This habit of discriminating is often a deeply ingrained one, and initially it may take a great deal of vigilance and discipline to break it. But it is ultimately essential. To be truly free emotionally, the tendency to resist and cling to emotions must be checked. All emotions must be responded to equally, with detachment—and ultimately without even a preference.

How can this deeply-ingrained habit be broken? Let's look more closely in the next two steps at how we tend to react automatically to emotions when they appear in our consciousness and what can be done to begin dissolving this habit.

4. **Allow Negative Emotions Simply to Be**. Simply allowing negative emotions to flow in without reacting to them is perhaps more challenging than not reacting to positive ones. Because they can be so painful, we naturally react to them in a way that we hope will get rid of the pain they appear to be causing. It's important to recognize these habitual reactions toward negative emotions because they do not get rid of the pain—and they do, in fact, keep us recycling back into it. These reactions usually fall into three categories: resistance to an emotion, indulgence in it, and attempts to fix it.

Resistance: Resisting a negative emotion can take many different forms: pushing it away, ignoring it, denying it, judging it, distracting oneself from it, fighting it, getting angry with it. All these maneuvers, far from dissolving the pain of the negative emotion, actually create even more pain. Just as we saw how resistance to physical pain can increase the pain, so resistance to emotional pain can compound it in a similar way.

First of all, if you look clearly at what happens to the emotions you've attempted to resist in one way or another, you'll see these emotions do not go away. They may go underground for awhile and give you some respite, but they do not disappear. And they usually seep out at some later time in a displaced and inappropriate way.

Besides being ineffective in getting rid of a negative emotion, fighting it can compound the pain. It requires a great deal of energy to resist something, and causes much tension in both your psyche and your body. You may not be aware of this if your resistive reactions to unpleasant emotions have become deeply habitual. But, if you take the time to stop the habit—even just once—when a negative emotion appears, you will be able to experience the beautiful release of tension you may not have even known was there.

Joseph was an engineer in his late forties who came to me with a massive amount of pent-up tension in his body. He told me that people saw him as an "up-tight" and "rigid" man of whom they were often afraid. They intuitively sensed the intense anger he had stored inside him and were hesitant to be around him, for fear he might "blow" at any time. He was aware of the amount of rage he was carrying around, but did not know what to do with it. The times in the past when he'd stopped resisting his anger and let it simply explode had been disastrous for him. People had been completely alienated from him; he had actually even lost his job a couple of times.

I asked him what he did to keep his anger in check. He told me he just kept a very tight rein on it. He did his best not to express it at all. If ignoring it didn't work, he'd try to tell himself how "evil" it was to get angry. If this didn't work, he'd often start eating voluminous amounts of junk food to try and stuff it down. Or he'd try turning on the TV to try and deaden it.

"Wow," I said. "It must take so much energy out of you, just to keep the anger from exploding."

"Yeah, it does," he replied with a pained sigh. "I get so exhausted."

I then suggested that he might perhaps stop resisting his anger. He immediately became very fearful. "Oh, I couldn't do that! I have to keep it in check. It's catastrophic when I don't!" He was only seeing two options: either he could resist his anger and hold it in, or he could let it explode. I explained that there was a third option: he could simply allow the anger to be, without expressing it. He could accept the feeling of anger as it appeared in him, not making it wrong or bad, and, at the same time, avoid expressing it in an explosive way.

This was a novel idea to Joseph, and it didn't seem possible to him. How could he just accept the anger, without having it explode on him? The more I suggested this was indeed possible, the more defensive he became. As I persisted, his anger began to rise. I decided at this point that I might as well help create a situation while we were together in which perhaps I could demonstrate what I was talking about, so I continued to push him further and increase his anger.

Finally I said, "You're pretty angry right now, aren't you?"

Rather loudly, he exclaimed, "You bet I am! You're a therapist—you're not supposed to be making me mad like this!"

"Why don't you take this opportunity right now to test what I've been talking about?" I knew I was taking a chance with this, because his anger at me was probably producing even more resistance to my suggestion. So I added, gently, "This kind of anger can feel pretty awful, can't it?"

"Yeah," he muttered, somewhat mollified. "I hate it. I hate it. I just want to kill people!"

"I can really see that, just looking at you. You know, I'm not suggesting that you kill people."

Despite himself, he smiled a small smile. "Well, what are you suggesting then? I don't get it."

With this opening, I began to speak again about simply allowing his feeling of anger to be—without doing anything at all with it. I suggested he close his eyes and relax his body as best he could. He did this and took a couple of deep breaths. As I guided him through the process of identifying and locating the anger, he found that it was a massive, throbbing, red "fire-monster" that had his entire body in its clutches. Even doing this beginning exercise had an effect on his body. I could see certain muscles in his face and his chest begin to relax.

As he finally began simply to observe the anger as it grabbed and squeezed at different parts of his body—and as he learned to keep focused on the anger itself, rather than the mental stories around it—he found that the monster began losing its vividness and strength. Eventually, after about fifteen minutes of keeping on track with this process, he finally reported to me that it had disappeared. I saw that he sat on the couch before me ten times more relaxed than I had ever seen him before. When he opened his eyes, relief shone in them. He couldn't quite believe what had happened.

Of course, this was not the end to all of Joseph's anger. As could be expected, it was to appear over and over again. But, as he began working with it in this new way, he found that there was no longer any reason for him to be fearful of his anger. His new approach of not resisting it—either through fighting it, attempting to contain it, or distracting himself from it—began to lessen the clutches of this monster on his life. He experienced who he was as so much more powerful than this form of energy called "anger"; simply accepting it and letting it be, his whole life was changing. He became visibly more relaxed. People weren't so afraid of him anymore. And for the first time he could remember, he wasn't letting anger—or fear of his anger—run his life.

No matter what emotion you stop resisting, you can have the same kind of results. Take depression, for example. You may be someone who has suffered from this debilitating emotion for most your life. Perhaps you're asking, "You mean I should just let the depression stay when it comes in? It'll take over, if I do—I know, I've let this happen in the past. I can't afford to let it ruin my life again like that!"

If this is what you're thinking, then, like Joseph, you are assuming that there are only two options with depression: either you resist the depression in some manner, or you let it take over your life. What I am talking about when I say "let it be" is not falling into it; this is a form of indulging in it (which I will address in the next section). I am not encouraging you to give in to the depression, nor am I suggesting you give up responsibility for how you're feeling. I am speaking only of stopping the reaction of resistance toward it—and simply letting it be, without reacting to it at all.

I am also not suggesting that stopping habitual patterns of resistance is easy or that it can be done overnight. Obviously, as in changing any ingrained habit pattern, it takes patience and time. But it can be done. Even if you can just begin the process, you will experience quickly the wonderful result of greater relaxation in your body. It can be such a relief to let go and stop resisting!

Indulgence in the Emotion: The second type of habitual reaction to negative emotions is to give in to them and indulge them. One way to indulge an emotion is to project it into action. If the feeling is anger, for instance, as in Joseph's case, the tendency may be to blow off steam at someone or something, in hopes that the pain from the anger will diminish or go away with this action.

We can sometimes get an immediate sense of relief in expressing anger like this. At times, if no one has been hurt by this expression of anger, and we are able to simply let go of it after we've expressed it, this can be okay. No great harm is done. But I think few people can actually do this with anger. More often, the same anger about the same thing shows up again later on, sometimes over and over again. Thus, acting out our anger this way obviously does not resolve it.

Similarly, acting out other negative emotions can also end up strengthening them. The reaction of bursting into tears over upsetting events is a good example. Again, like the brief expression of anger that is quickly released and forgotten, a burst of tears now and then can be harmless, and probably even helpful—simply as a release of pent-up energy. But so often, this reaction can become habitual and completely nonproductive; far from resolving the hurt, it can actually start a spiral of depression and despair.

A sensitive, fragile young woman came to see me a few years back. Theresa had been struggling with deep depression for many years, along with a sense of helplessness and anger toward many people in her life. Often she would report to me how, after something had happened, she just "bawled her eyes out," or that she had spent the entire night crying. When I finally asked her one time if this crying had given her any relief, she answered, "No—not at all. I felt worse. But I just couldn't help myself."

Somewhere along the line, Theresa had developed the habit of acting out her hurt, depression, or anger through bursting into tears. As so often happens with the habits we form, it wasn't doing her any good—but she just didn't know what else to do. The habit had taken over. I began talking to her about adopting a new response to hurtful situations. I suggested that instead of falling automatically into her torrent of tears, she instead become still and simply watch the hurt as it floated through her awareness. At the time, she looked at me very doubtfully. She nodded her head, but I knew that, like Joseph, she didn't believe that this could do her any good.

Fortunately, during our session a few weeks later, I had an opportunity to help her try out this new approach in handling hurt. As she talked to me about a situation during the previous week at work in which she had felt threatened and helpless, she began crying. Immediately, I suggested, "Rather than going into this same old reaction to your pain, perhaps you can simply close your eyes right now and become still." Rather reluctantly, she finally complied. She stopped crying and closed her eyes.

I said, "Just relax and watch your breathing for a few moments." Presently, I said, "Now scan your awareness and look for your hurt—it's probably settled somewhere in your body."

"Yeah, it's in my belly. I see it. It's kind of a grayish-pink." Suddenly I heard a catch in her voice, as she started to cry. I said, "No need to react to this hurt; just observe it. Tell me, how else can you describe it?"

"Well, it's soft and fragile. It's kind of like a cloud, a grayish-pink cloud." She paused, and then said, "I always feel this kind of hurt whenever anybody threatens me or tries to intimidate me...."

I gently stopped her in this thought process. I said, "No need to follow that thought about your hurt. You've gone over and over that one. You understand it well, how and why it happens. This has never resolved the pain. What I'm suggesting is that you simply stay still and watch this energy form as it sits in your belly—and just see what happens."

She frowned but began concentrating in this way. Soon she said, "It really hurts. It's tight and it squeezes the muscles in my belly."

"That's an important observation. This emotion called 'hurt' constricts your belly and causes it pain. Don't go off into anything else about this now; just keep observing. Tell me what is happening."

"I just keep thinking about all the times I've felt this hurt...."

"See if you can move out of that thought right now—just let go of it. It'll just take you for a ride. Come back to observing. What is happening to the grayish-pink mass of energy in your belly now?"

She was silent for awhile. Then she said, somewhat surprised, "It was there, really permanent feeling for awhile, but now it isn't there anymore."

"Is it somewhere else?"

"I don't think so. It just kind of disappeared...."

"How is your belly feeling?"

"Well, it's kind of relaxed now. It's fine." She opened her eyes and smiled a tentative smile. "That's really weird! It just disappeared. I'm not feeling hurt anymore." She was puzzled but very relieved. She had discovered, through direct experience, that simply observing an emotion, rather than indulging it, could have an amazing result. Given no energy, it simply fades and disappears.

This isn't to say that handling an emotion this way will get rid of it forever; undoubtedly, it will be back. If it has been a welcome guest in your consciousness and has been given lots of attention for many years, it will continue to return, as if attempting to recapture this pampered-guest status with you. But by persistently refraining from giving it the kind of energy on which it thrives, you will find that it eventually fades and has less and less pull on you. You will finally be able just to note the appearance of this guest on your doorstep, smile at it graciously, and then go on about your business, completely undisturbed by it.

Another way to indulge a negative emotion, besides projecting it into action, is to do what Theresa started to do several times during our process: to move into the "story" and begin analyzing it. We often react this way to a chronic emotion, with the hope that if we can just analyze it enough, we will eventually discover how to release ourselves from the pain of it.

With great agony, we find ourselves stumbling down memory lane, remembering all the times we've experienced the emotion and the drama that's surrounded it. Obsessively, we attempt to analyze how it all happened and what we could or should have done to prevent it. We then, in despair, often indulge in self-pity, self-doubt, and self-hate for how we've failed.

To pile on the pain, we also fearfully project into the future about it, as well. We fear the next time it's going to happen and wonder if we'll ever be free of it. It all becomes a horror story by the time we're done (if we ever are). And all this, simply because a negative emotion happened to appear in our consciousness!

Indulging negative emotions like this is ultimately responsible for the negative thought patterns and belief systems we develop in life. Because we have fed and nourished these emotions with so much energy, they get stronger and stronger and eventually become habitual. Automatically moving into the story around emotions is therefore really important to watch and release.

Attempting to Fix Emotions: The third type of habitual response people tend to have to negative emotions is to try to fix or change them in some way, in order to make them more positive. If you have spent time learning how to transform and heal negative emotions, this reaction may now be habitual for you. Trying to transform or heal an emotion might seem more "spiritual" to you than the other two reactions—resisting or indulging them; it may have a more pleasant and loving attitude about it. But it is ultimately as much a rejection of negative emotions as the other two approaches are. Its purpose is to change them, rather than simply allowing them to be.

Many techniques people use to heal negative emotions do seem to work. For many years, I worked with numerous processes to transform and heal my negative emotions. Doing these processes, and for a time afterwards, I usually experienced a great high. I'd forgive myself and others, and I'd reach into some really clear and loving spaces inside myself. Feeling free and clear at the time, I'd consider myself "healed" of the emotions.

There came a time, however, when I got honest with myself about this process. Occasionally, when I'd really be open and delve into some of those places where the negative feelings "used to be"— much to my horror, I began finding that those old emotions were still there. Anger at my mother for things that had happened forty years before was still in me, biding its time. Despair about my whole life was still alive and well; the unbearable loneliness from my childhood was still pushing at the door. What had happened to all the "healing" I'd done on these emotions?

Sure, the feelings weren't as powerful as they'd been previously, and they no longer seemed to be running my life, but they were still in there—and probably always would be. And they could emerge, I knew, any time my defenses were really down. It seemed that all the transformational work I'd done on them hadn't really done much good at all.

I wondered, finally, if I were alone in this predicament. I began an informal survey of friends who had also done a considerable amount of work on their emotions. Not surprisingly, most of them admitted (although somewhat reluctantly) that the same was true for them.

One of them, who had been a healer for many years, revealed that she had been somewhat alarmed by this fact for quite awhile. She had not only been working the metaphysical principles of emotional healing for many years on herself, she'd also been working them on many other people. And just as she was seeing her own "healed" emotions still causing her pain, she was also seeing this same occurrence with clients she'd worked with for some time. It was indeed a disturbing phenomenon, bringing serious doubt into her whole paradigm of life and how the universe worked; it also threatened her source of income. I knew that I was in a similar position; I completely understood her alarm. Becoming honest about my experiences of "healing" was shaking my universe. What did it all mean for me?

What I finally saw was that a new paradigm about life, emotions, and healing was necessary—one that could encompass and integrate the revelations of my honest inquiry inside myself. It had to include the realization that although methods of "healing" do often bring relief to people, they do not necessarily resolve negative emotions. They certainly don't get rid of them or completely defuse their ability to trip us up somewhere down the line, if we ever feel vulnerable or threatened enough to have them triggered again.

Perhaps the most important realization I had was that trying to "heal" an emotion was simply a polite way of rejecting it. And I wondered if perhaps it was the act of rejecting the emotions that kept them unresolved. Maybe what needed to be done was simply to accept them, just as they were. In fact, maybe the answer was no longer even to care what emotions were floating around inside me at all.*

---

*I am not suggesting that techniques for healing emotions are completely useless. In fact, for very deep emotional wounding, I believe they can be extremely helpful to reduce the suffering involved. It's just important to realize that healing techniques are limited and that eventually, once you have worked on healing your emotions for some time, it might be wise to abandon this attempt to heal this aspect of your ego-self—and begin truly to get free of the suffering that is being caused by your misidentification with your emotions.

As it turned out, this is exactly what has worked for me. When I finally began abandoning my urge to fix or heal negative emotions in any way, I began experiencing an enormous relief. I came to realize that there is nothing inherently wrong with negative emotions. They are essentially no different from the emotions I have deemed "positive," except that I find them unpleasant. Negative and positive emotions are simply different forms of the same energy.

After working successfully for some time with many clients using this new approach, it eventually became clear to me that we really need do nothing at all to change negative emotions. We truly can just observe them objectively and let them be. If they have been well-fed by us in the past, they will probably return for a while. But if we can stay neutral and non-reactive, they will eventually let up and move on out of our awareness. It can be such a relief to see this happening!

I once had a very aware client who had been coming to me for several reasons: depression, relationship problems, and career problems. Sharon had spent years, before coming to me, working on herself through therapy, twelve-step groups, and *Course in Miracles* processes. She knew herself well and had made good use of the information she'd learned throughout the years. She was certainly a much happier and more empowered person than she'd been ten years before. She just felt, at this point, kind of "stuck" in certain areas of her life.

In our initial months together, Sharon and I worked on how she could create a happier life for herself. Very enthusiastically, she'd go home after our weekly sessions and assiduously work on fixing and changing her life situations and her emotions so as to become a happier person. Then, at some point, I realized, enough was enough. She could do this forever. She had fixed and changed and fixed and changed so many things in her life, and although she had become a happier person, she was finding that there was always more to fix. It was endless.

At this point I started a new therapy with her that I called "So What?" Therapy. Each week when she'd come in describing a new emotional problem (or generally, it was an old one dressed in new clothes), I would inevitably say to her, "So what?" Or "Who cares if that's still happening? What difference does it make? It's not who you are."

The first time I did this, she was surprised by this new tack I was taking and somewhat perturbed. Her emotional problems were important to her, and she took pride in the work she'd done in fixing and balancing them. But then she began to smile. She had had important glimpses of her true Self and knew what I meant when I'd say she wasn't her emotions. But she, like anyone else who has worked for years on fixing their emotions, kept forgetting. She kept falling back into believing she was her emotions, and if her emotions weren't positive or "spiritual" ones, then she felt she needed to change them.

This process continued for several weeks, until Sharon would catch herself before I did, and she'd smile and say, "So what?" Such relief would flood her at these times, she'd laugh a beautiful liberated laugh. She was realizing she could finally put down the burden of having to constantly fix herself in order to be "spiritual" or happy—she could just be as she was. The ego-self that she kept trying to fix was ultimately imperfectible, and more importantly, it was not who she was.

She became one of my most delightful clients after that. We'd barely get seated across from each other, and she'd be beaming at me, knowing she really no longer had any problems to solve. Her only problem all along had been one of misidentification. Needless to say, she didn't need to come to see me for much longer.

The three habitual reactions to negative emotions that I have described—resistance, indulgence, and attempting to fix—are often unconscious and automatic. It is therefore important to bring them into your conscious awareness, so that you can begin to let them go and start creating a new response of simply allowing them to be. As always, this requires some practice.

At first, set up a "system" inside your mind in which a "bell" will go off every time you feel a negative emotion. When the bell goes off, it is a signal for you to watch your habitual reaction to the emotions—and then gently refrain from doing it, allowing the emotion instead simply to be there. Observe it, acknowledge it, and then leave it alone. In other words, let the negative emotion itself actually be your ally in dissolving it.

To avoid any misunderstanding, note that allowing an emotion simply to be does not rule out the possibility of also taking appropriate action concerning a situation that helped trigger the emotion in you. For example, upon noticing hurt in yourself due to a misunderstanding you've had with someone, you might decide to speak to the person in hopes of resolving it. Or, in the case of feeling anger because of having been taken advantage of, you might take action to make sure you are not taken advantage of again in that same way.

These are examples of appropriate *responses* to negative emotions (as opposed to the *reactions* I have been describing), that can work quite effectively to help relieve the suffering caused by the emotions. You can easily do them while you are also engaged in the observation process inside yourself.

5. **Allow Positive Emotions Simply to Be.** It can sometimes be just as difficult to allow positive emotions simply to be, without reacting to them, as it is to allow negative ones to be. The automatic tendency is to grab onto them and cling as long as possible. Attachment to these positive emotions, as well, causes suffering when they eventually leave.

It is necessary to be as neutral and non-reactive with positive emotions when they appear as with negative ones. As you learn to do this, an incredible sense of freedom can appear. You'll find that it doesn't in any way detract from the good feeling that positive emotions bring; it actually increases it. You'll no longer clutch at the feelings out of fear they might leave. You know they *will* leave, so there's no point in trying to hang on to them. You simply enjoy them while they're around, and then willingly let them go, when they go. You're free and flowing, no matter what's happening.

7. **Take Time to Practice.** If you come up against a negative emotion that you have given much energy in the past, it will naturally take more practice and time to let go of it. But I have found it can be done. Certain emotions that caused me tremendous suffering in the past, eventually appeared in a very anemic form and then hardly came around at all anymore. What was important was that, even if

they did come back, I was no longer upset by them. I could note their presence, and even feel them if I wanted to, but I did not enter into the familiar suffering about them.

One thing that actually became a fun game for me was that after I'd been dealing with certain emotions for some time, they began taking on the characteristics of little cartoon figures. For instance, my feeling of inferiority around certain people I admired started appearing to me in the form of a sad little cow that would traipse forlornly along, following after these people. Rather than getting angry or depressed whenever this feeling of inferiority would appear, I was now able to smile and have great compassion for this little cow. My fear of abandonment became a bedraggled little orphan girl who would stare at me with large sad eyes. Love automatically filled me when she'd appear.

When I've encouraged other people to see in which characters their negative emotions might appear, they've come up with such figures as scary comic-book monsters for their anger or hatred, or Cinderella-type figures for their sadness or despair. It can be fun to start playing with the characters in your mind and can be helpful to a point. But remember to use them only to defuse your energy on the emotions they represent, not to get caught up in a new creative story of suffering around them. Simply watch them appear, do their little dance inside you attempting to get your attention and energy—and then just disappear. Stay detached and objective.

Ultimately, it will not matter whether positive or negative emotions are present with you. If there's no more habitual reacting, no more discriminating, you're free to just allow them to be with you for as long as they happen to stay. Given no energy by you, they have no power over you. You come to realize that who you are is so much more vast and powerful than they are, that there's never any reason to be disturbed by any of them. They're just free-flowing energy floating through your awareness—all part of the wondrous play of consciousness on this level.

8. **Stop Identifying with Emotions.** This brings us to the last step in this process toward liberation from emotional suffering, which is to stop identifying with the emotions that come into your awareness. If you have become proficient in simply watching them objectively

and allowing them to be, this is relatively easy to do. You've begun to see, through direct experience, that you are something beyond the emotions that float through your consciousness. It is obvious how these flimsy, impermanent, and ever-changing things called emotions cannot possibly be who you are. The you that has been watching them all along has stayed constant and unchanging, no matter what emotions might be visiting you at the moment.

If you can fall deeply into this observer, this eternal witness of all that goes on in your life, you will discover the YOU that you have been seeking all your life. And emotions will never again cause you the kind of suffering they always have. You will then be well on your way to ceasing your identification with the emotional aspect of your ego-self.

Although simply allowing emotions to be and not identifying with them is ultimately the path to freedom from the suffering emotions can bring, this is often easier said than done. Because of our deep conditioning about emotions, much time and practice is usually required. Also we all have particular chronic and deeply embedded negative emotions that are likely to keep us in bondage. I will devote the next chapter to ways of dealing more intensively with these emotions.

CHAPTER FIFTEEN

When Emotions Overwhelm You

Every emotion, sensation, or energy faced purely and simply reveals eternal Self.

—Gangaji

T HE PROCESS DESCRIBED IN THE PREVIOUS CHAPTER of simply allowing emotions to be, without interfering with them, may sound helpful for when you're feeling ordinary, run-of-the-mill negative emotions. At these times, you're still able to be somewhat rational about them. But you may be wondering about the times you're feeling completely overwhelmed, out of control, or paralyzed with an emotion. You can't, at that point, just decide to observe it—it's too intense and overwhelming.

When you find yourself in this predicament, you need to get out of the mode of overwhelm before you can do anything else. The first essential step is to take time out to be totally present with yourself. This probably entails finding both the time and space to be alone. When you do this, you are already making an important statement to yourself; you are recognizing that you have to do something about your overwhelm, something different from what you are already doing. You are telling yourself that this overwhelming suffering needs to stop, now. If it is inappropriate to take time immediately to be alone, then take time just as soon as you can. Don't linger in your suffering any longer than you need to.

Once you have found the time and place where you can devote your full attention to yourself, I suggest two options: embracing the pain or surrendering to the pain.

Exercise: *Embracing the Pain*

The first option involves creating a compassionate and nurturing attitude toward yourself. It is usually difficult when you're drowning in a negative emotion to immediately come up with compassion toward yourself. So the first thing you need to do is simply turn your attention to your body.

Take a few deep breaths and let them out slowly. Then begin noticing where the emotional pain has settled in your body. This doesn't require any great concentration; it's usually pretty obvious—it's where your body is feeling the most constricted. Once this is ascertained, begin consciously to let go of the tension in these areas. Do this slowly, gently, by breathing deeply into them. Concentrate on freeing the energy, getting it moving. Become aware of how your body has been constrained and squeezed by the pain. If you can, send love with your breath into the areas of pain. You may not be totally successful at first in releasing all of the blocked energy, but just keep breathing into the constricted areas and releasing whatever energy you can.

If tears come during this process, let them flow. This can be helpful in the natural release of the physical tension. Do be careful, however, not to let this crying move into an indulgence of emotion, where self-pity slides in to take over. Don't let the dramatic story of your suffering become your focus. This is a distraction, and, although perhaps familiar and enticing, it will not ultimately release your suffering. As the first burst of tears subsides, let it go. Then move into the stillness that awaits you. Focus on how good it feels for the body to relax, after having held on to so much tension.

Next become aware of any judgments or criticisms that may be running through your head about yourself—either about feeling the emotion, about the situation that has brought the emotion on—or about anything. Turn off this "inner critic" voice inside you. If necessary, tell it firmly to shut up. This is a quiet time to be with yourself, in a nurturing, loving way. Take the time to embrace yourself (both in your mind and physically, if this feels comfortable). Maybe rock and stroke yourself, as you might a young child. If you have ever done inner-child work, this will probably feel familiar, and you will know how comforting it can be to be loving and compassionate with yourself.

Become aware that, as you are embracing yourself, you are also embracing your pain—both physical and emotional. Make sure you are including all of it; reject nothing that you are feeling. It is all part of *what is* at this moment, and all must be accepted, welcomed, and embraced.

In the midst of doing all this, you may find your mind urgently barging in, over and over again, with its stories about incidents and people who have caused your pain or about what you should do about this situation to set things straight. This is when you really need to take charge and not allow yourself to be carried away by this familiar reaction of the mind. It's very important at this point to stay centered and focused on your body and on giving yourself nurturing.

If your mind is insistent, you can tell it, "Later! We will go through all that later. Right now, I'm bringing a calm, loving stillness to myself." Then bring your focus back to your body and to giving love and understanding to yourself. There's no need to get angry with your mind for its interruptions; it's only doing what it's been conditioned to do. In fact, as you embrace yourself, be sure to include your mind (and even the inner critic!) in your embrace. Embrace ALL of you, just as you are.

This can be a very powerful exercise if you have felt overwhelmed by emotions and have also felt pummeled by your judgments toward yourself. You can realize that beating yourself up with judgments does nothing to release the hurt, anger, and pain you're feeling; indeed, it simply serves to pile more pain and guilt on top of them.

At this point, you will probably be experiencing a sense of relief and relaxation. It can feel so good finally to stop resisting the pain and to accept and embrace it. This is where people are often inclined to stop—and either go to sleep or find a distraction of some kind.

This can be a big mistake, because the core of the problem has not yet been addressed. You have only put salve on the symptoms. The problem is misidentification—you are mistaking yourself for a small and separate entity that can be overwhelmed by energy forms known as "emotions." Unless you go to the root of this problem, the same suffering is going to continue to come up, every time the same emotion is triggered.

Therefore, take the time, once you are somewhat still and re-laxed, to look more deeply into the reaction you had to the emotions when they appeared. This will require your mind—but not in an analyzing way. It's more of a gentle reflecting and inquiring process inside yourself. See if you can become aware of any resistance to the emotions you were experiencing. If you were in so much pain that you were overwhelmed, some resistance was bound to be involved, some attitude of rejection or pushing the emotions away. See if you can identify what resistances were involved. (Examples are pushing away, ignoring, denying, judging, distracting yourself, being angry at them.)

It is important to identify these reactions of resistance to negative emotions, because it is the resistance to the emotions that generally puts you into overwhelm—not the emotions themselves. When emotions are felt purely, without any resistance or mental stories put on them, they can usually be tolerated. This becomes clear if you can remember, for instance, times when you have simply experienced sadness—with nothing added to it. There can almost be a sweetness about it, when sadness is truly pure. It's only when judgments or stories are added to it that it becomes intolerable and eventually evolves into depression.

Sometimes you have to observe yourself very closely; resistance to emotions can disguise itself very well. Let's say, for instance, that when you went into emotional overwhelm, you had been experienc-ing deep hatred toward a particular person in your life. When an incident between you and this person triggered this hate, you sud-denly found yourself "over the edge." Your hatred was raging; you wanted to kill the person.

What you might find, in looking clearly at this later, is that you intellectually accepted the emotion of hatred; philosophically, you believed that it's okay to feel hatred—you're human and everyone feels it from time to time. But underneath this intellectual overlay, perhaps you were not truly accepting the emotion. It felt wrong and "unspiritual," so you were very subtly resisting or denying it. Or you may have been reacting to your hatred with some other form of resistance. Whatever it was, once you've brought yourself out of overwhelm, you can now just take note of it.

As you continue this process, check to see what other reactions you may have had toward your hatred. Another habitual reaction, as we saw in the last chapter, is indulging the emotion. Although this reaction may not seem to be resistance, it actually is. Both forms of indulgence—the attempt to release the pain in action and entering into the mind to analyze it—are forms of rejection. You are not simply allowing it to be as it is. Going into the mind and telling the story about the emotion is a strong habit for most people. If this is what you were doing when you were hit by overwhelm, take note of this.

Lastly, check for the third form of resistance to an emotion, which can flow very naturally out of analyzing the story: attempting to fix or change the emotion in some way. If you were also doing this, note this as well. There is no need to judge yourself for using any of these forms of resistance; simply observe that this is the way you have been conditioned to react to certain emotions.

Once you have discovered which of these habitual reactions of resistance you used to help create your experience of overwhelm, you can then learn how to catch them *before* an experience of overwhelm is created. You can begin to detach from the emotion, before it begins drowning you. Awareness of your automatic reaction patterns is, therefore, the key, along with discipline and commitment. You have to be so sick of your emotional suffering, that you will do whatever it takes to find your way through to the end of it.

The last step is to focus on all the different states you've found in yourself during this process; first you were in overwhelming emotional pain; then you were relatively calm and serene; then you were involved in thought processes in your mind; and now you are experiencing whatever is currently present for you.

Look at all these different "you"s. See that they've all come and gone. Take the time now to tune into what has *not* come and gone—the YOU that was there, constant and unchanging, throughout all of that drama. Move into that Awareness now, that silent, constant

Awareness that is always present—no matter what changes are happening in the inner landscape, no matter what emotional "weather" is occurring at the moment. And rest there. Know that this is who you are. You are not the suffering. You are not the emotions. You are not the thoughts about the suffering. You are that silent abiding Consciousness within which all of it is occurring.

Exercise: *Surrendering to the Emotion*

The second option, when you find yourself in emotional over-whelm, may take some courage, but I have found that it can have quite spectacular results. It is to simply surrender to the emotion you are feeling—to totally and completely give yourself to it. It's to experience it with *all* of you, holding nothing back.

Surrendering to an emotion like this may sound like indulging it, but it's actually quite different. Indulging an emotion is a reaction of giving up and passively letting it take over; it's falling into all the thoughts and stories about it, out of an automatic, self-destructive habit. Surrendering to an emotion, on the other hand, is an active, purposeful, and courageous decision to consciously dive into the middle of the emotion and totally experience it head-on. It's to ruthlessly let go of any resistance that you have to it, and openly investigate the emotion. Another way to put it is that indulging an emotion entails diving into your *mind;* surrendering to it involves diving into the *emotion* itself.

I gave an example of this process in Chapter 11, when I described working with the woman who dove into her fear of death. She wasn't quite in overwhelm at the time, but she was feeling the fear quite strongly. It can be even more powerful from a state of over-whelm, because you have all the more energy with which to dive in.

Paradoxically, the process entails taking just enough control of yourself—so that you can completely let go of all control. It involves making the conscious decision to jump into the very core of the pain—without thoughts, judgments, or analyzing. Your mind must be left behind, as you completely surrender to the feeling. And you must be willing to be consumed by it. Only with this kind of commitment can you truly discover what exists at the core of the emotion.

As I've said, this process can take some courage—or maybe just a large dose of desperation! But if you are truly sick and tired of feeling bullied by an emotion, this may be the step to take. Face it squarely; call its bluff. See for yourself if it can annihilate or devour you, as it's threatening to do. The results may startle and amaze you.

The first time I tried this on myself, when I really gave it my all, I was in the throes of a gut-wrenching reaction to something about which an old friend and I had been arguing. Familiar feelings of rejection and abandonment were overwhelming me. My mind was chasing around in circles, panicked, trying desperately to think of something I could do to put an end to my unbearable suffering. Surely there was some way I could fix or change this emotion, so I could find some respite! But I could think of nothing. A feeling of paralysis threatened to take hold of me, as enormous fear spread more and more deeply through my consciousness.

I had felt all of this countless times before. Each time I'd just wanted to die. It seemed the only way out. Even with all the ways I had learned to deal with emotions, I could never find anything that would even begin to dissolve the pain of this one. The best I could do was push it underground for awhile, by distracting myself with something else. Inevitably it reappeared the next time it was triggered.

This time, as I sat struggling with the unbelievable pain of profound rejection and abandonment, I decided maybe I should truly let go of my resistance to the pain and simply dive into it—consciously and purposefully—and see for myself what was actually there. Exactly what did it consist of?

Terror immediately arose as I decided to do this, terror of either being totally consumed—or of going insane. I wrestled with this for a few minutes, but then I just decided to do it. I was finally so weary of these emotions that I had to do the only thing I'd never tried with them before.

With my eyes closed, I carefully inched my way over to the mouth of the cavernous black hole of fear, rejection, and abandonment in the center of my gut. Terror truly took hold of me now; I was physically shaking. But I knew it was either dive in or face a lifetime of running from it. I was desperate.

Without thinking another thought, I quickly dove in, thrusting myself into the jaws of the beast. Immediately, my mind began grabbing at me: "No, no, don't jump—come back, we can figure this one out. You're going to die! You'll go crazy!"

There was a struggle for awhile, as I'd put my hand halfway up for my mind to grasp and pull me out. But then I became resolved. Either I was going to do this all the way, or forget it. Finally, ignoring my mind, I plunged into the center of the feeling of absolute abandonment. I completely let go and sank into its depths.

Profound blackness surrounded me. There was nothing there— just complete and overwhelming darkness. I was quivering as I held myself there and then did what I could to plunge ever more deeply into it. I soon found a sense of anger beginning to rise in me. I was yelling inside myself, "Show yourself, Abandonment! Damn it! Show me your teeth! What's the worst you can do to me?" Immediately, an image came to me: an ugly black monster with huge teeth. Snakes and scorpions were writhing around inside its mouth. Naturally, this was frightening, but, somehow, my facing up to it and demanding that it show itself had strengthened me.

My anger began building. I was shaking now with rage rather than terror. And yet I could still hear my mind doing new numbers: "You know, you should be expressing this rage to your friend. Look at what she said to you!" Or "This is silly. It's like a grade B horror movie here. What are you doing?" Or "Let's stop here. It feels good to be angry. Let's not go any further with this."

After following these thoughts for a few moments—and almost becoming convinced by them—I again pulled my attention back to where I was. After a moment's hesitation, I decided to hurl myself at the beast and simply let it have me. As I did this, much to my amazement, the beast disappeared. I had plunged into the middle of it, and nothing was there.

Nothing at all was there. Absolutely nothing. It was utterly depressing. All around me was a desert—the landscape only gray sand stretching on forever in every direction. The sky was gray, as well. Tears welled up inside me in seeing this. It felt as if this were really how my whole life had been—barren and empty. But I stayed alert with this; I was determined not to get sentimental and fall into a habitual state of self-pity. I dove instead ever more deeply into what was there in front of me—the barren sands of depression.

A few moments later, I emerged in a place that looked like a desolate moonscape, compete with craters and scraggly hard ground. It was all black—as if a fire had once raged there but had burned out and left cold, solid-packed dirt. Compared to this landscape, the desert had been a warm and friendly place! It was as bleak and God-forsaken a place as I'd ever seen. I sat there, unable to move. Profound despair had a stranglehold on me. And yet, I knew I had to do something. I certainly couldn't stay there. Sighing, I finally summoned up what little courage and energy I could and dove into one of the craters.

For a few moments, I felt almost suffocated. But then, much to my surprise and delight, I suddenly saw above me clear blue skies—beautiful, bright, and friendly skies, with puffy white clouds floating through them. I let out a long sigh of relief. As I looked around, I found I was in a garden—the most incredibly lush garden I had ever seen. Brilliant flowers bloomed everywhere in every color. Trees rose into the sky, with chirping birds flying back and forth through them. Colorful butterflies played among the flowers. Squirrels ran up the trees. Rabbits hopped around, chasing each other. This was, indeed, the land of Bambi—in vivid technicolor. Such joy arose in me as I gazed around!

I walked along a path through the garden and eventually came to a beautiful, serene, turquoise lake. I sat down on a log next to it, gazing into its depths. I felt as if I could stay forever. Amazingly, my feelings of fear, rage, and abandonment had been left far behind. A profound peace and contentment now filled me. I was ecstatic.

And yet, something kept pulling at me. A voice was calling to me, "Come deeper. Come deeper still." Somewhat reluctantly, I decided to see if, indeed, I could go any more deeply into what I was experiencing. I got up and dove into the middle of the lake.

As I slowly let myself fall ever more deeply into it depths, I soon realized I could breathe underwater. And as I relaxed more and more into it, a profound serenity began flowing into me—one far surpassing the one I had experienced sitting by the lake. This serenity began rippling through me with tremendous power. In a strange way, it felt as if it were pulling me apart—and yet it was an exquisitely pleasant and sensuous experience.

As I gave into it more and more profoundly, I soon found myself experiencing a sense of enormous vastness. I realized I was everywhere. I extended in all directions. The entire universe was inside of me. I was the Mother—the Source of all that is. Tears began streaming down my face, as I vibrated with the tremendous power and elation of this realization.

I thought back to the feelings of rejection and abandonment I had been experiencing so profoundly just a short while before, and they were like mist—unreal—so insignificant in the whole scheme of things. They so obviously had no power whatsoever over who I now knew myself to be, it was a joke! I began laughing, as the tears continued to stream down my face. Both laughing and crying, I now began to rock. My whole body rocked—and it felt as if the entire universe were rocking.

I sat there for almost an hour, blissfully marveling at what I was experiencing—and at what I had discovered. By finally facing the demons inside me—and fully surrendering to them—I had discovered what truly lay at the core of them: my Self. Then I realized that of course Self would be there; Self is everywhere, inside of everything. Why would it not be inside of my demons as well?

When I finally got up and walked into the other room where my friend sat, still angry and sullen from our argument, I simply smiled at her and went to put some water on for tea. I could see she was puzzled. The last time she'd seen me, I had been raging with helpless anger and pain. Now I obviously had no interest at all in engaging her about the issue we'd argued about.

I knew that something had definitely cleared in me. I was no longer terrified of feeling emotionally or physically abandoned by her—or by anyone. Such incredible freedom! I never again experienced the fear of abandonment that, up until that point, had haunted me. Sometimes a ghost of it appears in my awareness. But it has no power over me anymore. Since I finally saw it for what it was, it can no longer do anything to me.

As is clear, this process of surrendering to an emotion can take courage, persistence, and patience. But the value you can derive from it is beyond words. At the very least, you will have faced your *fear* of the emotion and will no longer need to feel bullied by it in the future. More importantly, you will likely discover who you truly are, beyond the emotion. You will find that you have indeed survived surrendering to it completely; you have not been annihilated or devoured. Indeed, you have found that who you are is much larger, much stronger than any emotion you could ever have.

The extraordinary discovery is that you can actually use your emotions as gateways into your Self—the very emotions that threaten to overwhelm and annihilate you! Through them, you can discover that Self truly is everywhere. Although seemingly hidden at times, it can be found, if you simply take the time and the courage to look for it.

There are probably many different ways in which you can handle overwhelming emotions. Most of them will likely give you a sense of relief. Some of them may even offer a healing of the emotion. However, what I am suggesting is that you take it one step further and go to the core of the pain, to the cause of *all* emotional suffering: your belief that you are a small and separate being who is subject to the power of emotions. If this is what you identify with, then you are doomed to suffer. Emotions will run you ragged, dragging you back and forth, inside out and upside down. They'll feed you horror stories. At times, they'll overwhelm and drown you.

The only way out of this is to know that who you are is the essence of Life itself. You are the very Source of all emotions. Without you, they have no life. An effective way to discover this is through understanding that there is no reason to try to control, manipulate, or get rid of emotions. Simply see them clearly for what they are— forms of energy that are visiting your consciousness. They have no inherent power except that which you give them. This is such good news! All you need do is let them be. You can watch them as they act out their scary little dances designed to allure and hook you … and then go on about your business, unperturbed.

Of course, even with all the experiences of Self you may have had, and with all these processes to help you, treating emotions like this may still be easier said than done, because of all the years of emotional conditioning you've had. In order to help you get your arms around this animal of emotional suffering even more se-curely—so that you can eventually release it for good—I will come at it from another direction in the next chapter. I will address the ways in which we are trapped in our emotions by holding on to our "story of suffering."

CHAPTER SIXTEEN

Letting Go of the Story

Mysteriously, in the ending of the personal story, completion and fulfillment are experienced.

—Gangaji

To truly experience emotional freedom, you must be willing to let go of your personal story of suffering. You must be willing to give up making your suffering important, and stop defining yourself through your story about it. You cannot detach from the suffering while remaining attached to the story about it. It just doesn't work.

Letting go of the story of our suffering is not an easy thing for many of us to do, however. We automatically tend to give lots of energy to it—we think about it, talk about it, grieve about it, ask people's advice about it, try to figure out ways to stop it. It's easy to begin believing that this story is who we are.

Metaphysical laws state very clearly that the more we focus our energy on something, the more we create it in our lives. I have always found this to be true. I think it is especially true in how we perpetuate suffering in our lives: the more energy we put into our stories about the suffering, the more we perpetuate it. In fact, if we look carefully, we can find that, because we have focused so much on our stories, we have actually created broken records in our lives: the same painful events and situations keep happening over and over again.

You may feel that you have good reason to put energy into your story of suffering. Perhaps you have worked hard in getting in touch with your suffering and in learning how to deeply experience your feelings. You have talked about your story to many people, analyz-ing it over and over again—believing that if you can just figure it all out, the suffering will be relieved. You may protest that you're not trying to perpetuate your suffering with all of this; you're trying to alleviate it.

Getting in touch with your story of suffering is, indeed, an important step toward emotional freedom. You need to know what has been keeping you in bondage. Attempting to fix the story by changing behaviors, attitudes, and beliefs can also be helpful. But if you've been at this process for some time and are still deeply caught in the suffering, you might want to honestly ask yourself: Do I truly want to be free of my suffering? Think for a moment: without this story, with what would you be left?

In some ways, stories are an important way in which we can feel special. They are a way we can feel valuable, important, and interest-ing. In fact, in some circles, the more juicy a person's story of suffering is, the more interesting and well-respected they are. I've listened while people actually try to one-up each other with their stories, as if to say, "You think *you've* suffered—wait till you hear *my* story!"

Note that nothing is inherently wrong with stories of suffering. They are, actually, often what gives color to life. Sometimes people have incredibly fascinating stories; they're exciting, dramatic, tragi-cally humorous. They can all be entertaining in their own way. But it's what we *do* with these stories that causes us suffering. It's how we use them to perpetuate the pain, how we stay attached to them and build our identity around them, that gets us into trouble.

Throughout the years of my counseling practice, I have had a number of "drama queen" clients. In some ways, these are the most difficult to help. So often their whole identity is caught up in the stories of all the suffering they have endured. Whenever I finally suggest that perhaps they are attached to their stories of suffering, they always protest that of course they aren't—they want to put an end to their suffering!

Diana was one such woman. She did, indeed, have a tragic story to tell. From the very beginning of her life, she seemed doomed: a harsh, alcoholic father and a schizophrenic mother; criticism, abuse, and abandonment all through childhood; one disfunctional relationship after another throughout adulthood; accidents and abortions and children out of wedlock. You name it—it had happened to her. It was understandable that she held onto her story of suffering—what else did she have in her life? Because of her early wounding, she had never been able to discover anything besides her suffering to help her feel important and valuable.

At first she could not even hear the suggestion that making her story so important was precisely what was perpetuating it. It took many long months of counseling before she could even begin to look at this possibility.

As we've seen earlier, anyone on a self-improvement path can make this erroneous detour and fall into worshipping their wounding. Usually, after some therapy or reading some self-help books, people will begin to look closely at how their story of suffering came into being. Then they will try to fix it some way. These actions can be helpful.

The problem begins when the attempts at fixing don't have the results people would like. Believing they just haven't found the right techniques or insights to fix the suffering, they go back and rehash the story of suffering—until it has finally become ingrained in their identity. To make things worse, the efforts to alleviate their suffering end up being woven into the story, strengthening it further.

The next step people will often take, after feeling unsuccessful in fixing their suffering, is to see their suffering as "spiritual lessons" they are here to learn. They adopt the belief that all their pain has a purpose: they are "growing and learning" through it. This may well be valid. This perspective can certainly make the suffering somewhat more tolerable. But, in the end, the solace it offers is limited. No matter how much reframing we do about experiences of emotional suffering—if we're honest about it, the suffering is still here. Our philosophy about it does not make it go away.

As we've seen in the last few chapters, emotional freedom can only really come about when we detach from the emotions themselves, and simply let them be. This is also what we need to do with emotional suffering as a whole: just let it go, let it be. And to let it go, we have to let go of the story we have about it.

Do You Really Want to Let It Go?

What it comes down to is asking yourself: Am I really ready to give up my personal story of suffering? Think about it honestly. Are you ready not to take it so seriously, not make it of such primary importance in your life? Are you ready to stop talking about it to people so often? Are you willing to stop thinking about it so much, analyzing it to death? And are you willing to see, once you've done all this, what might be left of you, without your story?

If you think you might be ready for this, here are some steps you can take to begin letting go of your story.

Exercise: *Letting Go of the Story*

1. **Understand that your story of suffering is about your ego-self; it's not about YOU.** It's the story that your ego-self has created about its painful reactions to the events and situations that have come its way since childhood. This story, in reality, has nothing to do with YOU. As Consciousness, the true YOU has simply stood by and watched the whole drama that the little ego-self has created. It has been compassionate and loving; yet, being utterly free, it has not been touched by the suffering.

    Even if you can't yet see the story from this detached viewpoint, just understanding on the intellectual level that this story is about your ego-self and not the true YOU can be a start.

2. **See your life as a story.** The next step is to begin seeing your life of suffering truly as a story—a movie, a drama, or a soap opera. This can be a fun process, one that can bring in humor and a sense of relief. Become the objective observer of this drama. Take time to look over the long expanse of your life, assuming a neutral attitude about it—as if it were the story of someone else's life.

    Now attempt to determine the important themes of suffering that have been woven into the story throughout the years. Look at the painful experiences that have happened over and over again; note the emotions and thoughts that have gotten triggered each time. Also become aware of who the main players in the story have been, the ones who have helped you to play your role as the sufferer.

3. **Write a summary of your life.** Compose a short summary of your story of suffering. Here's an example:

   This is a story about a woman who has felt misunderstood and unloved most of her life. Even when love is offered to her, she always manages to reject it, because she feels undeserving of love. She has felt lonely and unhappy most of her life.

   Or:

   This story is about a man who has rebelled against authority figures all of his life. This has gotten him into trouble time and time again—first with his parents, then with teachers at school, then with bosses and superintendents at work. He has also automatically rebelled against anyone he feels is smarter than he is. He has experienced enormous rage and suffering because of all this. He has never really felt loved, because he's always pushed the most important people in his life away.

4. **Find a broken record.** Now choose a particular theme within your story, a painful event that happens over and over—and determine specifically how the dynamics of this "broken record" work. Let's use the example of the woman who felt misunderstood and unloved most of her life. The woman who came up with this story wrote the following broken-record scenario:

   It all starts when I see someone I find attractive, and think I want to get to know them. Pretty soon I start feeling like I really want them to love me. So I begin doing everything I can to try to win this person's love. I do great things for them. I take care of them when they're sick. I give them support and nurturing when they need it.

   Quite often, as time goes on, the person will start showing signs of loving me. They become affectionate and warm. They do caring things for me. They even tell me they love me. But as soon as all this begins, I start feeling turned off by them. I think, if this person loves ME, how attractive or smart can they be? And I no longer want to be with them. I leave.

5. **See how you perpetuate the story.** Now that you understand better what your story of suffering boils down to, and how the

dynamics of a broken-record scenario work, it is time to ask yourself what you do to perpetuate this story. By this I do not mean for you to continue analyzing what happens in the story so that you can fix it or change it in some way.

I am suggesting that you step outside the story and see what you do with it that perpetuates it. For instance, what attitudes do you hold about yourself as the hero or heroine in the story? Judging yourself or your story will certainly keep the story going strong. Similarly, feeling pride or sentimental pity for yourself will perpetuate the story as well. Do you present this story to people as who you are? Do you talk endlessly to people about it? Do you think about it constantly? Or do you perhaps try to hide your story from people, out of shame?

All of these actions and attitudes about your story give energy to it and keep you attached to it, keeping it going in your life.

6. **Let go of the story.** The final step, after becoming aware of all you are doing to perpetuate the story, is to give up doing them. You will probably see how habitual some of the attitudes and actions are, and find them difficult to let go. Persistent vigilance may be necessary at first. The attitude toward your story needs to be an objective, dispassionate one—without judgments. And your actions need to reflect this attitude.

Giving your story this new treatment probably won't immediately stop the broken-record scenarios from playing out in your life. They will likely continue for awhile, simply because they are so familiar and habitual. However, you can begin robbing them of their vitality and pain by observing yourself while you're playing them out. Watch them as episodes in the soap opera you now have seen your story of suffering to be. See how boring, repetitive, and predictable they really are. Given no energy, they will eventually disappear from your life.

The important thing to remember is that your story of suffering is not a story about YOU. It's something your ego-self has invented. Have the courage to let go of it—even for a short time—and find out what is left of you, without a story of suffering to define you.

Exercise: *Starving Your Story*

You can try this as an experiment for just a day. During the entire day, watch both your thoughts and what you talk about to other people. Watch for any thoughts that have to do with what's wrong with your life and how you're suffering because of it. Catch all thoughts that have to do with how bad these things make you feel, all the times in the past they have happened, how they might happen again in the future—and how you need to fix any of it in any way. Note these thoughts, and the feelings that go with them, without rejecting any of them. Then turn your attention toward something else. Act similarly with any urge you have to talk to other people about your story: when the impulse arises, simply decide to talk about something else.

In other words, give your story of suffering a starvation diet for the entire day. See what happens. You may be amazed at the peace and freedom that are waiting for you, once you spend even a short period of time without this tired, old, familiar story. And then think about what it might be like to drop it for good!

Sally's Story

I once set up a psychodrama situation in a class I was giving, in order to demonstrate how to let go of the story. It turned out to be a fun and powerful learning experience for all of us.

First of all, everyone in the class wrote out their stories of suffering and then the dynamics of one broken-record theme within their stories (as in Steps 3 and 4 above). After all of them shared what they'd written, I chose a woman, Sally, to be our subject in the psychodrama. I could see she was very clear about what her story was and that she was also eager to learn how to let go of it.

Sally had been coming to individual counseling for a number of months, during which time she had been working hard to discover why she kept getting caught up in feelings of anger and resentment. We saw that she had developed many patterns of overextending herself to please others and then becoming resentful when they were not as considerate and kind in return.

We began working on how she could take responsibility for creating this situation and turn it around. A bright young woman and also very motivated, she began focusing on giving to herself more, not giving to others from an "empty cup," and not expecting others to fill the needs that she herself needed to fill. She was empowered through this work, and over all, more happy in her life.

Yet, she realized, no matter how much she'd changed and how vigilant she'd become, the same situations still happened. She wasn't as reactive in the situations, nor did she experience quite as much suffering in them, but they were still occurring. And she was getting truly sick and tired of them.

At this point, she was very ready to try a new approach. I asked her to read to us again her broken-record scenario. Here's what she told us:

> First, I decide to do something really nice for someone. Sometimes I actually bend over backwards to please them, even when it means I don't take care of my own needs in the process. But, at the time of doing these nice things, I'm usually feeling loving and warm toward the person.
>
> Then the person either ignores what I've done, or they actually criticize me for doing it, get angry at me, or feel hurt and resentful about what I've done. I am amazed and incredulous. I can't believe they aren't feeling appreciative about what I've done for them. I try explaining why I've done what I've done, and end up getting defensive about it.
>
> Then they get angry and even more critical. Finally, I get furious, yell at them, and leave—vowing never again to be nice to them.

After outlining this broken record so clearly, she described three people in her life with whom she was currently playing out the story. She told us about her brother, her husband, and her cousin, describing the situations she was in with each of them, what their personalities were, and what their basic messages to her were.

I had her choose someone in the class to play her part in the psychodrama. (She was going to be part of the audience, watching the "movie"). Then she chose three other people to play the roles of her brother, her husband, and her cousin. I explained that the rest of us in the class were going to be Sally's "friends"; we were accompanying her to watch new episodes in the movie about her life and to give her support about what she was experiencing in her movie.

As her friends, of course, we were all very familiar with her story; we'd all seen previous episodes of the story; we knew the plot and the themes very well. But we were looking forward to the new episodes that were going to be shown in a few moments—just as we might any new episodes in a soap opera.

Before the movie began, we in the audience talked about Sally's story. We mourned how she was always being misunderstood and unappreciated. She was such a good person, so nice and good to everyone—and look at how she was always treated! We passed popcorn and soft drinks to each other, as we sat and chatted among ourselves about Sally's story, waiting for the movie to begin.

Then it started. The actress playing "Sally" immediately fell into the role with great authenticity. Her anger and her tears were very real and palpable. The other players in the drama were also playing their roles quite convincingly. As is so delightfully common in psychodrama, all the players discovered that they'd been given perfect roles. In one way or another, they could relate only too well to them.

As the different scenes unfolded, and "Sally" in the movie began truly to become embroiled in her emotional struggle, we in the audience began to talk among ourselves:

"Oh, here comes the part where she gets hurt and angry!"

"Oh, poor Sally—people just don't understand her. She tries so hard to be nice to them, and look what they do!"

"Boy, the acting sure is good, isn't it? It really feels real!"

"Sally is such a good person—I feel so sorry for her."

It was apparent by this time how uncomfortable the real Sally in the audience was beginning to feel. Although she was laughing and joking about the story with the rest of us, she was beginning to see clearly how her story looked from the outside. She was, in effect, able to see it objectively for the first time.

What really struck her was how boring the story was, how repetitious and predictable. She was shaking her head, unable to believe that this was the story she had been putting so much effort into all her life—and that she had come to identify herself as the heroine of this story.

At one point, I stepped outside the psychodrama role I'd been playing and said to her, "Remember, Sally—this woman in the movie is not who YOU are. She's just a little ego-self that goes around in the world believing herself to be a separate, individual little being who has to figure out how to run her life. She doesn't know that you, as Consciousness, are here to do that job. And with this very limiting ignorance, she's doing her best to cope with what life is handing her. It's not easy! Have love and compassion for her. And, at the same time, don't get caught up in the illusion that she is who YOU are."

I could see the light in Sally's eyes shift, as what I was saying registered. She knew what I was talking about; she had had some important glimpses of Self in the past. All she needed to make the shift in awareness at this point, even in the midst of her pain, was a reminder of the Truth. She smiled and nodded. I could see her body relax some, as the final scene concluded.

At the end, the players bowed, and we all clapped and lauded them. They briefly shared their experiences in playing their roles. I then turned my attention to Sally and asked her to share what her experience had been. She told us how painful it was to see her story enacted so clearly—but also how elated she felt. Something had shifted inside her, she said; a decision had been made on a profound level that it was definitely time to drop this whole story. Although she had thought in the past that she had made this same decision, she realized now that she never really had. She had still wanted to cling to the story of the mistreated, unappreciated victim. Now she was utterly nauseated by it.

I told her I understood her reaction and I knew she could no longer play out this scenario in the same way. She now knew this was just a script she had developed somewhere along the way but no longer needed to follow.

I also cautioned her that this wasn't necessarily an easy thing to do; she would probably find that broken-record scenarios seem to have a life of their own. The process is similar to when a ceiling fan has been switched off; it takes a little while for it to completely come to a stop.

But at any time in the future, when she found herself in the same situation, she could to step back and watch it as a movie—just as she'd done in class. She could become the observer of the movie, as well as the heroine on the screen. In doing this, she would inevitably discover that the scenarios happened less often. More importantly, she would discover that she was really not touched at all by the suffering going on in them.

I described to her how I had experienced this with my own story in a number of situations and interesting things had happened. One time I was on the telephone with a colleague with whom I had had difficulty over and over again; we always seemed to miscommunicate about one thing or another. Typically, she would get angry—and I would assume all the blame and then end up getting defensive and hurt. I had tried numerous times to change this pattern—by not assuming the blame, not getting defensive, staying "neutral" in my explanations. I had also tried talking to her about our "problem," in hopes of resolving it together.

Although the situation seemed to get a little better for awhile, it was never really resolved. The pattern continued in one form or another, and I kept getting pulled into it. It seemed I had put so much energy into my role of suffering in this particular scenario that the pattern would not break. My identity was still hooked into that of the misunderstood victim.

Finally, I began to loosen my identity with this victim; I distanced myself just enough to just watch her as she thought her tiresome thoughts and went through her predictable defensive behaviors and explanations with this woman. Little by little, an almost visceral "unhooking" took place, along with the direct realization that this victim was not who I was but just a product of conditioning.

A short while later, as I was on the phone once again with the woman with whom I'd been having trouble, I started observing myself as the whole dynamic once again began to unfold. I observed what I was saying, what I was feeling, how I was reacting. Suddenly, I found myself becoming very bored with the whole scene—without the energy to even continue it. I stopped mid-sentence and was silent for a few moments. Then I said to her, "You know, I don't want to do this anymore. It's old; it's tiresome; it's a waste of time. I'll call you later." And I hung up.

Amazingly, we never entered into that dynamic again. Our miscommunications even diminished. The few times they did occur, the dynamic between us was very different. We each assumed responsibility for our part in it, and we very quickly cleared it up and moved on. I had had to see it very clearly—objectively—in order to get so bored with the story of it that I finally let it go.

Sally reported to me a week later that the same old dynamic with her cousin had happened again. However, she told me, throughout the scene, she had been able to watch it. Although it continued much as it always did, the suffering about it was greatly diminished. She knew she had finally seen the story of suffering so clearly and had become so bored with it, that it could no longer grab her as it had in the past. She'd also been able to see the pathetic humor in it all; her poor little ego-self was just doing what it had been conditioned to do.

I could see she was finally beginning to feel at peace about her story. She said she no longer was interested in even talking about it to anyone anymore. She no longer felt she needed to do anything to fix it, either. She just needed to continue viewing it as a movie that her ego-self was playing over and over again, and not give it much thought. She could just let it die a quiet death and put her attention into something more exciting and productive. She laughed with relief. After so many years of trying to fix her story of suffering, she was finally letting go if it!

As time went on, Sally realized something else very important, something I, too, had realized about myself and about many others with whom I'd worked: once you begin letting go of your story of suffering—beyond experiencing the relief of letting go of something so negative and painful—you also realize that you have made room for your true Self to begin shining through into your awareness. Without the clutter of all the emotions and thoughts about the suffering, there is suddenly space, an openness, for something else to become present. You find a peace, a harmony, a restful calm begin to pervade your consciousness. You realize that this is for you to rest in, to drop into ever more deeply—and to see where it takes you.

You may find that, even after you have begun truly to let your story of suffering go, your story starts finding new ways in which to allure you once again into following it. Don't worry; just let that be. Give it no energy. Just keep focusing on the peace and the calm and the spaciousness in your consciousness. When ignored long enough—and when seen clearly for what it really is—the story of suffering eventually begins to evaporate. It becomes clear what it was made of all along: your imagination. It can be really humorous to realize that you were at one time so troubled by something that was only imaginary!

CHAPTER SEVENTEEN

Experiencing Freedom Within Relationship

The Love that any two beings share is the Love of Self for Self ... all attraction is for the Self only, although appearances are deceiving.
—Papaji

T HE FINAL WAY in which I will approach emotional freedom is through exploring perhaps the most challenging emotional area that people face in their lives: relationships. No matter how many other emotional difficulties people have (with the probable exception of fear about survival), it is usually problems in their relationships that bring the most suffering. Intimate relationships with marital or romantic partners are especially challenging for most people, so I will focus on these relationships. However, most of what will be discussed can probably also be applied to any important, intimate relationship.

As we all know, creating and maintaining a fulfilling relationship with another human being isn't always easy. Most people make numerous valiant efforts; only too often, they fail. Always something is not quite right or satisfactory about what they create. I think most of us can look around at the marriages and partnerships with which we are familiar and see few (if any) we might call "good" or "healthy" relationships. Often we initially think some are very healthy and happy, only to learn later that tremendous suffering has been endured by one or both partners in the relationship.

The fact that people have stayed together in a marriage for many years does not automatically make these marriages "good" or "successful" relationships. It *is* possible that it signifies a healthy, mature quality the partners share—knowing how to hang in there through the difficult times they have together. But it can just as easily signify an unhealthy dependence and fear they both have of being alone. Think of all the marriages you know where the partners unbelievably have stayed together for years, while obviously hating each other and making each other miserable. Or the ones where one person in the relationship has "sold out" in order to keep the relationship together; they've decided they'll do anything—including negating what is most important to them—in order to hold on to the other person. It seems that as unhappy and unfulfilled as the people in these relationships may be, facing the fear of living alone feels like a worse alternative to them.

Many relationships, of course, have beautiful aspects about them. Deep love, acceptance, support, and appreciation are all profoundly present. But these have generally come about through many years of hard work, compromise, and sacrifice. And, inevitably, this isn't the whole story. Often other aspects of these relationships aren't so rosy.

Furthermore, even the most positive and loving relationships usually have one catch that cannot be transcended as long as the people in the relationship look to it as a main source of their happiness, security, and love: there is no guarantee that the relationship will continue past the present moment. No matter how many promises people in a partnership may make to each other about staying together forever, forces beyond their control can come in at any time and challenge these promises.

Life brings all sorts of surprises—accidents, unexpected situations, and unsought attractions—that can change a fulfilling and seemingly secure relationship overnight. Often the most devastating event is death. Whether conscious or not, the fear is always present that an important relationship could end at any moment through the death of a partner. With this death, the person would be alone again, without the source of love, security, and fulfillment they once had.

This realization can bring such immense fear that it is usually kept unconscious, but it is always there.

Hundreds of books have been written on how to be happy in relationships, books that tell us how to stay in them, how to leave them, how to fix them to make them more fulfilling. I think it's safe to say that most people who seek therapy end up (if not begin by) talking about their relationships. Either they are having problems in the one they're in, or they're not in one and would like to be. People obviously find relationships very important—but are continually dissatisfied with what is going on in that area of their lives. No matter how full of love and trust their primary relationship may be, they always want something more.

Addressing the Real Issue

This is so, I believe, because the basic issue in just about all relationships is rarely ever addressed: what most people are looking for in a relationship—a guarantee of love, security, and fulfillment— cannot be given by another person.

Often, at the onset of a romantic relationship, there is the illusion that this guarantee is, indeed, being given by the other person. People in love float around in sheer bliss, believing they have finally found the person who will fulfill their important needs. But ultimately this illusion bursts. It is discovered that this person is not, after all, giving what has been promised. This is when many relationships break up—when people realize that the partner they've chosen isn't going to give them the love, security, and fulfillment they were looking for.

This would be an important insight, except that, unfortunately, most people believe they have simply chosen the wrong partner. They believe that all they need is to find the right one who *will* give them what they want. They don't realize that no one else can actually fulfill their needs for them.

Some people in relationship, either through therapy or simply through personal insight, discover this truth. They realize that they have to fulfill their own basic needs for love, security, and a sense of wholeness. They can accept whatever their partner may be able to offer in these areas, but they know it is up to them to find the true fulfillment of these needs within themselves. Coming to this insight is an important step toward a truly healthy and mature relationship, and it can bring about tremendously rewarding changes.

However, this still does not go far enough. Most people, unaware of their own true spiritual nature, attempt to find the love, security, and wholeness they desire from within the meager resources of their ego-self. They learn to be good to themselves; they learn to love themselves as unconditionally as possible; they do important things for themselves; they develop rewarding relationships with other people; they develop new interests and new talents and skills. All of these things can be immensely fulfilling and take a lot of pressure off of a primary relationship.

If you have done such things in your own life, you have probably experienced this. However, even with all this going for you—if you're honest, you may realize that there is still an empty hole of desire and need that has not been filled by all these changes. There is still something missing. You have not, after all, truly fulfilled the need for feeling completely and wholly loved, the need to feel safe and secure in the universe, or the need for fulfillment and a sense of wholeness.

Perhaps you have again turned, out of habit and frustration, to your partner and your relationship to get these things that still elude you. Then you are back to square one, attempting to get from another ego-self what you as an ego-self have not been able to give yourself.

I had a friend, Joanne, who had been miserably married for almost fifteen years. Although unhappy almost from the beginning, she had never been able to leave her husband. She had spent many of the years in therapy, in reading self-help books about relationships, and in doing everything she could to improve the relationship. But she was as miserable as ever.

She finally came to the realization that all this time she had been focusing on her husband and the relationship, and on how both of them were failing her, and that this was what was keeping her in such a helpless position. Her feeling of helplessness, in turn, had evolved into a constant resentment and rage that she carried around inside. She finally saw why she'd been so miserable.

When she realized all this, it became clear to her that she needed to focus on herself and attempt to fulfill her own needs, since her husband wasn't doing this for her. I remember that she became hell-bent, at this point, in wanting finally to resolve the turmoil in her life that she had created around her relationship.

It wasn't easy, but she began turning around some old, ingrained habits in her marriage. She decided she was no longer going to bend over backwards to "keep the relationship together." In effect, she stopped pursuing her husband and demanding his attention so much. She developed her own interests, that didn't happen to include him, and developed a number of new and fulfilling relationships with people in the process. She decided to take the risk of finding a more interesting and challenging job.

She also began taking care of her body like never before; she joined a gym, took saunas and steam baths, and got weekly massages. Her therapy was no longer focused on fixing her relationship; it now centered on her and her spiritual growth. She began meditating every day and felt more and more balanced in every activity in her life.

Predictably, her husband began taking notice of this new woman in his life. He began missing all the attention she had formerly given him and the tremendous effort she had put into keeping their relationship going. As a result, he found it necessary to put his own attention and energy into this job for a change. Joanne, of course, loved this. All that she was doing for herself was giving new life to the relationship and was making her a much more attractive mate for her husband.

For a couple of months, I heard nothing but glowing reports about the state of her marriage—along with all she was doing to enjoy life more on her own. Then, I began noticing a slight sense of flatness about her and not much later, the familiar old depression.

She wasn't just backsliding into some of her old habits of looking to her husband for fulfillment, although some of that was happening, too. She was simply finding that this new program of self-improvement was not really doing it for her. The old emptiness would still creep into her awareness sometimes late at night, when everything was still. Despite all the attention her husband was giving her, and the fun they were now having for the first time, she still sensed the lack of true fulfillment deep within. She still didn't feel totally loved and cared about. In desperate tears, she came to visit me one afternoon, telling me all this. "After all I've done, I've still missed the mark. I'm still not happy. What's wrong with me?"

Your Ego-Self Cannot Give You the Fulfillment You Seek

The ego-self cannot give itself a true sense of love, security, and wholeness—and it certainly can't give these things to another ego-self. It simply is not capable of it. Its understanding of life and reality is based on illusion; it cannot even grasp, except perhaps intellectually, from where these qualities come. This is because ego-selves perceive themselves as separate, individual little beings, operating within a vast, often unpredictable universe. If honest and realistic, they know that their only real tool to combat the sense of helplessness that comes with this perception is the mind. And the mind is hopelessly limited when it comes to controlling the forces of the universe. Thus, the whole notion that the ego-self can provide us with a true sense of security and fulfillment is absurd.

No matter how much we may improve our ego-self—by changing attitudes, expectations, beliefs, and behaviors—it will never be quite enough. No matter how much we may demand that another ego-self give us what we want and need, we will never get it. No ego-self—neither our own nor someone else's—can give us the love, security, and sense of wholeness we seek, because it is incapable of doing this.

Although it might sound simplistic, underneath all other issues, the strife that occurs within intimate relationships stems from this one unrealistic notion—that two people are capable of fulfilling each other's needs for love, security, and fulfillment. Believing this, they issue demands that the other simply cannot fulfill, no matter how much they might wish to.

So what is the answer to all this? As usual, it lies in the realization that we are not this little, limited, ego-self form that cannot fulfill its own needs—but the true Self *which has no needs*. Who you are, in reality, IS Love, IS Wholeness, IS Fulfillment—you have no need to seek them anywhere from anyone or anything. Issues of insecurity, loneliness, and lack of self-worth don't even arise; they're irrelevant. As Self, you are already complete, whole, fulfilled.

If two people come together in partnership, truly realizing themselves as Self, there can be no strife due to unfulfillable demands. They simply give each other the freedom to be as they are. They can be loving companions, supporting each other to continue in their ever-deepening awakening to their true nature. They can assist each other on the physical level to make life in the world easier and more comfortable. They can have fun and share adventures together. They can even having exciting, passionate sex together. But that is basically it—no demands or expectations that the other cannot fulfill. Needs for security, happiness, and a sense of wholeness are already naturally taken care of through their awakened consciousness of who they are.

This may not sound very appealing to you; it may not even sound like a "real" relationship. Where is the romance? Where is the emotional attachment? These, for better or for worse, have disappeared, along with the heartache, the loneliness, the dependence, and the insecurity of believing yourself to be an ego-self.

There actually can be some sense of "romance" in a relationship between people who know themselves to be Self—but it is not the ordinary kind that is rooted in the illusion that the other person is going to fill all one's needs. It's a carefree, playful response to the magnetism felt between the two people. It's a light and whimsical courtship that is known to be a dance, a game—and therefore does not ultimately produce the disillusionment and disappointment that so often occurs when people finally fall out of love.

Perhaps the relationship I've described above sounds overly idealistic and unattainable. Yet I believe that people can create this relationship, at least to some degree, and really benefit from it. It's perhaps the only relationship in which each partner can truly experience inner freedom.

Moving into a Relationship of Freedom

The next question is how to get to a relationship in which both partners can truly experience inner freedom with each other. How do we get from the ordinary, run-of-the-mill, somewhat satisfactory relationship to one like I've described? There are undoubtedly countless ways to do this. One is to find your way toward deeper and deeper realization of your true nature. You can also take steps to deal with your relationship directly. I outline below some steps that might be helpful to you in this regard. Please note that they aren't strictly sequential. Some can be done simultaneously with others; others may have to be done over and over again.

1. **Focus on loving yourself.** This is where you need to begin. If you are not able to truly love yourself, you will not be able to create a conscious, free, and loving relationship with your partner. Ask yourself if you are being as loving toward yourself as you could be. If not, what can you do to be more so? Sometimes it can be hard to know how to be more loving, especially if you have been conditioned for a long time to be hard on yourself. You may really want to learn how to love yourself, but you don't know how to begin turning all your old habit patterns around.

There are many, many books written on how to do this. If you need some help in learning how to love yourself, it might be good to read a few. Books on how to heal your "inner child" are especially helpful. Also books on dealing with your "inner critic" are important. Most valuable, I have found, is becoming aware of the dynamic between your child and critic, and learning how to bring harmony between them.

The simple message offered in all these books is to stop doing those things that are unkind and harsh to yourself, and begin doing those things that reflect love, gentleness, and understanding. Stop allowing the critical parent voice inside your head to beat up on you, stop listening to its judgments against you. Take care of your body; eat well, get exercise, and be gentle and nurturing toward your body. Own and feel your emotions. Do what you can to heal yourself on all levels. Take responsibility for your own well-being; make it a priority. Don't give to others from an empty cup. And most importantly, perhaps, accept yourself exactly as you are. (See the list at the end of this chapter for suggested books on learning to love yourself.)

Learning to love and accept yourself is an important step in creating a healthy relationship with yourself—and an important one for creating a free and conscious relationship with a partner. Keeping this focus of self-love in mind while taking all the following steps will make them both easier and more effective.

2. **Begin focusing on all the positive aspects of your relationship.** Rather than focusing on what's wrong with it, what's missing, begin looking at the positive aspects. Become aware of all the good qualities your partner has, and focus on your love for him or her. Become aware of what you have to feel grateful about. Let your love and your gratitude flow through all your communications with your partner—and watch the miracles that can occur in the environment you are creating.

3. **Stop blaming your partner for your own unhappiness.** Once you experience more love for yourself and focus on your love and gratitude for your relationship, it is time to take the next essential step. Stop looking at all the things your partner is or is not doing that are "making" you unhappy. Blaming keeps you in a helpless position. It gives the power over your happiness to the other person, because you are dependent on them to be or to act in a certain way so that you can be happy. Since you have no control over them, you feel helpless—and this produces anger and resentment. It is therefore necessary to take back the power you have given your partner and to use it yourself to begin creating your own happiness.

Be careful, however, when you remove the blame from your partner, that you do not then place the blame on yourself for your unhappiness. I think we are all conditioned to believe that if there is something "wrong," then blame must be placed somewhere for it. This is not so. No blame at all needs to be placed anywhere. Blaming anyone, including yourself, is counterproductive.

What *is* productive is to step outside of the blame paradigm altogether. Understand that taking responsibility for something is not the same as taking blame for it. Taking responsibility is claiming the empowerment to do something about it.

4. **Pull back your demands and expectations.** Become aware of how you may have been expecting your partner to fill certain needs you have, such as happiness, security, and a sense of wholeness. Realize that doing this is not part of your partner's job. He or she actually *cannot* do it. Only you can do it.

The love you are undoubtedly looking for is unconditional love—which assures you that you are loved simply for who you are, no matter what you do or what may happen. It's a love you don't, in any way, have to earn; you are loved because you are you.

This kind of love cannot come from someone's ego-self. The love of the ego, on its own, is always fraught with subtle or not-so-subtle demands. For you to "earn" the love you want, there are conditions that you must be a certain way and do certain things. If you don't, then the love is threatened. At the very least, the demonstration of the love is removed until your behavior changes. Ego love is also typically entwined with a sense of possessiveness, which brings its own conditions.

Unconditional love, which can only come from the Self, is what we all really want. In rare situations, a person is actually able to give this to a partner in an ongoing way. It's important to distinguish, however, between unconditional love that emanates from a true awakening of the Self—and a feeling that may seem the same but is actually co-dependent attachment that says, "You can do anything to me, even abuse me—but I will always love you." This isn't truly free, unconditional love. It is an emotional attachment to a person, rooted in self-denial. Attachment is often mistaken for love.

Of course, most people in a healthy and mature relationship experience love for each other from time to time that is truly unconditional. When attuned to the consciousness of Self, this true love flows forth naturally toward the partner. Generally, however, people are not able to sustain their attunement to Self all the time; thus the unconditional love they feel for their partner comes and goes. If you are depending on this kind of love from your partner, especially all of the time, you are bound to experience disappointment and resentment.

The sense of security and safety that you may be seeking from your relationship also cannot be given to you by your partner—simply because no one can have any real control over future events. The best that can be given are expressions of feelings in the present moment.

For example, rather than a promise of "I will never leave you," we can say something like, "Right now, I feel I never want to leave you.

I certainly do not ever want you to be hurt." However, as accurate and realistic as these statements may be, they do not take care of a person's basic need to feel secure and safe in the world. The fulfillment of this need, too, must be sought elsewhere.

Seeking a sense of wholeness from your partner must ultimately be unfulfilled. Your partner cannot give this to you; you must find it within yourself. You may have experienced what seemed like a sense of wholeness with your partner. Perhaps it has come as a feeling of "merging" with him or her. This can be a very blissful experience. Maybe, at the time, you felt as if it were fulfilling your need to feel whole. But has it ever lasted? Do you actually have any control over "making" it happen again? And did it truly give you the feeling, deep within yourself, of finally feeling completely whole?

The merging of two ego-selves, no matter how profound and fulfilling it may be, cannot provide the true feeling of wholeness each partner seeks, because, by their very nature, ego-selves are limited and imperfect—and illusory.

You may believe that the merging you have experienced with your partner wasn't one of ego-selves coming together, that a higher spiritual consciousness was present. This may well be so. But the problem remains of controlling the process of merging and making it on-going. These experiences cannot be controlled, and therefore, to depend on them for a sense of wholeness is bound to bring disappointment and frustration. Another more reliable source must be sought.

Letting go of these expectations of your partner may not be easy at first. So much of our conditioning has told us that a partner is an intimate relationship is "supposed" to provide us with happiness, security, fulfillment, and wholeness. And yet, as we've seen, not only is it not our partner's job to do this, he or she is ultimately incapable of doing it.

So it is important to be realistic. Don't have expectations that are doomed to be unfulfilled. Know that your needs can only be fulfilled by awakening to your own true nature, and focus your attention on this Reality. Then, if your partner happens to be tuning into the consciousness of Self at certain times and is able to bring a sense of happiness or fulfillment to you, this will be the "icing" on your cake—the cake that you yourself have made. Icing makes a cake more delicious, but it is not necessary for the cake's existence.

5. **Stop trying to fix or change your relationship.** At this point, at least for awhile, see if you can take your focus off trying to do anything at all about your relationship. Allow things to be the way they are; allow your partner to be the way he or she is. Ignore the urge to have to fix or change anything.

Of course, if simple, obvious things occur to you that will improve something between you and your partner—things that come easily and naturally—then, by all means, do these things. But if the problems require much thought, if you find yourself getting involved in blame and hurt and anger about them, or if there are issues that you've gone around and around with in the past, then abandon all thoughts for now about trying to resolve these problems. They'll just get you back on the merry-go-round of dissatisfaction about your partnership. Begin, instead, to center your awareness on yourself.

6. **Explore your emotional attachment to your partner.** It's now time to begin exploring more deeply within yourself to find the more subtle ways in which you are creating attachment—and therefore suffering—in your relationship.

First ask yourself the question: "What does being in relationship mean to me?" (If you're married, you can ask, "What does being married mean to me?") How attached are you to being in this role? What does being in this role mean about you? What would being out of the relationship or marriage mean about you? Would you somehow feel less of a person if you were not in this relationship? Become aware, in general, of all the judgments and values you place around being in relationship (and in the particular relationship you're in). Answering these questions will help you see the attachment you have to the relationship. It will also reveal to you how much of your happiness is dependent on your relationship and on how things are going in it.

Next, face your worst fears about your relationship: Ask yourself: "What if my partner leaves me?" Face this possibility squarely; don't push it away. What would this really mean? Without dwelling morbidly or sentimentally on it, without falling into self-pity about it, just look at what feelings it brings up. Observe them objectively, as described in Chapter 13. If there is fear, allow yourself it feel it, without resisting or rejecting it. Find out honestly what the worst thing could be about your partner leaving you.

Now ask yourself, "What if my partner were to die before I did?" Again, have the courage to face this possibility. Just sit quietly for a while with this question, and allow your feelings and inner truth about the issue to surface. What would it mean? What would you feel? What would you do? Where would you go? Then answer the question honestly: would you be able to go on without him or her? Would you be truly devastated?

What about the possibility that your partner might choose to continue being with you, but he or she decides to have affairs with other people? Again, this is not something to dwell on in a morbid, fearful way. Staying still within yourself, simply ask yourself the questions: What would I feel and think about this? What would I feel this means about me? What would I do? How would I handle it? Could I stand to stay in the relationship?

Now face any fears you may have about possibly wanting to leave your partner. Although you may think at this point you'll probably never want to leave, certainly you have had thoughts at one time or another of wanting to leave. Maybe the challenges you've experienced in the relationship have gotten too difficult at times. Maybe you occasionally feel bored with your partner. Maybe you've felt attracted to someone else.

Or maybe you'll be the one to die first. How would your partner react to any of these situations—and how would you feel about his or her reactions? Would you feel responsible for his or her feelings? Explore all of these questions. They will reveal a lot to you about your attachment to the relationship and your partner—and show you the degree of emotional freedom you have in this whole area.

If you are finding these questions difficult to face, and your inclination is just to pass them by without exploring them, this may be an indication of your general fear of being alone. This is, then, where you may want to start. Ask yourself, "What does being alone, without an intimate relationship, mean to me?" Discover what judgments and values you have about people who are single, without a relationship. In particular, what would this mean about you? Face whatever fears you have about being alone.

Do you know if you could make it on your own, if you need to—physically, financially, emotionally? How dependent are you on your partner in these areas? How does feeling dependent feel to you? You may believe that you have no choice except to be dependent in one way or another, but, if you're honest, you'll see that you always have a choice. There may come a day when you'll have to be independent, whether you want to be or not. And you will see that you can be.

Facing the fears that asking all these questions can evoke is very important. It does no good to keep them hidden in your subconscious mind. You are probably going to have to face them sooner or later, anyway. You might as well do it now, so the fears don't run you.

Perhaps more importantly, facing these fears can also take you out of your immediate situation and give you a view of the larger picture of your life. In this larger picture, you can see that all events, situations, and relationships in your life come and go—and yet, YOU remain. You continue, with or without a partner, in or out of a relationship. Experiencing this perspective can bring a peaceful sense of spaciousness and timelessness—as well as a knowing of who you are in Reality, beyond all issues or questions around relationship.

7. **Focus on awakening into Self.** Once you have done all the preliminary psychological work of balancing the ego-self, you can then focus on awakening more deeply into your true Self. You can, of course, have this focus throughout your explorations of your ego-self attachments; indeed, it is always helpful to keep the Self in mind while you explore your ego-self. But once you begin to get clear about how your ego-self operates, it is easier to turn more fully to your awakening into Self.

There are many ways in which you can do this. Everything I've described thus far (and in subsequent chapters) can be helpful. Focusing on experiencing glimpses of the Self is a start. Review how to recognize Self in your everyday life. Take the time to prolong the glimpses you do have. Cultivate an environment and a life-style that are conducive to becoming more and more familiar with the Self. Create and be faithful to a meditation practice. Attend spiritual gatherings, classes, *satsangs*—whatever will "light your fire" spiritually.

Begin to observe how attached you are to the roles you play in life, and learn how to become more detached from them. See how you identify with your body and with your emotions, and begin detaching yourself from this identity. Take steps to become more of an observer. Open yourself to experiencing yourself as pure Awareness.

See if, as time goes on, you can begin trusting your true Self more to take care of you. See if you can surrender your sense of control over your life. Try accepting your life as it is, surrendering to it. See what happens.

As you begin to do all these things, your relationship with your partner will undoubtedly be affected. Wonderful new experiences between the two of you may begin happening. You may inspire your partner to begin doing some of the same things you have been doing. There may develop a greater closeness and alignment between you than ever before.

However, other changes may also happen. If your partner is not open to growing and expanding his or her awareness into greater awakening in the way that you are, your doing this may at first cause some waves in the relationship. Your awakening into greater freedom can't help but upset the status quo. But if your relationship has its foundation in Truth, it will weather this rocking and become stronger.

If you are fearful that your awakening process may destroy or break up your relationship, and you find yourself closing down your own inner process because of this, you might really want to look at this. What are you choosing? What are your priorities? Is staying in your relationship at all costs worth it to you, even if it means shutting down your own spiritual awakening process?

It's important to ask yourself these questions. But be careful not to fall into an unnecessary "either-or" position about it, thinking you have to choose immediately either your own awakening or your relationship. Sometimes it just takes time for a relationship to catch up to one partner's awakening process. Wait and see. Don't put pressure on your partner or on your relationship to conform to some new concept you have about what they should be like. Give your partner freedom to be who she or he is. Focus on love and acceptance. Focus on awakening.

Your partner may soon be making his or her own awakening just as much a priority as you're making your own. You can then become companions along the road of awakening, giving each other support in your explorations. If this doesn't happen, so be it. Either way, if you are on your way to emotional and spiritual freedom, you can't lose. You are becoming more and more aware of who you truly are. And you will continue to benefit from this, whether you happen to be in or out of an intimate relationship.

* * * * *

There is no doubt that intimate relationships are challenging. They can show us only too well in what ways we are not free emotionally, and how attached we are to our emotional identity. But, for that very reason, they are tremendously valuable. We can use our relationship as a forum in which to become progressively freer; we can use it to help us learn to detach from our emotions and the suffering they can bring when we identify with them.

Experiencing greater and greater emotional freedom is immensely rewarding. Learning to simply observe our emotions and let them be—without resisting them, indulging them, or trying to fix them—is an important step toward this freedom. Letting go of our story of emotional suffering is another. And gaining freedom within our relationships is still another key. As we gain a detachment and freedom with our emotions in these ways, our awareness becomes less and less cluttered. With this clarity, we can then begin to deeply experience the Self as it shines through into our consciousness more and more clearly.

Suggested Reading

Affinito, Mona G, *When to Forgive*. Oakland, CA, New Harbinger Publications, 1999.

Alexander, Chris, *Creating Extraordinary Joy*. Alameda, CA, Hunter House Publications, 2002.

Baldwin, Martha, M.S.S.W., *Self Sabotage*. New York, NY, Warner Books, 1987.

Bennett-Coleman, Tara, *Emotional Alchemy*. New York, NY, Harony Books, 2001.

Berne, Eric, *Games People Play*. New York NY, Ballantine Books, 1964.

Bradshaw, John, *Homecoming*. New York, NY, Bantam Books, 1990.

Branden, Nathaniel, *The Art of Living Consciously*. New York, NY, Simon & Shuster, 1997.

Burns, David, M.D., *Feeling Good*. New York, NY, Avon Books, 1980.

Burns, David, M.D., *Feeling Good Handbook*. New York, NY, Plume Books, 1990.

Domar, Alice D., Ph.D., *Self Nurture*. New York, NY, Penguin Books, 2000.

Epstein, Mark, *Going On Being*. New York, NY, Broadway Books, 2001.

Hay, Louise L., *Gratitude*. Carlsbad, CA, Hay House, 1996.

Jeffers, Susan, Ph.D., *Feel the Fear and Do It Anyway*. New York, NY, Fawcett Columbine, 1987.

Kusher, Harold S., *When Bad Things Happen to Good People*. New York, NY, Quill Books, 1981.

Morton, John, *The Blessings Already Are*. Los Angeles, CA, Mandeville Press, 2000.

Pittman, Frank, *Grow Up!* New York, NY, St. Martin's Griffin, 1998.

Prend, Ashley D., *Claim Your Inner Grown Up*. New York, NY, Penguin Group, 2001.

Sorenson, Marilyn J., Ph.D., *Breaking the Chain of Low Self-Esteem*. Sherwood, OR, Wolf Publishing, 1998.

Weisinger, Hendrie, Ph.D., *Dr. Weisinger's Anger Work Out Book*. New York, NY, Quill Books, 1985.

Whitfield, Charles L., *Healing the Child Within*. Pompano Beach, FL, Health Communications, 1987.

CHAPTER EIGHTEEN

How the Mind Gets Us in Trouble

The mind cannot know what is beyond the mind, but the mind is known by what is beyond it.

—Nisargadatta

*I*DENTIFICATION WITH OUR MIND is probably the most difficult identification of all to see clearly, and is, therefore, the most challenging from which to detach. It may be especially difficult if you have a strong intellect that you have spent years developing; you are naturally going to be hesitant to give up your identification with something into which you have put much effort and about which you have developed pride. But, to attain true freedom, it is ultimately necessary to see clearly that you are not the mind and to be willing to give up your identification with it.

It's important to understand, however, that there is nothing inherently wrong with the mind. Many people, as they become aware of the hazards of identifying with the mind, make it into an enemy, something to be gotten rid of in some way. Assuming this attitude is actually falling prey to one of the many tricks that the mind can perform: dividing itself up into separate parts and then creating battles between these parts. We do not have to get caught up in this game. We can simply watch it—and all the other games and tricks and cartwheels the mind performs—without identifying with any of them.

The mind is actually an amazing and wondrous object to observe and study. And when used properly, it is an extremely effective tool. Its ability to create and traverse countless realms, many of which remain mysterious and uncharted, is vast beyond measure. It creates thought in countless different varieties: concepts, ideas, images, memories, projections, beliefs, values, opinions, morality systems, judgments. Like a super-computer, the mind receives information from the senses and instantaneously analyzes, categorizes, labels, cross-indexes, stores, and downloads. Indeed, when used to help us negotiate this three-dimensional physical world, it is an indispensable tool.

It's when we identify with this tool, however—when we believe that it is who we are—that we get into trouble. If we are identifying with the mind, certain aspects, functions, and qualities of the mind can keep us from clearly experiencing the Self. It is therefore important to be aware of them and the suffering they can cause, as you detach yourself from your identity with your mind.

Confusing the Mind with the Self

One of the challenging qualities of the mind is the very subtle nature of thought. It is so subtle that it can be very easy to confuse a thought we have about the Self with the experience of the Self. At times we may have very lofty thoughts about spiritual matters that can give us a sense of freedom and joy. These thoughts are undoubtedly infused with the grace of the Self and are certainly wonderful to experience. But it is important to remember that if we are involved in thinking thoughts—no matter how beautiful they may be—then we are not fully experiencing Self, which is an experience that is beyond conceptual thought.

Part of the difficulty in knowing the difference between thought and the experience of Self stems from the fact that many spiritual paths do not even address this difference. In fact, their teachings only deal with the "spiritualizing" of the mind, without any reference at all to the direct experiencing of the Self. They emphasize thinking certain thoughts about "God"; they teach ideas about higher, spiritual "realms"; they encourage certain rituals in order to focus the mind toward loftier ideals; they dictate certain behaviors in order to cleanse the mind. Thus people following these paths are generally not aware that there even is a Self they can directly experience, let alone that there's a difference between the mind and the Self.

The process of spiritualizing the mind can be an important step on the road to true Freedom; the mind must become clear and focused on spiritual thoughts before true and frequent glimpses of the Self become possible. However, ultimately, it must be understood that thought about the Self is not the same as directly experiencing the Self. And it is this direct experience that must be pursued.

I was once sitting with a group of friends in a meditation circle. We had just meditated together and were sharing the experiences we had had during the meditation. A good friend of mind, Jim, began speaking. Immediately the whole group became rapt in what he was saying. He described in simple yet eloquent terms an exquisite experience he had just had of the Self. His eyes were shining, and his face was suffused with a bright glow. The energy of love was radiating from him toward every one of us, as he described the quality of unimaginably blissful peace he had experienced and the rapturous joy that had pervaded his whole being.

As usually happens when someone is directly transmitting the energy of an experience of Self, the rest of us were soon feeling a quickening of our awareness of Self. Because his very presence was fully suffused with the grace of the Self, it was causing an experience of awakening within each of us sitting with him.

Then something very subtle began happening. It was hard to put a finger on just when it began, but, at some point, I felt a slight shift in the energy in the room and noticed that everyone's attention was beginning to drift away from him, as he continued to speak. The feeling of rapt attention was gone, and people seemed to be back in their own worlds, thinking their own thoughts. The "magic" that had been present just moments before had very subtly dissipated.

Perplexed by this, I began listening very closely to Jim as he continued to speak about his experience. Suddenly, it became clear to me what had happened: he was no longer directly describing his experience from where it had happened; he was now analyzing it from within his mind. It had been a very subtle switch. He was using many of the same terms and phrases he'd been using previously, but the energy was different. It was now mental. He had slipped through the very subtle doorway from the experience of Self into the realm of the mind.

Just as I realized this, Jim seemed to also. His voice drifted off in the middle of a sentence and then he was silent. Everyone's attention was immediately back with him. Somewhat puzzled and sad, he said, "I lost it, didn't I? I'm back in my mind. I'm thinking about my experience, rather than just being it." He closed his eyes at this point, and the rest of us did also, attempting to call back the Silence we had "lost" by falling into the mind. Although we were somewhat able to recapture the exquisite sense of stillness his expression of Self had brought to us, it was not quite the same.

When we began speaking again awhile later, we realized that, as disappointing as this experience had been in one way, we had all learned something very important about the subtle and tricky nature of thought and how it can masquerade so cleverly as Self. The dead giveaway, we realized, is the mental energy that an expression of the mind brings—and the lack of true inner stillness. We realized how important it is to pay attention to the subtle energetic shift the mind brings when it begins to analyze an experience with Self, rather than allowing the experience itself to speak directly.

What is important in seeking the experience of the Self is to realize that it is much closer to you than your mind is. As close as your thoughts may seem, you need to look more closely; the Self is not as far away as your thoughts are. Indeed, there is no distance at all—it IS you. To discover this, look inside to where the thoughts are coming from; follow them to find their source. Ask yourself: "Who is it that is thinking these thoughts?" See what you discover.

Another "gateway" into Self through using the mind is to realize that you can perceive the mind. You can watch it, you can talk about it as something you have, something that is separate from who you are. Therefore, it stands to reason that your mind cannot be who *you* are; you are the perceiver of it. So ask yourself: Who or what is it that is perceiving the mind?

The Mind Creates the Illusion of Duality

If you have had profound glimpses of the Self, you have likely experienced a blissful sense of Oneness with all that is—a knowing that everything that exists is of the same essence, that it is all one Consciousness.

The world the mind lives in, on the other hand, is one of duality: there's "me"—and there's everything else. In fact, the mind perceives reality as an infinite number of pieces; everything is defined and separate from each other. It does not see, and cannot truly comprehend, the Oneness that exists for the Self, except as a mental concept.

This basic misperception of Reality that the mind holds can cause us a number of problems. Perhaps most importantly, it can cause feelings of separation, lack, fear, and loneliness. If we believe ourselves to be a separate, individual being in the world, something apart from all other people and things, and separate from God or Self (or whatever other term we use), there can be enormous suffering. Especially when people or things we believe we need are taken from us, we can experience an unbearable sense of loss and helplessness.

Other times, the sense of separateness can bring up deep anger and hostility in us, if we are feeling that we don't have what we need in order to be happy. Especially if we see others who have those things we think we need or want, we may experience greed and conflict with them; these feelings, in turn, may push us toward crime, violence, and even war. This is very important to understand: all of these negative feelings are based on an erroneous understanding of the nature of existence. They arise from a belief in the illusion that we are separate beings, existing apart from everything else.

Another difficulty of duality arises when the mind takes the pieces it sees in the world—all people, objects, ideas, feelings—and creates polarities among them. Some of these polarized concepts are useful to us in communication with each other about the world: for example, such terms as "big" and "little," "cold" and "hot," "boy" and "girl" are quite essential in our everyday communication.

However, other polarized concepts are much less useful and, indeed, often cause many problems. Some of the worst of these concepts are "good" and "bad" and "right" and "wrong." Polarities like these tend to cause conflict because people have formed beliefs around them and find it necessary to oppose other people, things, and events that do not agree with the beliefs they have adopted.

Other polarities that people often create and cause themselves distress with are "spirituality" vs. "money," "spirituality" vs. "sex," and "spirituality" vs. "the world." Neither money, sex, nor the world is opposed to spirituality, and none is inherently wrong. All of these concepts, including "spirituality," are simply concepts, emanating from the mind. Yet people tend to believe that they are real and experience all sorts of guilt, shame, and confusion due to this belief.

To live and function in this world effectively, it is necessary, of course, to act as if duality exists. We generally need to treat the things the mind perceives as if they are separate and defined objects. However, this can be done while at the same time holding the knowing inside that, in Reality, there is no actual separation between anything that exists. There is only the one Consciousness.

The Mind Gets Caught in Time

Still another way in which the mind functions that can prevent us from clearly experiencing the Self is the way in which it lives in time. The Self lives outside of time. Indeed, an important aspect of many glimpses of the Self is the sense of timelessness. The Self lives in a dimension where time simply does not exist. There is the knowing that everything is taking place in the Eternal Now, the Present Moment; there is no past, no future—and really no present, either.

In fact, when experiencing Self, you can become aware that time is something that the mind has simply made up. It might be difficult at first to see time as an invention of the mind. Most people assume that time has its own inherent reality. But a direct experience of Self will give you the understanding that it doesn't; it is simply an idea that has been created by the mind.

Time itself is not a problem. It has its useful purposes; it is certainly helpful to us in functioning on this physical level. Indeed, coordinating events among all of us humans on the planet would probably be impossible without the idea of time.

However, we can get into trouble with the concept of time when we allow our minds to get caught in focusing on it too much. Too often, we become so involved in our memories of the past that we bring them forward to create the same situations over and over again. There's little space for new and spontaneous experiences to happen. Furthermore, getting so involved in the past and the future, we often end up missing the present altogether. Rather than living in real life, we're living in our minds.

Most importantly, by getting so involved in time in general, we miss out on experiencing the eternal Now. We cannot get there from the past or from the future. We actually can't even get there from the present, if this "present" is just another place on the continuum of time.

So how can we get to the Home of the Self—with its exquisite sense of timelessness—while living in this three-dimensional world that seems so dominated by the concept of time? If you feel stuck in this time-limited world, and find yourself swinging back and forth between the past and the future, and experiencing the subtle suffering that this circular and exhausting ride can produce—here are some steps I have discovered that might help you get off of that ride.

Exercise: *Accessing Timelessness*

1. First of all, bring your attention completely into the present and observe your physical surroundings. Look all around you at the objects in your field of vision. Observe the details of these objects, their colors, their sizes, how they occupy space.

2. Now become aware of your body. How is it feeling? Notice how it is occupying space. Take some deep breaths, and feel them in your body. Observe your thoughts and your feelings; don't follow or resist them at this time—simply observe that they are present.

3. Take in the whole gestalt of where you are and what is happening at this moment in time to this mind-body organism with which you currently identify. See it objectively, as if you were standing outside of it. See it sitting, lying down, standing, or

moving through space—whatever it is doing. See it turning its head and taking other things into its field of vision. Watch it moving its hands. Observe its thoughts and feelings as they float through the mind.

4. Now see this entity as it moves through time. From moment to moment, see how it continues, but somewhat differently in each moment. Physical, emotional, and mental changes are constantly happening.

5. Become aware of how strange a phenomenon time actually is. The present continuously becomes the past, and the future continuously becomes the present and then the past—all in just an instant. Quietly observe how time is doing this. Is there truly any difference between the past, the present, and the future? Are they perhaps all the same thing? Do these concepts even have an inherent reality of their own?

6. Become aware of who you are as the observer of this thing called time. Who or what are you? Where are you existing? Does time exist there?

Finding a doorway into the experience of timelessness can be an important step in having a direct experience of Self. It can bring a sense of restful, and even blissful, peace. You can realize that the stressful pressures that you create in your life around time are totally unnecessary, because time itself is fictitious.

In fact, the more you can live your life from within the realm of timelessness—and learn to trust it—the more you can realize that things in life have a way of working out smoothly, synchronistically, without any intervention on your part. Time is never an issue. You neither have too much nor too little of it. You're always right on time that is best for everyone. There is always enough time for everything that really needs to happen. Everything flows spontaneously in a natural way.

The Mind Claims Spiritual Experiences as Its Own

A fourth thing the mind tends to do that creates trouble for us is to take an experience we have with Self and claim it for its own glory.

Quite often, if allowed, the mind will look at an experience we have with Self and begin to think, "Wow, see how spiritual I am." Although the mind actually had nothing to do with the experience, it moves in to claim ownership of it. Indeed, it can actually begin believing it has created the experience itself.

I often have to chuckle, when I watch my own mind doing this with an experience I have had with Self. It not only uses the experience to glorify itself, it gets busy analyzing it thoroughly. It begins devising formulas on how I can have the same experience again, and draws up maps on how I can get there. It actually thinks it has some control over making these experiences happen. The image I get at these times is that of a young child who believes that because he has decided to fly his kite, he has made the wind blow.

As charming as this quality of the mind can be, however, it is necessary to stay aware of this tendency to take over that which is completely out of its realm of understanding. It really is incapable of understanding what Self is. The mind is only an object that is appearing within Self. As such, it can be aware of itself and of other objects, but it cannot be aware of what its own Source is—except intellectually, as a concept. This is not true understanding.

Remember, the next time your mind begins analyzing Self or an experience of Self that it can only know Self as a concept. Don't be satisfied with this. A concept cannot nurture you or give you the true peace and fulfillment you are looking for. Only a direct experience of the Self can give you this.

* * * * *

There are two other important aspects of the mind that tend to get us into trouble and can keep us identified with it. The first is its chattering nature, its tendency to be repetitious and overanalyzing. The second is its tendency to create and follow desires.

Since both of these tendencies of the mind are rather complex, I will devote an entire chapter to each of them in the following pages.

CHAPTER NINETEEN

Stilling the Chattering Monkey

All misery is created by the activity of the mind.
Can you let go of words and ideas, attitudes and expectations?

If so, then the Tao will loom into view.

—Hua Hu Ching

*H*AVE YOU EVER NOTICED how many thoughts you think that are repetitious, boring, and unnecessary? I once heard that a group of scientists studying the mind concluded that on the average we think about 60,000 thoughts a day. This statistic alone is somewhat amazing. But what is really interesting is that they also concluded that almost all of these 60,000 thoughts are thoughts we have previously thought!

As you become more aware of your own thought processes, you will probably find that you can corroborate the conclusions of these scientists. You may find, in fact, that most of the thoughts you think are actually useless, habitual distractions that aren't helpful or purposeful in any way. They are just chatter— irritating noise. Although many of the thoughts may revolve around a problem you're trying to resolve, you'll undoubtedly find that they do not resolve anything; they are simply recycled thoughts.

At other times, you may find, much to your embarrassment, that some of these chattering thoughts are simply habitual, defensive

177

reactions to ancient criticisms. You're still explaining to your mother, for instance, why you left the dirty dishes in the sink overnight, or you're still trying to show your third-grade teacher that you're not really lazy—you just didn't have time to get all your work done. Similar thoughts are the arguments you are still having in your mind with people who are no longer even in your life.

Aside from being boring and pointless, all this chattering, conditioned thinking can get in the way of experiencing the peace and stillness of the Self. Indeed, our minds can get painfully noisy at times, especially when there is an obsessive quality to our thinking, an out-of-control feeling. Quite often, a variety of painful emotions weave their way through this obsessive thinking, pulling us into a morass of psychic sludge that feels impossible to get out of. The Silence of the Self feels a million miles away.

A woman in a class I gave complained about her noisy, chattering mind. I asked her to demonstrate what her chattering mind could sound like by getting up in front of the class and speaking her thoughts out loud. I also directed her to use exaggerated body postures and facial expressions to reflect these thoughts. Here's a simulation of what she came up with:

> *Oh God, how am I going to pay the bills this month? I never have enough money. I've got to get a new job. Oh, but I don't want to get a new job. But I've got to get some more money somehow. How am I going to pay the bills? I've got that doctor bill, and my car insurance is due. Should I get a new job? I can't get a new job. I can't afford to get a new job at this time. Maybe I should go back to school. No, I can't afford to go back to school. I need to get a new job. But I need to pay the bills first. How am going to pay my car insurance? Without a car, I can't even go to work. I have to go to work. But I hate my job. I wish it paid me more money. I'm going to get sick, worrying like this. Then I'll have to go to the doctor and I'll owe him even more. God, I can't even pay my present bill. How am I going to pay my bills this month?"*

The rest of us were in stitches by the time she finally wound down. It all sounded so familiar. And for some it was only too painfully familiar. What a waste of time and energy this kind of thinking is!

If you have become aware of the pointlessness and the pain of this type of thinking in your own mind, you may have attempted to do what many people do: "make" your mind shut up. You probably were not very successful—at least for very long. Papaji says that trying to force the mind to be quiet is like holding a dog's tail in an attempt to straighten it: as soon as you let go, it curls upward again. The mind cannot be forcibly held in a quiet place for long.

Learning to Quiet the Mind

A number of things can be done to coax your mind into becoming quieter, so that you have a chance to slip past it into the Silence. A quiet mind is much easier to ignore than a noisy one.

1. **Body Relaxation Exercises:** There are all sorts of body relaxation exercises you can do. One is to sit or lie down, close your eyes, and take a few deep breaths. Then begin focusing on one part of your body at a time, consciously relaxing the muscles in that area. You can start with your head and work your way down to your toes, or vice-versa. You can use the imagery of calling in white light or energy from the earth to help the relaxation process. Another way is to briefly tense each set of muscles very tightly as you focus on them, and then let the tension out, allowing the relaxation to flow in. These relaxation exercises accomplish two things: they relax your body, and they also relax your mind, helping it to become still.

2. **Physical Exercise:** Physical exercise or sports can also relax the body and the mind. It pulls your energy and attention away from your conditioned mind and focuses it on your body and movement, releasing it from the chattering "tapes."

3. **Changing your Environment:** Sometimes all it takes to move your mind out of habitual thinking is to physically go somewhere else more conducive to a quiet, meditative state of mind. This may be obvious, but it is sometimes surprising how the obvious doesn't always occur to us when repetitious, habitual thinking has us hooked.

4. **Focusing on Something Present:** Something that can be done immediately, wherever you are, is to focus your attention on some object close at hand, and look closely at the details of it. If you can,

pick it up in your hands and feel it, smell it, listen to it. Observe how it occupies space. Focus on the space around it, the space between it and other objects close by. Concentrating on something concrete, even for a short period of time, can quite effectively break conditioned thinking by bringing your attention into the physical world.

5. **Listening to Music:** Sometimes you can find music that will help to quiet your mind or jog it out of its circular ruts. This could be quiet, meditative music—or it might be loud, rhythmic music that invites you to start moving or dancing. Either way, it's shifting the energy out of your conditioned mind and loosening and freeing it.

6. **Working with your Hands:** Finding something to do with your hands that requires mental concentration can be still another way to break free of habitual, circular thinking. This can involve working on a creative project that brings you joy and a sense of accomplishment, or it can simply be attempting to fix something physical that is broken. What is important is to pick something that demands your concentration. If you your mind can still wander while you're involved in it, it may not work; the conditioned thinking may just grab control again.

The second group of suggestions involves inwardly redirecting your mind in some way, to coax it into a quieter space.

1. **Focusing on Rational Problem-Solving:** Find a problem that needs to be thought through in a rational way. This might include figuring out how you're going to get your car to the mechanic's tomorrow and then negotiate the rest of the day without a car. Something practical like this can redirect your mind out of painful habitual thinking about some emotional problem into functional thinking, such as deciding whom to call to take you to work, when you need to leave in the morning, and so forth.

Another example of redirecting your mind might be planning a vacation—deciding where you want to go, when you'll be leaving, where you'll be staying. In other words, you're still using your mind, but you're directing it into new and fresh areas of thinking that are not laden with heavy emotion, and involve issues that are relatively easy to resolve. Just switching the mind's focus like this can be such a relief!

2. **Listening to Visualization Tapes:** There are a great variety of tapes and CDs on the market today designed to assist people to relax and become more mentally still. Many of them include suggestions to induce an alpha state in the brain, which naturally relaxes both the body and the mind. Others contain positive affirmations about many situations in life to assist in changing limited thought patterns. Playing these tapes can calm and quiet your mind, without demanding a lot of effort on your part.

3. **Meditations That Require Concentration:** Doing any type of meditation that requires concentration can be a very effective way to quiet the mind. Some that I've found to work especially well are various breathing meditations found in yogic traditions, hatha yoga postures, T'ai Chi, and chakra visualizations. Many of these are not only designed to quiet the mind, but also to direct one beyond the mind into the Silence.

4. **Witnessing Thoughts:** This is a meditation much like the process described in Chapter 13 of observing the emotions. It involves simply watching thoughts as they come into your mind, without following them and without resisting them—just letting them be. You can become aware of how thoughts, like emotions, are simply a form of energy. They really are not inherently "your" thoughts—they're just thoughts. There's no need to claim them and make them our own.

This can be a very powerful exercise when done with painful, habitual thoughts in which you feel caught. By moving into the observer's perspective, you immediately take power from them. You're not following them on their old, familiar pathways into further thoughts; you're not resisting or judging them; you're not indulging yourself in the emotions the thoughts evoke. You're simply watching them, letting them float by in your awareness. It might take five or ten minutes of persistently doing this, but, by the end, you will find that you have effectively stopped the broken record of thinking.

5. **Opening Your Mind:** If you find yourself stuck in thinking about a problem, take a moment to close your eyes and visualize your mind actually opening up wide. One way you can do this is to picture your mind as a flower that is slowly opening up its petals, all the way.

In this new, vast space you have opened up, suddenly you become aware of how much is inside your mind; the problem you have been caught in is just one small bit of energy floating through this space. You can choose to focus in on it, if you wish—or you can choose to focus on many other things as well. A great many thoughts and images and memories are floating around in this enlarged, open container known as your mind. Become aware of all of them.

Now focus on all the space in between these mental objects. There's so much space—just quiet, empty space—uncluttered by any energetic form. Feel the draw of these empty spaces and allow yourself to be pulled into one of them. Feel the relief of floating around in your own mind, in and among all the thought forms, images, memories, emotions, and concepts. Now watch yourself actually floating *through* them and seeing how they actually have no substance at all.

If you relax long enough, you may find yourself floating through one of the doorways into the consciousness of Self—where you will lose all sense of being an individuated self at all.

All of these exercises are designed to quiet the mind. They distract it just long enough to get it out of a habitual, conditioned rut, so that you can then redirect it into a quieter space. When done with attention and sincerity, they can be quite effective and bring great relief from the chattering mind. However, I encourage you not to stop here simply with a quieter mind. Instead, take the opportunity you now have to slip past the mind, beyond it, through it—to where you really ultimately want to go: to the true Silence within you.

Another thing you may discover in doing these exercises is that it really does not matter if your mind is chattering or not. The key is not to focus on the chattering, but to look beyond it—to the stillness that exists, no matter what the mind is doing. This stillness is no more bothered by the mind-chatter than the ocean is bothered by the waves. You can just let the chattering be, while seeking more deeply beyond it to discover what is always still, peaceful, and never-changing.

Once in this silent Consciousness, you will find that any thinking that appears is fresh, inspired, and creative, springing directly from within the Self. Such a joy this kind of thinking can bring—and how entirely different from the old, stale, conditioned thinking our mind so often produces!

Exercise: *Discovering the Inner Voice*

A last exercise will not only assist you to quiet your chattering mind, it will also help you to resolve in a new way a problem that has been going around and around in your mind. Here are the steps involved:

1. Think of an issue that you have been wrestling with, perhaps for some time, that you have not been successful in resolving.
2. Formulate a clear question out of the issue. This can be a simple question, such as "Should I quit my job?" or "Where should I move?" Or it can be more complex, such as "Why do I keep falling into the same painful pattern with my boss all the time?" Or "What am I doing that keeps alienating my girlfriend?"
3. Now take pen and paper and write down what the problem is all about, what you have thought about it, what you have done about it, what you are confused about. Include the following kinds of things:
   a. How did this problem originate? What did you do? What did other people do?
   b. The decision(s) you feel you need to make about it.
   c. The pros and cons about each decision
   d. What are your feelings about the problem?
   e. What ideas do you have about trying to resolve the problem? Which, if any, have you already tried? What effects have these actions had?
   f. What will happen if you don't resolve the problem? What are your fears? How is not resolving the problem affecting others?
   g. What self-doubts and self-judgments do you have about yourself for not being able to resolve the problem? What does having this problem in the first place mean about you?
   h. Anything else your mind has hashed out about the issue. This step is designed to give your mind total freedom to express all

the work it has done in regard to your problem. Let it list all the ideas it has thought and all the analysis it has accomplished, until it feels totally heard and appreciated—and willing finally to be somewhat quiet about the whole issue.

4. Now put your pen and paper aside, sit back, and close your eyes. For a few moments, think about all that you have written. Even allow yourself to get lost for a bit in this thought. Become aware of your body and the tension it is feeling as you think about your problem. Tune into whatever emotions you may be feeling. Become aware of the discomfort and pain that thinking about a problem like this can produce. Be aware of all the effort and energy you are using.

5. Now drop all thoughts about your problem and what you are creating by trying to resolve it through your mind—just be present here and now. Take some deep breaths and let them out slowly. Bring relaxation and calm into the muscles of your body. Call in white light through your crown chakra at the top of your head and let it flow into every cell of your body.

6. Step back into the observer perspective and begin watching any thoughts that pass through your mind. Remain still as they float through, without following them anywhere, and without resisting them in any way. You may wish to picture yourself lying comfortably in a hammock looking up at the sky, watching your thoughts as they float by, much as you might watch clouds. Or perhaps you can visualize yourself snorkeling in a clear, calm bay, quietly watching your thoughts swimming by, as you might fish. Simply observe them from this calm and detached place.

7. Now drop down to a place of deeper and deeper silence. Just let go and fall back into yourself, into a place where there is no past, no future; where there's no need to plan, understand, or resolve anything. Everything's fine just as it is. There's only awareness in the here and now.

Effortlessly, stay present here, observing the thoughts, images, and emotions that may be passing through, controlling nothing. Keep focusing on the present moment, on the Silence, the Nothingness, the blissful Emptiness. Feel the peace of this place, where nothing needs to be done or changed, where everything is perfect, just as it is. Continue to drop more and more deeply into this space.

8. Now, from deep within the Silence, allow your question about your problem to come into being. Watch it as it forms and becomes a thought. Stay calm and detached as it develops into the full form of a question. Let it float there in your awareness, putting no energy on it. Do not start calling in your mind to tackle it again—just let the question be there.

9. At this point, simply become as open and receptive as you can. Have no preconceptions about how an answer should come to you—or even about getting an answer at all. Just remain still and open, and see what happens. People receive answers in a multitude of ways. Sometimes it will come as a quiet voice, speaking words. Other times, as a visual image. Still other times, as a simple feeling or knowing—or even as a sensation in the body. There is no set, prescribed way answers come to us from the Stillness.

   It is possible you may get no answer at all at this time—simply a sense of knowing that the time is not right. If this happens, you might be disappointed—but don't follow that emotion. Focus instead on what else this feeling is telling you.

   Is it telling you when the right time will be for you to know the answer? Is it perhaps asking you to simply trust that all is proceeding perfectly, according to a higher plan? Is it encouraging you to let go of your will and trust this plan? Perhaps it's answering a deeper question you didn't even know you had. Or it's giving you information about something altogether different that is really more important. Remain still and listen with an open heart. Experience deeply what is being offered to you.

10. As you continue to rest in the Silence, ask yourself, "Who is listening to the Silence?" Truly look to see who it is. Then ask, "Who is asking this question?" Don't struggle to come up with a mental answer to these questions. Simply wait and see what you experience.

11. When you feel ready, open your eyes. Keep focused on the peace and the Silence you have been experiencing. Then ask yourself, "Who opened these eyes?"

12. Now look down at your hands. Move a finger. Ask yourself, "Who moved this finger?" Then become aware of your breathing, and ask, "Who is breathing?"
13. Now ask, "Who am I?"

You can do this exercise again with other questions in a much faster way. Just take some time with pen and paper to empty your mind of all its noise and chatter about your problem, so that it will let go of its anxious grasp on it. Then relax your body with some deep breathing, and begin dropping down into greater and greater Silence. As you become still, simply observing what may be passing through your awareness, ask your question again. See what comes to you. I have found that the more I do this exercise, the more clear and specific the answers are that come to me.

Something that becomes evident is the love that is always present in the voice within the Silence. Unlike the mind's voice when dealing with a problem—which is always fraught with some kind of fear—the answer I am given from within the Silence is always loving, calm, unworried about anything. It is full of trust and clear knowing that everything is moving along just perfectly. Sometimes there is counsel to do something specific or to behave in a certain way. Other times, there is a great deal of information about what is going on with me and others involved in my life. But often there's simply a gentle encouragement to be patient and trust what is happening.

The love and the authority of this voice are so powerful that it is easy to trust what it is telling me. Seeing how accurate and wise the counsel has been over time, rarely do I have lingering doubts.

The pain of an obsessive pattern of thinking can be acute. It can feel like a veritable prison from which you can't escape. Therefore, it is important to learn how to escape from this prison—just to find relief. Don't stop with the relative peace and calm; move more deeply, whenever you can, into the profound Silence that resides inside you. Rest there as often as you can, as constantly as you can. Bring this Silence to every activity you perform. Bring it into your mind. Let it begin to infuse your mind with its sweet and blissful presence—and watch your whole life transform.

Thought is just thought. It does what it knows how to do. There is no reason to tie yourself to it and let it drag you around after it, as it plows ever more deeply into the depths of doom and gloom, or into the fields of irrelevance and inanity. Don't waste your time thinking a thought that really has no purpose—especially if the thought isn't at least a pleasant thought!

Use the mind appropriately, for what it does well. It's especially effective for solving practical problems. It can analyze how things function in the world. It can be really good at pulling ideas apart philosophically—this can actually be great entertainment. It can also be very effective in manifesting creative ideas in the world. With anything practical, functional, and objective, in fact—the mind can be a true wizard.

For all the rest, it is wise to rely on the Silence—your true Self—to run your life. It is so much more effective—to say nothing of more restful! The Self is really what is in charge; you might as well let go of your attempts to control anything in your life, and jump on board and enjoy the ride the Self is giving you!

CHAPTER TWENTY

Rejecting the Ego's Game Plan for Happiness

When you pursue pleasure, you court pain ... pain will come in its wake, as surely as night follows day.

—Robert Powell

*H*AVE YOU EVER NOTICED that no matter how many desires you fulfill, you are never quite satisfied? How many times have you believed that if you could just have that one more important thing in your life, then you would finally be happy? Maybe it's more money, a bigger house, a newer car, a better-paying job, a new refrigerator— or any of the millions of things that look like they can finally give us the happiness that always feels just out of reach. But then, when you've finally gotten that thing, the initial sense of contentment just doesn't last. There is always something more that you want before you can really be happy.

Perhaps at some point along the road of pursuing desires, you realized that the happiness you were seeking wouldn't ever by satisfied by material things. So you began desiring the more subtle things in life, such as more harmonious relationships, a more fulfill- ing job, a deeper sense of security, or a greater sense of personal power. Maybe you even became aware that what you really needed to attain these more insubstantial things was to improve *yourself* in some way. So you began reading self-help books, going to therapy and other self-exploration workshops and trainings. Perhaps in doing these activities, you began experiencing a greater sense of happiness.

But maybe you still weren't satisfied. Your life was better, but you still weren't feeling a lasting sense of fulfillment; you were still yearning for more. Then maybe you turned to spirituality, thinking that what you were really yearning for was even more subtle than empowerment, harmonious relationships, or fulfilling work. You began learning to meditate and perform other spiritual practices. Again, these probably proved helpful; a deeper sense of contentment appeared, at least some of the time.

Maybe since then you have even had some profound glimpses of the Self, peak experiences of bliss and freedom. But perhaps you are now discovering that your desires haven't stopped. You now want more of this peace, bliss, and fulfillment. You want more glimpses of the Self—longer and more profound ones. And your desire for these things is now driving you just as hard as it ever did for anything else in the past. In fact, you are actually feeling just as much unrest, dissatisfaction, and lack of fulfillment as ever.

Perhaps, at this point, you are wondering: Why is this? Why hasn't my pursuit of fulfilling my spiritual desires finally brought me the fulfillment and peace I am seeking? If you have gotten this far along the path of pursuing desires, sometimes you undoubtedly feel frustrated, angry, despairing. Perhaps you have even reached a point of apathy about ever wanting anything again.

Believe it or not, feeling all this is actually good news. As uncomfortable or distressing as it may be, you are now probably ready to begin seeing the incredible lie that your ego-self has been feeding you all along: that the way to happiness and fulfillment is through following your desires.

Understanding the Nature of Desire

The truth is that *fulfilling desires cannot bring lasting happiness, peace, and fulfillment; on the contrary, it actually produces more suffering.* It does this through continually creating more desires, which are never-ending. Desire feeds on itself. Fulfilling desires breeds more desire.

Contrary to what the ego believes, grasping after what seems pleasurable and trying to avoid what seems painful is not only an endless task, it is also a fruitless one. It can never be done successfully for any length of time. This is because, as we've seen before, pleasure and pain come in the same package. You can't have one without the other. Many centuries ago, Buddha gave us this very message. He stated very simply that desire creates attachment, and attachment creates suffering. Do away with desire and attachment, and peace and happiness naturally appear.

Although this message may not be readily understandable, you can learn to see it clearly for yourself. Take some time to examine closely the suffering in your life. You will see that, in the midst of the suffering, desire is always present—desire that things be somehow different from how they are. See also how, because of the desire, attachment, expectation, demand, and fear are also present. When you are caught in any of these qualities, there can be no true inner peace.

In fact, true peace only happens when we are completely empty of desire. It is true that happiness can appear when we finally fulfill a desire. It may last a moment, or perhaps an extended period of time. But it always comes to an end. The happiness we experienced in fulfilling our desire was not due to what we gained; it is due to the state of desirelessness we have finally achieved. *It is the lack of desire that gives us the feeling of peace.*

Desire is a hungry ghost. It's always after MORE—more things, more power, more security, more knowledge, more love. It's never satisfied. If we continue to give it these demands, it only gets stronger and continues to want even more. We need to realize that nothing in form will ever satisfy this ghost and bring us true peace. All things, however gross or subtle in substance, are merely reflections of what we all ultimately want: true inner freedom, peace, oneness, perfection. Only waking up to the Self will give us all this.

Finding Freedom from Desire

Of course, it is one thing to understand the whole dynamic of desire and to see the lie we've bought about it, and an entirely different thing to get to the point of being able to let go of desires and the endless pursuit of them. This habit of chasing after desires must be one of the most deeply ingrained habits we all have. Yet there are some things you can do to begin the process of freeing yourself from your fruitless pursuit of happiness in this wrong direction. The following are suggestions that may help get you started in this process.

Exercise: *Experiencing the Feeling of Desire*

Become aware of exactly what holding desire in your consciousness can do to you. You can do this by closing your eyes and focusing inward for a few moments. Tune into an important desire you have—perhaps one you've had for quite awhile. Feel the sense of lack and the feeling of discomfort or pain you generally experience when thinking about this thing you want but don't have. Don't go off into all the stories about it—simply feel the sense of need and lack that are present.

Now step back slightly from this and see more clearly just what this energy of desire is creating in you. See the discomfort, the unrest, the irritation it produces. See the suffering that comes from this sense of not feeling full, whole, and complete. Be aware of your body. Note how having this feeling of desire actually prevents you from being totally relaxed. It keeps wanting to drag you into the future when you hope to have this thing you don't currently have; or it's dragging you into the past, attempting to discover a way stashed somewhere in your memory in which you might fulfill this desire. Desire won't let you be; it keeps gnawing at you, demanding to be fulfilled. Experience this painful sense of discontentment, and see clearly how desire is causing it.

Seeing desire for what it is isn't necessarily easy. You may be tempted to believe that the suffering you are experiencing is coming from not having what you desire. But investigate closely. This is the lie you've bought. It is not what is true. It is the desire itself that causes you the suffering. It takes a ruthless resolve, born of utter weariness with the pursuit of happiness, to truly see this.

Exercise: *Becoming Aware of Your Desires*

After experiencing the true nature of desire and the trouble it causes you, take an inventory of what your important desires are by making a list of them. You might wish to list them in categories, such as desires around your job, your primary relationships, your material possessions, traveling, money, etc. Take time with this list. Allow your mind to empty all of its desires onto the paper. When you feel complete with this, sit back and look over your list. Become aware to what degree you are caught in the trap of desire.

Following are four exercises to help clarify how you may be hoping that fulfilling your desires will finally create the happiness you long for.

Exercise: *If Only . . .*

Look carefully at each of these things you desire. Become aware of the happiness you believe you might create in fulfilling them, by completing the sentence: "If I only had _____, then I'd be happy." Then think carefully about the situation. Would having that thing alone do it, or would there just be more desires that would crop up, once you had it? Remembering times when you finally obtained what you'd been desiring can be helpful. How soon did dissatisfaction set in after you'd fulfilled those desires?

Example: I once had a friend, Nola, who tended toward depression. She often complained that she and her family lived in too small an apartment. She really felt that if she and her husband could only afford to move into a house, all her problems would be solved.

She had dreamed for a number of years about moving into a house in a particular neighborhood. Finally, an opportunity to buy a house there arose. It was a house that looked perfect, like one in which she had always pictured herself living. She was absolutely elated, beside herself with hope and anticipation. Her desire might finally be fulfilled. After a number of weeks of offers and counter-offers, they finally signed a contract for it.

At this point, Nola could talk about nothing else. Her entire life revolved around this house, and about how wonderful life was finally going to be. For weeks, she was entirely wrapped up in all the details of the move.

After they'd been moved in for about two weeks, I received a call from her. I was amazed at the depressed sound of her voice. "The upstairs tub leaks, and it looks like we have retile the whole thing. And our next door neighbors are so noisy—we had no idea. And the house is so big. I realize that cleaning it is going to take me a good hour longer than our apartment ever did. I'm feeling a little overwhelmed. I really want to get a housekeeper, but Ted doesn't know if we can afford it."

The scenario is, of course, familiar. Whenever we get something we've asked for, we always have to be prepared to accept what goes with it. Nola had spent years desiring something and had finally gotten it. She may have had a few days of enjoying the state of desirelessness she had finally attained around her living situation—but then a whole new set of desires began to besiege her, once again dragging her down into the state of restless discontent and depression she'd been in before. Like most people, she didn't realize that this was because of the new desires that had moved in with her. She kept believing that she simply needed to fulfill these new desires.

Exercise: *What Do You Want?*

This exercise helps you see through the desire you think you have. Using your list of desires, pick an important one and answer these questions about it:
- What do you want?
- What would you gain, if you had that?
- If you had that, what would you gain?
- If you had that, what would you gain?

Keep asking this, until you feel you've hit a bottom line with it.

Example: Here's how a woman responded when I asked her these questions:

What do you want? An intimate relationship with a man.

What would you gain, if you had that? I guess I would feel I was special and important.

If you had that, what would you gain? I would feel loved, cherished.

If you had that, what would you gain? (with a sigh) Then I could relax, really relax.

If you had that, what would you gain? I could feel safe. I would finally feel safe. (Her voice wavered some with this one.)

If you had that, what would you gain? (pause, as she started crying) I could finally experience peace—total peace. God, that all I want. Just deep, inner peace....

We did this exercise with a few other desires she had—all very different desires. To her surprise, each time her bottom line turned out to be peace, or something very close to it. You may find you have a similar experience. Perhaps your bottom line might be joy or freedom or love. The point is to become aware of what it is you *really* want, of what it is you are truly searching for through pursuing these things you believe yourself to be desiring.

Will pursuing your desires give you what you truly want? Now look closely at how you are going about trying to fulfill this true desire that resides under all your others. Ask yourself honestly: Is pursuing these desires I think I have really going to give me what I actually want? Again, think back into your past for a moment. How many times have you fulfilled similar desires, hoping to gain your true desire? How many times has this plan failed? When will you finally be weary enough to see clearly that it doesn't work? When will you be convinced that something else must be tried?

I realize that these questions may not be easy to answer. Some part of you may still be convinced that fulfilling desires—even just a few important ones—will give you what you really yearning for. For example, if you are someone who has never really had fulfilling work and have been yearning for this for a long time, it might be difficult for you to be convinced that finally finding fulfilling work isn't going to bring you the kind of happiness you seek. Or you may be someone who has never really experienced a close, intimate relationship with someone, and very much would like to have one. You might truly believe that finding this kind of relationship would finally give you what you've been looking for your whole life.

If there are areas of your life like this, it is understandable that you would be convinced that following an important desire would bring the fulfillment you seek. If this is the case, it may be necessary for you to follow these desires further until you can fulfill them—and then see what you experience. Some desires have been fed so well for so long, that they just won't let go. So you may need to follow them through to their end, to see for yourself where they lead you.

If you have followed and attained many desires in your life—and realize that you are still feeling unsatisfied, restless, and unhappy—then perhaps you are ready to try some suggestions designed to help free you from the whole trap of desire itself.

Exercise: *Looking for the Boundary*

Close your eyes and relax. Breathe a few deep breaths. Bring into your awareness the desire for something very important to you. Get in touch with the discomfort (stemming out of the feeling of lack) that the desire brings up for you. Now become aware of what you believe fulfilling this desire would bring to you—happiness, peace, love, joy, or whatever it is. See if you can find the boundary that separates you from having or being this quality, right here, right now.

If you discover a block or boundary, investigate it closely. What is it made of? Does it really have any substance? Is it anything more than a mental concept—some idea or belief? Is anything real actually preventing you from experiencing joy, peace, or happiness at this moment? Check and see. Take an honest look to see if you can just let go of any mental ideas that prevent you from experiencing what you wish to be experiencing. Discover what is present when your desire is removed. You may be surprised—because nothing of any substance is preventing you from experiencing the peace, joy, and love you wish to experience. There can't be—because you ARE these qualities.

How can anything prevent you from experiencing who you naturally are? You are the very essence of joy and peace and love. All you need to do is drop any ideas you have about not being these things, and let go of the desires you've created about them—and discover immediately what is already there, waiting to be experienced.

Example: A lovely girl of seventeen, Amanda, came to see me for counseling due to problems she was having with her mother. Amanda had always experienced her mother as harsh and un-nurturing, and longed desperately for someone to understand and love her. She had never known her father, and there didn't seem to be many relatives around who spent much time with her. Although she did have some friends at school, in many ways she was a very lonely girl.

About a month after she'd started seeing me, she met a boy her age with whom she immediately become emotionally involved. They had a fast and intense romance that lasted about three weeks, until he abruptly left her and began dating a friend of hers. Amanda was devastated. She had thought she had finally found someone who could love and understand her.

She came to a session with me the day after her boyfriend had left her. The weight of her depression and despair was palpable. She talked and cried for awhile, expressing the pain she was feeling, but didn't feel much better. She finally said, "All I want is to feel loved. That is all I want … I just want to feel loved…."

I nodded with compassion. I knew that this was what she wanted and needed. Gently, I suggested she close her eyes and attune herself to her body to see what she was feeling. She immediately told me about the constriction in her chest and solar plexus, and the heaviness she felt throughout her body.

Then I asked about the emotions she was feeling. With tears, she told me she was feeling lonely and sad. Then she added, "I feel totally abandoned by God. So alone … and unloved.…"

"What you want to feel is that you are loved?"

"Yes! Really loved. I want to feel it all through me, really know it. I want to feel safe and warm … that I will always be taken care of.…" Quiet tears were falling from her eyes.

"Of course. You want to feel entirely loved, protected, and safe. What I'd like you to do, Amanda, is right now look for the boundary between you and that feeling you long for of feeling loved. Look to see what it is that is separating you from this feeling."

She looked puzzled for a moment. And then she said, "Well, there's nobody to really love me. I mean, I'd feel loved if there were somebody I knew who really loved me."

"Okay, so what's separating you from the feeling of being loved is the idea that someone needs to be with you who is loving you. That's what is standing between you and feeling loved?"

"Yeah, I guess."

"Try to see this clearly. There's you, and then there's the feeling of being loved that you can see somewhere away from you. And in between you and this feeling is this idea, this thought, that you need someone to love you in order to feel loved."

"Yeah, that's right. I can see it. It's like looking over at that feeling of being loved through a mist."

"So, all that's separating you from feeling loved is this idea that looks like mist?"

"Yeah. It's just there, blocking me. God, I can almost feel the feeling of being loved.… I want it so badly. But it's over there. Like in a land I'm not allowed to go in, or something."

"Why don't you see what happens if you simply walk through that mist toward the feeling of being loved?"

A few moments passed, and then I saw a sweetness appear on her face. Very softly, she whimpered.

"What's happening?"

"Oh," she sighed. "I'm in it. I'm in the feeling. Oh my God … it's so sweet. I feel like I'm being rocked like a baby in God's arms.…"

Tears flooded her eyes. Her face indeed had transformed into that of a baby. "It feels so warm and safe ... there's so much love. It's like I don't have to do anything ... I can just be loved for who I am...." She was now sobbing and could say no more.

After a while her crying subsided, and she said softly, "You know what's so amazing is that it isn't even like I'm being loved anymore. It's kind of crazy, but I've kind of disappeared into God ... it's more like I AM love. I feel so full. My heart—you should feel my heart. There's like this pressure all around it—but good pressure. It's soft and vibrating and kind of filled with this light...."

It was amazing to me. By simply looking closely to see what appeared to be blocking her from feeling loved, Amanda had gone, in a matter of minutes, from total despair to a deep knowing of who she really was.

This experience, of course, did not entirely eradicate her yearning to find someone to love her. Being so young and without the experience of being truly loved by someone, she was still going to pursue that desire. But what she had experienced in our session became a powerful reference point for her in discovering the true source of the love that she yearned for. She now knew she could contact this source inside herself—and that her own true nature was Love, itself.

Exercise: *Observing Your Desires*

This is the same basic practice as observing emotions and thoughts as they enter your mind. It involves simply observing desires as they come into your consciousness—and doing nothing about them, except witnessing them. It means not resisting, judging, or suppressing them in any way, and it means not indulging or pursuing them, either. It's just a matter of letting them be.

Like other thoughts that come into your mind, desires are just forms of energy that you have given a lot of attention in the past. As you give them this new treatment of simply observing them, they will undoubtedly pull on you even harder at first. Just hold steady.

As you give no energy to them, they will begin to lose their strength and power over you.

Redirecting energy from desires: There is one desire that some teachers of the direct path tell us is beneficial: the desire for true freedom, for the full awakening to the Self. Although this desire too ultimately needs to be dropped, it can be used at first to propel us toward the experience of awakening.

When this desire first appears in you in a powerful way, it is an important signpost telling you that you are headed toward full awakening into your Self. This is indeed a blessed event. When you discover that this desire for freedom is your only desire—that freedom is all you really want—this is truly a happy day! This is when freedom will begin pulling you Home. At this point, all you need do is completely surrender to this divine pull.

To get to this place, you need to focus your attention and love on your desire to fully realize Self. When it appears in your awareness, give lots of energy to it. See it as a flame you are fanning. Do everything you can to build this flame, to make it grow hotter. When suffering appears, throw it into the flames. When desire for anything else comes, throw this on the flames as well. Redirect the energy of the desire into your desire for freedom. Then watch the flames of this one desire burn away the desire for anything transient and illusory. It can be truly liberating!

Example: I once worked with a woman, Milana, who found herself in dire financial straits. She was recently separated from her husband, and she was attempting to build a real estate business from scratch. Money was already very tight, when she suddenly found she had many large expenses she needed to pay almost immediately. A sense of panic about this threatened to take hold.

I had been coaching her to simply observe feelings as they arose, and I now encouraged her to observe the panic. This was successful to a degree, but after a while she began speaking about a deep desire to be financially free. She believed that so many problems could be solved, if only she could attain financial freedom.

I asked her to become aware of the power she was giving this desire every time she gave it attention. She exclaimed, "You're right!

Whenever I think about it, it then comes into my mind more often, and soon it's monopolizing my attention. It's all I can think about. I give it an inch; it takes a mile." She added that sometimes, along with the thoughts, came such a deep longing and such a sense of suffering that she felt she was going crazy. It was like she was drowning in her feeling of need and lack and helplessness.

I remembered what Papaji had said about throwing all desires for transient objects into the flame of the one desire to realize Self. I suggested that she try this. She closed her eyes, and almost immediately, she said, "It's like a bonfire inside me—my longing to be done with all this, just to be free. God, I just want to be free! Wow, I can really see and feel the fire!"

"Okay, see if you can allow it to grow, to intensify."

She was silent for a moment and then moaned, "It's so huge already; it's eating away at my insides."

"Okay, now focus for a moment on your desire for financial security. Find it inside you."

"All right ... yeah, I'm back to that."

"Good. Now take that longing and throw it on the fire."

I could see for a moment that she might be drawn into giving that longing some energy and attention again. Then her face suddenly changed. It's hard to describe her expression—surprise, pain, joy, all at once. And then tears. I sat quietly with her for about five minutes as she wept. I could see her whole body trembling with release.

When she was finally able to speak, she told me that an incredible burning for true freedom had occurred at the moment of throwing the desire for financial security onto the fire—that it was like throwing something flammable onto it. Her whole body felt an actual burning; heat was coursing through her veins.

She was still stunned by what had happened. Then she said, "This yearning for my true Self is so intense and so painful—and yet it's so sweet. All I can do is surrender to it."

We sat together for awhile, not saying much. She continued to report that the fire was burning inside her. I suggested that she could simply observe the fire, rather than feeling consumed by it. She fell into a gentle, quiet, relaxed state of being. "The fire's out," she reported. "I feel so warm and tingly."

I suggested she look around inside her for the desire for financial security. She said she could not find it. All that was there was peace. "You know, it's strange. I just have this knowing now that I will always be taken care of.... I really don't have to worry any more."

Of course, this wasn't the end of worry thoughts about finances for Milana. But she was handling them very differently now. They didn't grab hold of her so furiously as before. She didn't pay as much attention to them. She said they kind of flitted through her consciousness, like pieces of tissue paper floating on the breeze, but did not stay long.

This process of throwing all desires into the one true desire for the Self can be a very powerful experience. Papaji tells us it can be used as a vehicle that can take us to full realization of the Self. The very yearning itself—as painful as it can be at times—is simply our Self calling us Home.

Desires will probably always be with us. Like other thoughts, and like emotions, they're simply part of the human psyche. But what can change is our response to them. We have no obligation to follow them or put energy into fulfilling them. We need not obsess about them until they are satisfied. We can simply let them be.

It does no good to try to suppress them. This will not work. But we can understand them and see how they function. We can begin to see clearly how trying to satisfy them simply continues our misery, disappointment, and discontent. This is the first step in becoming free from desire.

From there on, it's simply a matter of not giving them much attention when they arise—except to watch them or redirect their energy into our desire for total awakening to the Self. Given this treatment, they will eventually fade and weaken and become no more than part of the passing show within your consciousness.

You will begin to see that you can be happy no matter what is going on in your life, no matter what desires are fulfilled, what you have or haven't achieved. You'll find that you can experience true inner peace, no matter whether pleasure or pain is present in your life; you'll see that both of them are actually irrelevant to your experience of peace and contentment. They are merely phenomena passing through your awareness. They come and they go. You need not resist or grab onto them. The peaceful, joyful fulfillment that you are experiencing—indeed, that you ARE—is untouched by it all.

Summary

In the last few chapters, we have explored a number of ways in which the mind can keep us in delusion, convincing us that it is who we are. We saw how the subtle nature of thought can make it easy for us to confuse it with the nature of Self. We explored how the mind's creation of time tends to keep us out of the Now, where we can experience Self. We also saw how the mind tends to claim spiritual experiences as its own, deluding us into thinking that it has control over them.

We then explored the chattering nature of the mind to see how its constant flow of thought can keep us from experiencing the peace of the Self. And last, we explored how following the desires that our mind creates can produce a profound trap that keeps us in continual dissatisfaction and unrest, preventing us from experiencing the peace and happiness that we inherently are.

It is important to stay aware of all these potential traps our mind is constantly setting for us. We have fallen into them over and over again—and will continue to do so, even knowing what they are. Deeply-ingrained habits can be hard to break. But with persistent vigilance and practice, they can be weakened and broken. As these habits are broken, little by little, our identification with the mind begins to weaken and eventually fall away.

The mind is perhaps the most difficult aspect of the ego-self from which to detach. It is the one to which many of us have most attached our identity. But we must let go of our identification with all aspects of the ego, if we are to truly realize who we are. Many teachers of the direct path state that when we see clearly what we are NOT, then we are able to begin seeing what we ARE. The second section of this book has been the study of what we are not—the ego-self.

When we can begin to see the ego clearly and attain a degree of detachment from it, the Self that we truly are can begin to shine forth naturally and become self-evident. The ego-self, in one way, can be seen as simply a lot of clutter than needs to be cleaned up and put aside, so that the Self can be seen clearly. The Self is always present; we just can't always see it because we are focusing on all the clutter.

As you earnestly seek the Self and detach your identity from the ego-self, you will discover the ego slowly becoming a pale shadow of what it was, a translucent presence that you can simply ignore. As this happens, you realize the humorous paradox in the whole process of "letting go of the ego": that, in actuality, the ego never even existed. All there has been all along is Self. The ego has been a finely wrought illusion that we've mistakenly believed to be real. In Truth, it's all been a dream.

SURRENDERING
TO THE SELF

CHAPTER TWENTY-ONE

Accepting Life as It Is

What is needed is simply to take things as they come, reacting in the way one feels to be right, interfering as little as possible. Then things will come out of their own accord, and Grace will flow unimpeded.
—Arthur Osborne

THE THIRD STEP on the path of letting go is learning to surrender your life to the Self, trusting that it will take care of you in the best possible way. Eventually, it entails relying entirely on the Self and giving up all attempts to control your life. If you have devoted a great deal of your life to trying to get in control of it, this decision to surrender control may seem a frightening prospect. But it need not be. The surrendering of control can be done slowly through a process of testing and watching, at a pace that is comfortable for you.

Remember that when I speak of surrender, I'm not talking about a defeatist attitude of giving up, nor am I speaking about becoming inactive and passive. I'm referring, rather, to allowing a higher source—your Self—to guide you and decide what is to be done in your life. It entails an attitude of acceptance, letting go, allowing, and relaxing; one in which all struggle, resistance, and manipulation are released. In essence, it involves responding to life with a natural ease, trust, and flow.

The theme of surrender has been present throughout this book in a number of specific ways. I've described how a feeling of surrender can greatly enhance experiences of glimpsing the Self. I've talked about letting go of the identification with the ego-self, letting emotions and thoughts simply be, and letting pain and suffering be. I've also described many different ways in which you can let go of resistance and simply accept what is.

This third step on the path, surrendering to the Self, entails moving into fully surrendering your life as a whole to the Self. Learning to do this involves two processes. The first is seeing clearly the situations present in your life without any added "clutter" of emotions, beliefs, or desires, so that you can simply accept them as they are. The second is learning how to release the impulse to control the events in your life, and truly begin trusting the Self to guide you through your life.

Seeing Clearly What Is

One aspect of surrender that is important to develop is simply accepting whatever comes into your life. This doesn't mean you have to *like* everything that happens or passively put up with it for the rest of your life; you simply need to *accept* it—without judgment or resistance. This involves first being able to see it simply as it is, as clearly as possible—without superimposing any beliefs, desires, fears, judgments, emotions, or projections into the future about it—and then, very consciously and purposefully, accepting it, allowing it simply to be. After you truly accept it, then you are in a clear place to see what—if anything—needs to be done with it.

Exercise: *Practicing Acceptance*

1. Write down the things in your life you tend to worry and struggle about a lot. These are the things you spend energy either resisting or trying to change and improve. First list things about yourself: physical, mental, or emotional qualities that you don't like and you're trying to change; and addictions, obsessions, or other behaviors you find undesirable. Then list situations occurring in your life that you tend to spend time worrying about, resisting, or trying to change. From each of these lists, choose an important item.

2. Now close your eyes. Relax, take some deep breaths. Become aware of your body and note where you feel relaxed or constricted.

3. Bring to mind the item from your list of worries about yourself. Let this quality or behavior come fully into your awareness, and allow your mind to begin its process with it—the worrying, the analyzing, the resisting, the judging, the struggling to get control over it. Become aware of the energy you are expending on this issue, in trying to get control over it. See the effort it takes, how tiring it can be.

4. Now look closely at this thing about which you have been concerned. See all the stuff that you have attached to it: all your judgments, beliefs, emotions, desires, fears, guilt, shame, and projections into the future. Open your eyes, and write down what all these are.

   For example, let's say you've chosen a behavior that you call "overeating." In looking at your judgments about this behavior, you discover that you have many: you consider it bad, wrong, and weak. You believe that because of this behavior, you are overweight and you look like a "slob." Because of these beliefs, you also have a lot of emotions attached to the behavior: sadness, shame, anger, and hurt. Your fears and projections into the future say that you will never be able to stop this behavior and that you will eventually become totally out of control and enormous. Of course, this all leads to a desire to get rid of the behavior, to somehow overcome it.

5. Now look closely at what you've written down. Feel the heaviness of it, the clutter it creates in your mind, the pressure in your body. Become very clear about the fact that all this is stuff that you, yourself, have attached to this behavior or quality with which you have been struggling. See clearly that none of it is inherently, naturally there. The behavior or quality is simply what it is.

6. In realizing this, see if you can now begin to remove from the behavior or quality with which you've been struggling all the mental and emotional stuff you have attached to it. Pull away all the judgments, beliefs, desires, fears, and emotions you have

about it, and simply see the behavior or quality as it is. Look at it dispassionately, as something that seems to appear with some members of the human species, some of the time. This is all it is, in reality. All the other stuff around it are things you've added to it.

Learning how to look clearly and dispassionately at something like this is what Krishnamurti calls "choiceless awareness"—an art that involves seeing something as it is, without projecting anything onto it. To eventually become free, it is necessary to learn how to practice this art with all things, both outside and inside yourself.

7. In seeing the quality or behavior with detachment like this, now try simply accepting it as a fact in your life at this time. Take a deep breath, relax, and attempt just to let it be. Let go of the struggle to get rid of it or to improve or change it. Let go of your will about what *should* be happening about it … and just allow it to be as it is. Know that this behavior or quality is simply a part of the personality structure of your ego-self. It is not who you are. Your ego-self is not perfectible. Quit struggling under the illusion that you have the power to perfect it.

Feel the relaxation that can come in when allowing what is to simply be. This doesn't mean that you will never do anything about it or that nothing about it will ever change. It's simply giving up, at this point, the struggle you have created around it. It is also an allowance for the possibility that there is an important reason for this quality or behavior in your life at this time about which you are not yet aware.

8. Now repeat Steps 3 through 7 of this exercise with the situation in your life about which you worry a great deal. See that situation clearly as simply a situation that members of the human race sometimes encounter to which you have added judgments, fears, emotions, desires, and beliefs.

Then remove all this clutter from the situation—and move into acceptance about it. Let it simply be for a while. If there is something to be done about it, let this be revealed to you from within the Silence. Experience the relief and peace that comes with this kind of simple acceptance of what is.

You can do this process with as many things about yourself and your life as you wish. The more completely you can accept yourself and the situations happening in your life, the greater freedom you will begin experiencing.

It's No Big Deal

I was once working with a woman named Maria who had been diagnosed, as an adult, with attention deficit disorder. She had been making some progress in understanding the symptoms of this disorder and in making certain behavioral changes to become more effective in her life. But she kept getting caught up in her judgments about the difficulty of keeping organized and neat in her life. We decided to see if we could go further with her judgments in this area than just talking about them.

I had her close her eyes, take some deep breaths, and become aware of her body. I asked her to allow herself to begin contemplating the qualities of disorganization and messiness she observed in herself.

"Oh God," she moaned. "I hate thinking about it. All this stuff comes up for me. It feels awful. I feel my stomach beginning to clench. I see my apartment and my office at work just piled up with papers and stuff. Boxes I haven't unpacked yet from months ago. I don't even know where this month's bills are. I've worked so hard on this, but it doesn't seem to be getting any better. I'm such a slob, when it really comes down to it."

"You have some harsh judgments of yourself about it, don't you?"

"Yeah, I do. I'm so messy and disorganized, it's amazing I can live my life at all. Sometimes I leave dirty dishes in the sink for days. I don't ever make my bed—I never have time in the morning. I'm a pig. I'm really lazy, I guess." Tears appeared in her eyes, as she said this.

"So your judgments of yourself about being disorganized include that you're a slob and a pig and that you're lazy."

"Yeah, that about sums it up," she said glumly.

"What other beliefs do you have about this trait of yours?"

"Well, I really think that something's wrong with me. I mean, most people aren't like this. They don't have this kind of problem. So I guess I believe that I'm deficient in some way."

"And what kind of emotions do these beliefs and judgments bring up for you?"

"Shame, mainly. I feel ashamed and guilty. And I guess a lot of anger about it, too. I remember my mother really ragging on me about it all the time, when I was growing up. And hurt—I couldn't understand why she couldn't just understand me and accept me the way I was. I never understood why messiness and being disorganized were so awful."

"Tell me, does fear also come up for you when you think about your messiness and disorganization?"

"Oh yeah! Sometimes I'm afraid I'm going to lose my job. My boss gets down on me for misplacing things and not remembering certain things. I get really scared. I also get afraid that if I keep losing my bills, that I won't pay them—and they'll turn off my phone or something."

"And what desires do you have around all this?"

"To get rid of it, of course! To get better about it, learn how to get organized and stay that way. Oh, and I want people to understand it better, that it's hard for me, not that I'm lazy. I want people to get off my back about it."

"So you've got a lot of stuff that goes on inside you about your trait of disorganization."

"Yeah, a lot!"

"Get in touch right now with the heaviness of all this mental and emotional stuff that hangs around inside you, attached to this one trait that's been called 'disorganized.' Feel the energy you put into thinking about it and dealing with feelings and desires about it. See how all this weighs on you."

She was quiet for a few moments, then said, "Gee, I'm feeling so depressed. There's so much stuff in me around this thing, isn't there?"

"You know, the trait of being disorganized is simply a psychological trait that some members of the human race seem to carry. Some humans have it, others don't. Other humans have other traits.

We all have traits, characteristics—some we find pleasant, others unpleasant. But there is nothing inherently good or bad about any of them. Disorganization is simply the opposite of organization. There is nothing bad or wrong with either one of them. Sometimes people find disorganization unpleasant or inconvenient—but that's simply their reaction to it. In itself, disorganization is simply a trait that appears in certain people—who knows why?"

She was silent for a time. Then she said, somewhat hesitantly, "Yeah, I can see that, I guess...."

I continued, "And all this stuff you've put on it—your judgments and beliefs about it being bad and you being deficient, your emotions of shame and guilt, your fears and your desires—all this is just stuff you have attached to it. None of it has to be there."

"You mean, I could just let all this stuff go?"

"Yeah—you can try it right now. See if you can just remove, at least for the time being, all the mental and emotional stuff from this trait of disorganization you happen to have, and just look at the trait dispassionately. See it clearly for what it is—just one of many characteristics this personality structure of yours happens to have."

"Wow, that really feels different. I mean, just to see it like that. It's no big deal."

"Right. It's just what it is. Now see if you can move into an attitude of acceptance of this trait known as 'disorganization.' Just accept it as it is. Let it be okay for you to have this. You can still try to do something about it, if you want. But you can let go of all that heavy stuff that was attached to it and decide what's best without all the struggle about it."

I could see her face begin to relax in a remarkable way. Her furrowed brow smoothed out, and her mouth visibly let go of its tension. She said, "Wow, what relief I'm feeling! It's like I really don't have to do anything about this whole thing if I don't want to, do I? It's my characteristic—who says I have to change it, if I don't want to?" She suddenly laughed. Then she added, "Besides, it's not ME, anyway, right? It's just a way my mind happens to work. What's the big deal?" She laughed again.

After letting her rest for a time in the relief she was feeling, we then began to gently problem-solve around some of the problems her disorganization had been creating for her in her life. I was amazed at the clarity and detachment with which she spoke about these things. From the state of profound acceptance she had reached about it, she was able to think effectively in a relaxed manner. I had never experienced her like this before when we'd talked about this issue in her life. There was no heaviness about it, no struggle. It could have been someone else we were talking about.

Although she continued to deal with the issues around her disorganization, from that point on she never again seemed to really struggle with it. She could laugh at herself, make jokes about it. As she had said, it was "no big deal."

CHAPTER TWENTY-TWO

Learning to Trust the Self

God never forsakes one who has surrendered.
—Ramana Maharshi

O NCE YOU HAVE BEGUN THE PROCESS of surrender by seeing clearly what is present in your life and accepting it as it is, then it is time to learn truly to trust the Self as it guides you through life. It's time to trust that whatever is happening in your life is absolutely perfect for you, right-on-target for assisting you to fully awaken to who you are. It's time to begin releasing all attempts to control the events in your life, and instead welcome what is coming forward within the flow.

Giving up Trying to Control Your Life

In the West, two beliefs seem to be prevalent concerning life and the control we have over it. The first is that we do have control (at least some) over what happens in our life. The second is that by taking control of our life, we can find happiness. These beliefs are important to explore and question, because they are often assumed to be facts about life or statements about the Truth, rather than simply beliefs. And, like all beliefs, they may not, in fact, represent what is actually true.

If you hold the first belief—that we have at least some control over our lives—you might wish to explore the question: How much control do you really have over what happens in your life? Do you really know that what you do has a causal effect on what happens? How do you know that everything that happens isn't simply pre-destined? Things may appear to go a certain way because of what you do, but how do you know it isn't the way things would have gone anyway? Perhaps you have simply aligned your will to that which was going to happen anyway, and it just looks as if you've caused it. Furthermore, do you even know that your decision to do something wasn't already destined to be made, even before you thought you were making it? What do you know for sure about any of this?

The answer to these questions, of course, is that you can't know. There is no way to know how much control, if any, we have over our lives. There is no way to prove it either way. This is the old debate between the ideas of "free-will" and "predestination" that can never be proven through any scientific or intellectual process. The assumption that we have control over our lives is simply a belief and therefore may not be fact at all.

The second belief that is often assumed to be the Truth stems from the first belief. It is that by attempting to control our lives, we may be able to find happiness. If you hold this assumption, it, too, is important to explore and question. Do you know beyond a doubt that this is true? Has your attempt at controlling your life brought the happiness you've experienced? These questions also, of course, cannot be answered in any way that will satisfy the intellect. But again, it is important to see that the belief is not based on anything that can be proven, and therefore may not be true.

I went through most of my life confusing my beliefs with the Truth. I really thought that, by constantly focusing my attention on what needed to be improved in my life and on how I could change or fix myself, the situations I found myself in, and the acquisitions I had, I could bring myself the peace and happiness I had always sought.

It wasn't until I began hearing the spiritual teachings about surrender that I was stopped short on this never-ending, fruitless path of struggle. These teachings contend that we, as egos, are actually not in control at all. The Self is completely running the show. It is a delusion to believe that we can have some kind of control.

The teachings also state that we basically have two choices in how to approach life. The first is to try to control things that are happening: resist what we don't want and try to cling to what we do want, and struggle constantly to improve our lot in life. The second choice is simply to accept, flow, and trust what is happening in our lives, to allow the Self to guide us, trusting it will let us know when and how to act, and generally just to sit back, relax, and enjoy the ride. In essence, the teachings say that if we can just stop trying to control our lives and trust what the Self is bringing forward for us to experience, we will find the peace, relaxation, and happiness for which we are looking.

If you're like most people I know, this is much easier said than done. Your conditioning around trying to gain control over what happens in your life is probably quite powerful. Fears around helplessness, abandonment, and survival are likely well-ingrained in your psyche. I have, therefore, come up with some guidelines for how this process of surrender can be approached.

Feeling for the Flow

In considering the decision to release the controlling efforts in your life, you may well be asking: *So if I'm not trying to control things, what do I do? Do I just become a passive observer, allowing anything to happen in my life?*

The answer is no. You begin intuitively feeling for the "flow" in your life—what you are naturally and effortlessly being guided to do—and cooperate with it. It involves being open and trusting, and being willing to do whatever you are called upon to do.

This entails maintaining a constant awareness of your inner guidance. As I described earlier, inner guidance can come to us in many ways, and it is important to find the ways in which we best receive this help. It may come to you as an inner message that you hear; you may sense or feel it energetically; you may see images that point the way. Or you may just come to "know" what it is you are to do or where you are to go.

If you find something happening in your life that is unpleasant or does not feel "right," you can use the exercise I gave in Chapter 18 to determine the right action:

> *After pouring out onto paper all that you have attempted to do about the situation and all that you've thought about it, close your eyes and*

take time to move deeply into the Silence within you. Drop down, past all
your thoughts and emotions, and become still.

From within this Silence, now ask in a clear and unattached way:
"Does anything need to be done about this situation? Do I need to do
anything to change it at this time?" Be still and simply let the answer
come naturally, peacefully to you. Be open to receive whatever it is.

What you're essentially doing in this process is getting a sense for where the flow is. What course, if any, feels effortless, natural, and flowing? You may get the message that there is something you need to do, or there may be nothing to do. Simply be open to receive whatever comes to you from the place of deep stillness within you.

If something does need to be done about the situation, you will feel a clear and natural energy there with you to do it. The action will be part of the flow. It will feel effortless; it will feel *right*. If there is nothing to do about it—at least at this time—you will sense that clearly. There will be a knowing simply to let things be. Either way, there will be a sense of peace, clarity, and relaxation present. Your whole body and sense of being will feel aligned with it.

If, in this process of opening to inner guidance, confusion appears—or if fears, desires, doubt, or analyzing slip in—you will know that you have moved back into your mind. Without judgment about this, once again drop deeply into the Silence beyond the mind. Then begin again to ask what, if anything, needs to be done about the situation with which you've been struggling. Stay relaxed, unattached, and open. Be accepting of whatever comes forward into your awareness.

Bypassing the Traps of the Mind

On the path of letting go, the art of going within to receive inner guidance is essential to practice and eventually master. However, inherent traps are involved in the process, and they are important to observe.

One of the major traps is listening to the guidance coming from your conditioned mind, rather than from the Self. The thoughts coming from your conditioned mind can often feel as if they are effortless and flowing and natural. In one way, they *are*, simply because they are so very familiar to you. You've thought them so often for so long, they feel flowing and natural to you

If you investigate them closely, however, you will notice that these conditioned thoughts have an old, stale feeling to them. There's a dead energy about them—unlike the fresh, spontaneous, alive energy that ideas from the heart of Self carry. Ideas from the programmed mind are furthermore often steeped in fear of some kind. Thoughts from within the Silence lack this fearful energy. The messages have a confident authority, as well as a sense of loving support.

For example, let's say you are standing in a room when an earthquake suddenly hits, and you panic, wondering what the best thing might be to do. You may immediately get the message inside you: *Quick—leave! Run out the door!* This message might, on the surface, seem to be a fearful one. But if it is coming from the Self, while having a feeling of urgency, it will also have a sense of calm and firm authority, rather than fear. It will convey to you a sense that you are being loved and protected. For this reason, it will be easy to quickly obey.

The key to distinguishing between messages from the Self and messages from the conditioned mind lies in the energy and feeling of the message. The conditioned mind carries old, dead energy with it, along with an underlying sense of fear. The Self communicates with a fresh, spontaneous, alive energy and "speaks" with a firm and loving authority—however small and faint the "voice" may sound when we're first tuning into it. A simple rule of thumb is seeing if the message you're getting is infused with fear or with love.

A second trap we can fall into when learning to distinguish between the messages coming from the Self and those from the mind is falling prey to wishful, hopeful thinking. This kind of thinking can feel loving, joyful, and positive—and dupe us into believing it must be coming from the Self. Of course, sometimes messages from the Self will match your hopes and wishes in a situation. This can create an incredible feeling, because the plan that the Self has for you is in alignment with what you are personally hoping.

The trap lies in believing that your wishful, hopeful thoughts are always coming from your attunement with the Self. Sometimes this

220 Surrendering to the Self

is not the case. Sometimes you hope that a certain path or action is the right one and try to make it happen, simply because it feels good; all the while, a small, still voice is telling you that a different situation needs to take place. You may feel compelled to ignore this small, still voice because it sounds "negative"—but in reality, all it is doing is telling you something different from what you want to hear. It can be very tricky.

Essentially, what you need to do when earnestly seeking true guidance from your Self is be unattached to what you will receive. Leave all preconceived ideas and hopes behind, and simply be open to whatever guidance you receive. It demands a deep commitment to following the will of the Self, wherever that may take you.

At the same time, if you are open to trusting the Self and giving up your personal will, you will find that the guidance you receive from the Self will feel right to ALL of you, including your mind, your emotions, and your body. It will make sense. Even if you do not hear what you'd like to hear, if you're honest, you will know that it simply feels right.

Taking "Baby Steps"

Learning to tune into inner guidance is a very subtle art: it's a process of learning to trust the Self as it communicates with you—and yet stay grounded and practical. It's an art that needs to be practiced and learned through testing and leaning into the guidance you receive. And it's a skill that takes a while to develop. Trust happens over time. In part, this trust happens naturally, as you have more experiences of your Self and become familiar with it. It is also something that you can consciously develop through taking "baby steps" in that direction.

You can take these steps by beginning to relinquish your attempts to control your life. Become aware of these attempts and refrain from making them.

You can also take baby steps by accepting what the Self is bringing you in life. Look to see what is already in your life—what situations, relationships, and "issues" are present—and move into acceptance of all these things, without adding resistance or judgment to them.

Lastly, you can take steps toward trusting the Self by beginning to depend on it to guide you, take care of you, and give you what you need when you need it. Begin trusting that you are taken care of perfectly, in the way that is best for you at this time.

You can take these steps in different ways. One way is to take a day at a time, letting go of all conditioned urges to control what is happening. Simply go through the day, watching this urge to change, manipulate, direct, or fix things—and not acting on it. Just accept everything that is, exactly the way it is—and see what happens.

If, after awhile, it feels natural, effortless, and flowing to do something in particular, then gently move toward it. If it involves a struggle or resistance, don't do it. Don't act out of a belief that something is "wrong" or "bad" and needs to be changed; simply do it as a natural action emerging from the peace deep within you. There's a gracefulness with this; it's like doing a flowing, effortless dance with the Self, following its lead, trusting it to take you where you need to go.

Another baby-step approach into trusting the Self is to take one area or issue in your life with which you have been struggling and begin a slow process of letting go of your attempts to control it. Come into an attitude of acceptance about it, the way it is. Then become very alert to what your Self may be guiding you to do about it, if anything.

If the action—or lack of it—that the Self seems to be counseling you to take feels too drastic at first, then again, intuitively lean into it. Slowly follow what is emanating from the peaceful Silence within you. Watch closely what happens. If fear comes up for you in following the counsel you've received, drop back into the Silence, and be alert for messages.

Learning to trust this process takes some time. Start slowly. Begin with the less significant issues in your life, so that it's not too frightening.

Floating Down the River

The process of learning to trust the Self is something like being in a boat on a river. Usually in life, we're busy paddling away in our boat, attempting to guide it in the direction in which we think we want to go—to this shore or that shore, away from rocks and trees and branches, trying to go more quickly or more slowly. We are always somewhat anxious that, if we give up our tense vigilance and effort at paddling, we may get pulled someplace we do not wish to go. Sometimes, in doing all this, we get to where we think we want to go. Sometimes we don't; the flow of the river is too strong, and we end up overshooting our desired destination, getting snagged in branches, ramming into someone else's boat, or getting caught in a whirlpool.

If we don't get where we think we want to get, we often become angry, disappointed, or hurt. We curse the river and bemoan the fact that our boat and paddles are inadequate. Or we curse the other people in their boats who have somehow been lucky enough to have gotten where we wanted to go. We feel victimized and helpless. Maybe at some point, realizing that this attitude is getting us nowhere, we'll renew our efforts to overcome the river's flow. Often, after doing this over and over again, we just plain get worn out and let our boat drift for a while, feeling defeated and apathetic. Then panic ensues, and we start madly paddling again, trying to force our boat back in the direction in which we wanted to go. All this can be so tiring!

The process of trust can begin when we have the courage to stop paddling for a while, at a time when it looks relatively "safe" to do so. We simply put down our paddle and just let the boat follow the flow of the river for a while. In doing this, we have the opportunity to feel the natural flow of the river; we can see clearly where it is taking us.

Once the flow is quietly experienced for a time, then perhaps we can begin cooperating with it. We can gently paddle in the same direction, while staying sensitive to any subtle changes in the course of the flow.

There can be such a peace in this process of just floating down the river, barely paddling, trusting the flow. You can relax and enjoy the view and the gentle breezes. You become aware that if your help in paddling is needed, you'll know. It is an automatic, effortless, and natural action. Your ride down the river becomes pleasant and peaceful, as you fully experience the river and the views on either shore.

Surrender Doesn't Mean Doing Nothing

I wish to make it clear that surrendering to the Self does not mean that you avoid taking any action. It may involve less action than you are used to and spending more time simply *being*. But it also involves some action—action that is in accordance with the natural flow of things. What you will probably find is that the actions you do take in this approach to life are actually much more effective than those that spring from your conditioned mind and emotions.

I once had an experience that demonstrated this to me very clearly. I lived for a short time with several housemates. One of them was a man who was planning to live with us for just a few weeks. None of us knew him or really liked him much—but little did we know how disturbed a person he would turn out to be.

One day, when I happened to be home alone with him, he suddenly had what looked like a psychotic break and became violent with me. I had been sitting quietly at my desk in my office, when he began arguing about something with me. Because my response was not to engage him in arguing, he became enraged. He threw a chair at me and yelled, over and over, that he was going to bash in my face. I was shocked, aghast, and terrified. My conditioned mind was anxiously yelling two different messages to me: *Get up and run* and *stand up and fight back.* Things to yell back at him were also charging into my mind with an incredible force.

Thankfully, I had the awareness to do none of those things. In retrospect, I think any of them might have only increased his rage. Instead, I very quickly dropped into a place of stillness, silently pleading for guidance. What immediately felt natural was to continue sitting where I was and simply look him in the eyes, silently sending him love. I could see the expression on his face immediately become puzzled and uncertain. The longer I gazed at him silently like this, the more he backed up and seemed to lose momentum. He eventually stopped yelling, dropped the chair that he had raised to throw at me again, and walked out of the room.

Very thankful for this turn of events, I was able to reflect on what had happened. I felt such gratefulness! And how effective it had been to rely on the Self to guide me in response to the violence being thrust in my direction—rather than my conditioned mind and emotions.

Fully Cooperating with What Is Happening

I realize that being willing simply to follow what our inner guidance is telling us to do is not always so easy. I know this only too well. Things have happened in my life since I started on this path of letting go about which I was initially not at all enthusiastic. I experienced the pain that my resistance to the flow brought me. I also experienced the incredible relief and joy that inevitably comes with the letting go of resistance.

One such experience was singularly educational for me. I had been traveling and writing for awhile without bringing in an income, and I finally needed to settle down and make some money quickly. For a number of reasons, I wasn't able to develop a new counseling practice at this point. I needed to find a job—one where I'd be working for someone else.

This was not a happy prospect for me. I hadn't worked for anyone else for quite some time; I'd enjoyed working for myself and working the hours I chose. Now I was faced with having to do what someone else wanted me to do—and doing it for eight hours straight. This was quite a challenge.

The only job that came in the flow—naturally, effortlessly, and feeling "right"—involved sales, something not only completely foreign to me, but also difficult. Every time I'd feel for the flow in regard to taking this job, it would surprisingly feel right. Although my mind was highly doubtful and resistant, I continued to inwardly hear and feel that it was what was arriving at my doorstep within the flow of my life, and that I should take it.

At first, because the job felt so right, I was enthusiastic about it. I was cooperating with its arrival in my life the best I knew how. But it soon became apparent that the job was going to be quite difficult for me. I was not a natural salesperson; I didn't like the idea of trying to manipulate people into buying something, even when it was something I felt would be valuable to them.

Little by little, my resistance grew, and, more and more, my suffering grew. Doubt pervaded my mind constantly; how could something within the flow feel so difficult? Yet every time I'd go within and question this, I got the message that it was absolutely right-on-target for me. It was perfect for me at this time.

I couldn't figure it out. After a week and half of pulling myself out of bed in the morning and forcing myself to go to this job and doing the minimum I needed to do to keep the job, I finally got very quiet one night and inwardly asked, *Why is this so difficult and painful? What am I doing wrong?*

Feeling a wave of incredibly sweet love pass through me, I heard the message: *Your pain comes from your resistance. Yes, you are accepting this job that has come present in your life, and you are cooperating with it— but only 98%. The two percent resistance is what is killing you. Let go of this two percent and see what happens. You will experience joy beyond your imagining. You will actually begin loving the job. You will eventually even want to stay on past the time you've said you would.*

On hearing this, I was very doubtful—to say the least. I could imagine perhaps experiencing some relief if I were to give up my resistance. But joy? Actually loving the job? Wanting to stay on past the time to which I'd committed? Give me a break, I thought. Those things couldn't possibly happen.

Then I heard a further message: *You see, even the cooperation you have been giving to this job has been very passive. You've been saying, "Oh, okay. If this is what I'm to do, I'll do it." And you've been dragging yourself, along with your resistance, to do it every day. Trusting the Self to bring in what is right for you entails more than passive acceptance; it demands your active cooperation and full participation in it, as well.*

My resistance to what I was hearing was brought up short with this message. I was reminded of a story I had once heard about an Indian monk. This monk was coming home after a trip to a nearby village, when he saw smoke and fire rising out of his hut. He could see that his well-meaning neighbors were running back and forth, pulling his furniture out of the hut and bringing water from the river to throw on the fire.

Much to their amazement, rather than helping them in their endeavors to save his hut, the monk began throwing the furniture back into his hut and blowing on the flames to encourage the fire. Then it started to rain, and the fire began abating. Immediately, the monk ran to the river to fill a bucket with water and throw it on the fire.

I loved this story when I heard it. The monk had such complete trust in what was happening that he not only accepted it, he cooperated and jumped into total participation with it. In reflecting on this story, I realized what I had to do. If I were to totally accept and trust what was happening in my life, then I would have to actively cooperate with my job and fully participate in it.

This entailed completely changing my attitude from passively going along with what was happening, to saying: *Well, it looks like a sales job is here for me to do. I guess that's what I need to do: really become a salesperson! I'm going to get in there and sell this product to people, and, furthermore, like any good salesperson, I'm going to make good money doing this!*

I walked into work the following day, still feeling somewhat doubtful about the whole thing. But I was determined to give it a try. Mustering great enthusiasm, I started my first day as a salesperson eager to make a sale with every customer with whom I spoke and make lots of money in the process. Much to my amazement, before long, an incredible thing started happening. An upsurge of joy began bursting through me with every call. I was experiencing profound love for every customer with whom I spoke. I was feeling unabated enthusiasm for the product I was selling—and, needless to say, I was selling!

Deciding to give my full cooperation, participation, and enthusiasm to what was appearing in my life at the time was the key. This could only happen with my decision to completely trust that what the Self had brought into my life was right and accurate for me, whether I could understand how this could be or not.

What a relief to feel I could truly put all my trust in what the Self was bringing forward for me! Not only did the job work out well for me, but, as predicted, the time came when I not only was willing to continue the job, I was hoping that I could continue it on past the time I had originally said I'd do it.

Staying in the Now

In many ways, the process of trusting your life to the Self simply involves staying in the Now as much as possible and avoiding projecting into the future with any thought about what might happen. It's amazing how much of our conditioning keeps us dwelling on the past and on the future—and how we often miss out on what is actually happening in the present moment. For this reason, it is usually necessary to keep consciously (yet effortlessly) alert to living in the moment as much as possible.

If you're someone who tends to constantly make plans, you might try living more spontaneously. Begin trusting that what you will need to know and do in the future will come to you at the right moment for everything to turn out in the best way possible.

When you feel you do need to plan for something, see if you can first move into the Silence within you, dropping past the mind with all its ideas and fears and beliefs, and become still and open. Then ask what needs to be planned and done to prepare the way. You will find that the plans that emerge are not only clear and to the point, they take little effort to accomplish.

You may also discover that nothing actually needs to be planned—that the event you're foreseeing will just appear naturally, without your having to do anything about it. This approach to planning for the future allows for a great deal of spontaneity in life— and a refreshing unpredictability. It allows you to experience a sense of "magic," as you watch everything working out just fine, without your interference. Synchronicities abound, perfectly orchestrated events occur, and everything seems to flow in an exciting, harmonious way.

To really allow this to happen, however, it is necessary to be unattached to outcome. It's necessary to step out of all expectations, demands, and anxieties about how things are going to work out, and begin to trust that there is a bigger picture that you may not be able to see at the present time. It's a matter of seeing that a "hand" is guiding you through your life in the perfect way, bringing events, situations, and people forward in the way that will best help you awaken to the greater reality of who you are. It may not look like it at the time, but later on, you will be able to see that this is so.

In recent years, I have had much experience in living my life with this trust, and I am infinitely grateful that I have had the courage to do so. A while back, I received a very strong inner urging to give up the life I had created in Boulder, Colorado—one I had loved—and move to Maui. This meant giving up not only my home and all its furnishings, but also my beloved mountains, the counseling practice I had developed, my dog, and a large network of friends.

I truly did not know why it felt necessary to do all this; on the personal level of desire, this was not appealing. Yet every time I would check inwardly, I knew this is what I was to do. On a very deep level inside, when I'd think about the move, everything in me felt aligned. Every time I'd think about staying, I'd feel a powerful "NO!" course through me; I'd even feel somewhat nauseous.

So, despite my personal misgivings and fears emanating from my conditioned thinking and despite my personal preferences, I decided to follow the inner guidance and take off for Maui—a place I'd never been before and where I knew virtually no one. I had no known opportunities for work there, and I had very little money, after paying off debts, to tide me over until I could decide what to do with my life and bring in an income. In some ways, it felt as if I were stepping off a cliff into the total unknown.

Yet I did it. I sold almost everything I owned, jumped on a plane, and landed in Maui. It was amazing to experience the flow into which I had jumped. Everything worked out. Within days, I was living in a beautiful home; I had a car and all the other things I needed to start a new life. It was a much simpler life than I had been living, but that felt good.

The more I trusted things would work out smoothly, the more they did. The more I put this approach to life to the test, the more I realized it worked. Synchronistic events happened almost daily. I'd wake up with a delightful sense of expectancy every morning, wondering what was going to occur for me that day. I was becoming more and more aware of the higher wisdom that was planning and guiding my life.

Once in awhile, I'd fall into a sense of fear, wondering what I had done with my life. Had I stupidly thrown everything away? Usually, I'd immediately drop into the stillness and again know, without a doubt, I had done what was right. There were also times, of course, when certain things didn't seem to be going "right." I wasn't getting what I wanted, and situations in my daily life were uncomfortable. Although I usually became disgruntled and irritated at these times, rather quickly I would generally surrender to what was happening—and peace would blessedly return again.

I was seeing how the whole break with my past had been just perfect. By doing what I had, I was now experiencing a trust and flow in my life like I never had before. I was realizing that my Self truly knew what was best for me—and all I needed to do was trust it and rely on it more and more to take care of me in the best way possible.

I was directly experiencing that Home for me was where I was, no matter in which geographical location I might be. I was realizing I could actually be comfortable anywhere, if necessary. But most importantly, the only thing that really mattered to me anymore— that I awaken more deeply into the reality of who I am—was happening in phenomenal ways. My identification with ego was falling away rapidly, and I was standing naked within the void, not knowing at all who I was in any of the old ways of knowing myself.

As frightening as this could be at times, I knew that, within a moment, I could always be aware of the presence of Self with me, enfolding me with love, guiding me with utmost care. If I took the time to melt into the embrace of the Self, realization that there was no separation between us would inevitably occur. Indeed, there was not two of us at all. There was simply Self.

The Process of Surrender Is On-Going

Once you begin surrendering your life to the Self and trusting it to take care of you in the best possible way, you will find that this is an on-going process throughout your life. You will find yourself surrendering to many situations each day; indeed, the feeling of surrender continues to happen in every moment. It's not simply a new attitude that you bring into your life; it's the entire context in which your life can be lived. Surrender begins suffusing your consciousness with each breath you take. It's a sumptuous nectar that flows through your awareness, creating a sweet peace and serenity in all that you do. You begin floating through life, freely, naturally—trusting all that comes to you. There is truly nothing like it!

IDENTIFYING
WITH THE SELF

CHAPTER TWENTY-THREE

What to Expect
as Time Goes on

The true spiritual quest is not necessarily comfortable. Many people begin the quest searching for comfort. But however you begin it, what is finally revealed is depth of being that leaves all notions of comfort and discomfort behind.

—Gangaji

*T*HE FOURTH STEP on the path of letting go is to experience a shift in identification from the ego-self to the true Self. This is also the goal of the entire path. For most people, this shift is a gradual one that happens naturally, as they begin focusing more and more on their experiences of Self, on detaching from the ego, and on surrendering to the Self. As time goes on, the shift becomes increasingly apparent, especially once the Self has been deeply glimpsed and experienced.

I have watched my own process closely since the shift took place, and I have also been in close touch with a number of others who have been doing the same. In comparing notes with them, I have discovered certain experiences that are very similar. These experiences also match many that others have written about. I will describe these experiences, with the thought that you, too, may be experiencing some of these things.

The process is twofold. On the one hand, exquisitely beautiful experiences happen more often as you are lifted into the Self's Grace and begin to be carried along by it. On the other hand, some of the most difficult and challenging experiences can also happen. At times you can feel deeply steeped in either one experience or the other, and other times, paradoxically, you can be experiencing them both simultaneously. For instance, you may find yourself in an extremely painful situation—and yet experience tremendous love and peace.

A similar paradox may take place as well: you may, in one moment, be fully experiencing yourself as the ego-self, and then, in the next, purely as the Self. It's as if you are waking up, falling asleep, then waking up again. Or you may experience yourself to be both the ego and the Self at the very same time. I remember when I first began having this experience; it was rather crazy-making! But the reality is that both experiences are real at this stage. The ego identification is dissolving; yet it is still claiming you, especially in certain situations. So there is this back-and-forth, up-and-down process that takes place.

One way to understand this is that the identification with the ego—and then the re-identification with it, even after one's true identity has been experienced—is simply a process in which a long-standing habit is being broken. It takes some time to fully break this habit.

Experiencing the Bliss

The experiences of truly knowing yourself to be the Self can be ineffably exquisite. As I described in the last chapter, when you begin surrendering your life to the Self, a magical quality can begin permeating your every experience. Delightful synchronicities happen daily; circumstances have a way of turning out even better than they might have, had you planned them yourself. Life takes on a charmed quality. You walk through your life with a sense of wonder, beauty, and awe. You experience a sense of wholeness and peace for the first time in your life, a sense that the deep, aching yearning you've always had has finally been fulfilled.

Indeed, there are times when it seems that every moment is suffused with a golden joy; simple sensory experiences become excursions into exaltation; and the entire world is a promise of exquisite adventure. In fact, you can see, as Douglas Harding puts it, that your whole life is "woven with blessings," and that your heart is "busted wide-open for loving."

In many ways, it's as if you've begun living in a whole new universe or dimension. A sense of timelessness moves into your experience. Every place you go, you feel at Home. Glimpses of your true nature come so often, they become your ordinary experience. There is a constant sense of peace, like a quiet hum or current, that runs through your awareness. Sometimes, when not much is going on, this hum is in the foreground of your awareness; other times, when you are engaged in some activity, it is more in the background. But it is always there, like a peaceful lake you can dip into at any time.

A greater sense of detachment appears. The world becomes more like an entertaining show in which you are both participating and watching. As you begin seeing your story of suffering more clearly as the illusion it is, you may find that your sense of humor suddenly expands and breaks through into the direst of situations. It becomes delightfully difficult to take anything very seriously anymore.

The sense of detachment can eventually become so profound that you become aware that you are really not doing anything at all. Your body and your mind may be actively doing a lot, but who you are is quite detached from this activity. Nisargadatta Majaraj describes this experience quite eloquently in *I Am That* (p. 243):

> I appear to hear and see and talk and act—but to me it just happens, as to you digestion or perspiration happens. The body-mind machine looks after it, but leaves me out of it. Just as you do not need to worry about growing hair, I do not need to worry about words and actions. They just happen and leave me unconcerned; for in my world, nothing ever goes wrong. In a certain way, life simply becomes easier to live.

There's a knowing that everything is being taken care of for you, so there's less to worry or concern you. There's less doing and more simply being. You approach most events with a relaxed and yet curious attitude, wondering, as a child might, what life is about to bring forward for you to experience. And you trust that it will be for the best, whatever it is.

Riding the Waves of Ego Dissolution

All of this can be abruptly punctuated with experiences that are extremely challenging and demanding. There may be periods when you think you have "lost" your awakening and wonder if you were ever awake at all. You may realize that your life, as you once knew it, is in the worst shape it ever has been in; in fact, it appears to be falling apart on you. Negative thoughts and feelings abound in your consciousness; depression moves in. You experience what I call "gray nights of the soul"—where everything becomes lackluster. You feel as if your life is going nowhere; it's totally bleak and uninteresting.

When you stop to realize what this process of shifting identification is all about—the "death" of the ego—this can all make sense. It's no surprise that it gets rough at times! As you see things that used to be so important to you either falling away or being ripped from you, it can be greatly disconcerting. Your old sense of who you are is no longer holding together; it's dissolving into the nothingness that it essentially is. It's like being someone who has jumped from one cliff, hoping to reach another cliff across a chasm—but is currently in no-man's land, without either foot on the ground. This can be terrifying at times.

In *The Wisdom of Sri Nisargatta Maharaj* (p. 84), this "limbo" territory is described well:

> There are always moments when one feels empty and estranged. Such moments are most desirable, for it means the soul has lost its moorings and is sailing for distant places. This is detachment—when the old is over and the new has not yet come. If you are afraid, the state may be distressing; but there is really nothing to be afraid of. Remember the instruction: Whatever you come across—go beyond.

To add to the confusion that this experience of shifting identification can bring, something else happens as well. This is the occasional onslaught of what are known as *vasanas*—conditioned tendencies we all have in our subconscious mind that must be brought into conscious awareness and then released. If we truly want freedom, then all these things must surface and be let go.

At times, it may feel like stuff is just coming out the woodwork. Habitual reactions and patterns you haven't seen for years suddenly reappear out of nowhere. This can bring great distress, if you're not prepared for them and if you take them seriously and think you have to do something with them—like changing or fixing them.

As Gangaji puts it in *You Are That* (p. 122), all these latent tendencies are "coming up for *satsang*." They need to be freed.

> By opening the gate of surrender, suppressed subconscious beliefs, the demons that have been denied for eons, often appear.... If you recognize these ... demons to be mind-created, what power can they have? Latent tendencies arise to be burned up in the light of Truth.

All you need do with them when they appear is watch them. Be aware of them, identify them. Don't give them any energy. Don't judge yourself for them or fret about them. Just allow them to express and then release them. Learn even to welcome them. You'll see that they simply vanish, sometimes surprisingly quickly. What might have taken weeks or months in the past to clear out of your consciousness might take only hours or days.

It's as if the Grace of the Self has been flowing into you over a period of time, like a trickle of clear water into a bucket, loosening up guck that has been stuck in there for centuries. The guck at the bottom is eventually bound to float to the surface. Just observe it as it does, until you become filled with this Grace and your consciousness overflows, allowing the unwanted debris to spill out. That is really all that is happening.

Part of what may be making this process of shifting identity so rocky is that your ego is finally seeing what's up and is making last-ditch efforts to regain its hold on you. It's madly trying to cling to old identities, as it sees them dropping all around you. It's chasing after old, worn desires that you have already seen will take you nowhere. It keeps trying to usurp the throne inside you, where the Self has been reigning more and more often. It does this in many ways but mainly through claiming your awakening as its own. It will even see its own death as something it is achieving! It's like a mad king who has been dethroned but has not yet been put to death—and it is busy thinking up new plots and schemes to reclaim its sovereignty.

Another part of what is happening is that perhaps the bliss you experienced so much in the first "honeymoon" days of awakening seems to be less present. This may be because what once felt like an extraordinary experience of bliss to you has now become your ordinary baseline of experience. You got used to the high your awakening gave you at first, but like all highs, it has slowly dissipated.

As I discussed in earlier chapters, you need to realize that the high is not IT. It's not truly what you're looking for. The state of true realization, as described by masters who have been experiencing it for many years, is not an on-going state of ecstatic bliss. It is rather a natural, peaceful, detached reality of being. States of bliss, although usually very important in a person's awakening process in the early stages, are not the reality of being in which true fulfillment occurs. Although they do continue to occur, often more frequently, even after full awakening, they are experiences that come and go—like all experiences. Thus, if you have been expecting the ecstatic highs to remain, you will likely be disappointed or upset, believing you've "lost" your awakening.

Something else that may be contributing to your hard times as your identification shifts is the illusion that once you begin waking up, difficulties in life will eventually disappear. This is not true at all.

Teachings of the direct path tell us that the body-mind organism has past actions that need to be balanced, no matter what—until the day the body drops. All kinds of things happen, whether you're waking up or not. The important difference, however, is that while it is all going on, YOU CAN BE FREE. You can stand amidst any situation that your body-mind self has been destined to experience, and simply watch it dispassionately, knowing fully that none of it is happening to YOU. That is the monumental difference.

Surrendering Is the Key

The true key in all of this is that any time you find yourself in the midst of suffering, you can simply ask yourself: *To what am I holding on? To what am I attached? What desires am I still chasing? What am I still resisting or running from? To what outcome am I attached in this situation?* And when you realize what these things are, let them go—surrender them. You will find no true peace until you cooperate with the process of allowing the ego to die in the way it needs to. Trust that your Self knows what it is doing in all this. Let go of your need to control any of it.

As time goes on, you will get the hang of this, and you'll find that it becomes easier and easier to ride the waves of ego dissolution as they roll in. And at the same time, the beauty and joy that flow into your life become so powerful that the rough times are experienced, at worst, as small irritants in your life.

Aside from this, your detachment becomes such a natural, ongoing state, that it really doesn't matter, after awhile, what is happening in your life. You're simply watching everything from within a center of peace, as the dance of life whirls delightfully around you. You find, as time goes on, that you have actually never been bound at all. You have never even suffered. You have always been free.

CHAPTER TWENTY-FOUR

Keeping Focused on the Self

Meditation must be continuous. The current of meditation must be present in all your activities. With practice, meditation and work can go on simultaneously.

—Annamalai Swami

ALTHOUGH THE PROCESS OF AWAKENING ever more deeply into the Self is one that happens naturally, according to its own rhythm, there are times, as I've described in the last chapter, when you can feel as if your awakening is losing momentum. You sense yourself unhappily drifting back into the trance-like dreamworld of the ego. If you have been enjoying a time of deeply experiencing yourself as the Self, this can be distressing.

It is helpful at these times to know what you can do to refocus your attention on the Self and your quest for ultimate Freedom and keep more purposefully on track. The following are things that have assisted me to keep focused on the Self that you might also find useful.

Letting Go of Desires and Attachments

One easy way to keep focused on the direction you wish to go is to begin watching the desires and attachments that are still running your life. You may even want to take an inventory of what these are, from time to time—places inside you where you're still caught in the illusion that something in form is going to bring you peace, freedom and happiness.

You can catch yourself trying to *create* happiness through achieving or acquiring something, rather than *discovering* it to be already existent—no matter what circumstances or situations are happening, no matter what thoughts you are thinking, what emotions you are feeling. You can remind yourself that happiness is your natural state, your birthright. You need not do or find anything new or different to discover it. Redirecting your focus like this can really be helpful in reminding yourself of where your happiness truly lies.

Maintaining an Attitude of Surrender, Acceptance, and Receptivity

A powerful reminder of the Self is keeping focused as much as possible on an attitude of acceptance and surrender. When you wake up in the morning, open yourself to the Grace of the Self. Expect miracles and magic to happen—and yet welcome all that may happen on that day. Trust what the Self has in mind for you to experience; recognize the perfection in all that is.

If possible, consciously open yourself so that the Self can live life through you. When you feel resistance come up in a situation, or you see that you are trying to assert your own personal will—let go. Allow the Self to step forward and guide you. Become receptive, open, and accepting. This attitude, as we've seen over and over again, is one that can bring you into alignment with the Self quite rapidly.

Staying Vigilant

Daily life has a way of constantly pulling us out into the world of objects, desires, thoughts, and emotions. If you are not alert and vigilant, it is easy to succumb to your old, habitual ways of living. It's a trite saying that the price of freedom is eternal vigilance, but when it comes to the quest for true Freedom, vigilance is, indeed, the price you pay. This path toward Freedom is a very conscious one: it demands that you not passively allow your conditioned patterns, habits, and desires to run you. It calls for constantly remembering the Self and consistently deferring to it.

At the same time, the vigilance that is needed is not a wary, fearful attitude—but rather a free and effortless one. You need to be watchful and observant, but not tense—much like a cat watching a mouse: totally alert, yet gracefully relaxed. You watch for old tendencies to arise—conditioned desires, reactions, and thoughts—but you do not act on them; you simply watch them. (Or, if you do end up acting on them, you can then simply observe yourself doing this.) Developing vigilance like this can be freeing, but to become a habit, it must be practiced.

Keeping Focused on What You Are—or on What You Are Not

Teachings of the direct path tell us there are two different— apparently opposing—ways we can keep focused in our quest for Freedom. I have used both of them with much success. The first is to focus, as constantly as possible, on the Self: Think of it, feel it, breathe it, live it, as often as you can during the day. See everything as expressions of it. Do those things that keep your attention focused on it. If you are not experiencing it directly at the moment, then act as if you are. In all situations, keep bringing it back into your awareness.

The second way is simply to focus on what you are NOT— remind yourself that you are not these things, and let go of them. It's a matter of realizing that there is really no need to do anything with the Self—only with the "clouds" (the thoughts, emotions, and bodily sensations) that obscure it. Focus on calming and quieting these things, so that what you really are can shine through. Either of these approaches can work, because, with both, the attention is on the process of getting free of the illusion of what you are not and realizing that which you are.

Constantly Moving into Detachment

Another focus that can be helpful to keep you "on track" is detachment. No matter what is happening, you can always be more detached about it. You can step back in your awareness and watch the "passing show." This can be both the outer show going on around you or the inner one in your mind. I have described a number of specific ways in which to do this in previous chapters on detaching from the body, emotions, and mind that can be helpful. Watching life from this perspective can be a powerful reminder of what is real.

Letting Go of the Doer

Often in the midst of daily life you become involved in a mind-activity. It's easy, in this involvement, to believe that the body, which is so busy moving and thinking and feeling, is who you are. It's easy to fall prey to the notion that you are the doer of all the activity. With this belief comes identification with the body, mind, and emotions, and inevitable suffering.

Therefore, it is helpful to continually remind yourself that you are not the doer. Step back and simply watch as things are being done. See who is *really* doing the doing. Discover that really no one is doing anything. There is no separate, individual doer. All is simply happening.

Maintaining Earnestness in Your Quest

Sometimes you might feel yourself drifting in your quest for Freedom because your degree of earnestness in this quest has waned. It is very important to watch the state of this quality in your consciousness. Teachings about self-realization often state that it is our earnestness that will lead us to realize permanent freedom. It can be helpful to ask yourself during times of waning interest: How serious am I about this quest? How much do I really want Freedom?

Then see what you have been doing that has pulled you away from the powerful intention you may have felt at one time. Have you been following other desires? Have you settled for a temporary, watered-down version of happiness? Have you stopped taking time to be in the Silence every day? Stopped reading books that inspire you? Become aware of these things that have pulled you out of your earnestness in your quest—and begin reversing them. Begin doing those things that will again light your fire.

Developing a Willingness to Let the Ego Fade Away

A powerful way to give yourself a "push" into deeper awakening is to look at your willingness to leap into the Unknown and allow the ego to become "dismantled" or to "fade away" in whatever way it needs to. Develop your willingness to experience whatever is necessary, to let go of whatever is necessary. Be willing to see and drop all illusions you may have about yourself. Let your life as you know it collapse around you, if this is necessary. Be willing to become a "nobody," without any identification that your ego can hold on to.

In essence, be willing to give up everything that you think you are or have with which you have identified yourself and made yourself feel worthy. Be willing to give up everything and surrender to every situation, no matter what it is—with no holds barred. Become naked and vulnerable before the Self, ready to sacrifice whatever is necessary to attain the true freedom you desire.

Truly taking this attitude can seem reckless and terrifying. Yet I can tell you from personal experience, and from hearing from others I know, that you can reap great and powerful rewards. It's a choice to leap into the chasm, the void—knowing nothing about what will be there—and yet trust that the Self will catch you. It can be an action you take once, with all of who you are, being open to experiencing an enormous shift in who you are. Or, if this is too scary, it can be done in a particular situation, to test the process. If you have the courage, I highly recommend either way.

Focusing on Being

A final way I can suggest to get back on track when you feel yourself drifting is to focus on simply being. Catch yourself in your busyness, both outer and inner. See how much of your activity is really necessary and see if you can simply stop and be for a while. Rest your mind. Let go of all thoughts for a time and just bring your attention to simply being.

According to direct path teachings, just resting in Beingness like this is true meditation. It's being still and quiet in your mind. The more you can do this throughout your day, the better. In *The Truth Is* (p. 136), Papaji states, "True meditation does not begin and does not end. In fact, the true art of meditation is to always meditate. There is no place to arrive, there is nothing to do. Meditation is simply to stay Home as Being."

Specific Exercises You Can Do

The following are specific exercises that I've found or devised that might be helpful in "charging" your "spiritual battery."

Exercise: *Seeing Everything as the Self*

As you move through your day, approach everything and everyone you meet as simply another aspect of your Self with whom you are coming face to face. Rather than seeing another person, for example, as something separate from you—see him or her as a form that is interacting with the form with which you have generally identified, but see that the two forms are actually both a part of YOU. They are both appearing in YOU, coming together, then leaving each other. Experience yourself as this greater YOU, watching both forms interacting within YOU. Feel the love you can have for both forms equally, as parts of YOU.

You can approach objects in the same way. See this form with which you generally identify approaching this other form, one that is perhaps less "sentient." Again, both forms are a part of YOU. You are the Consciousness within which both forms arise and exist.

Ramesh Balsekar, in *Consciousness Speaks*, describes this process in a slightly different way. He states that realizing the Self is, first of all, realizing that all the forms in the world that we call "people" are really just puppets being manipulated by one Great Puppeteer—and then realizing that you yourself are that puppeteer. If you can keep this realization going consistently throughout a day, it can be amazing how clear and powerful your identification with Consciousness can become.

Exercise: *Keeping Focused on "I Am"*

Keeping just the idea of "I am" focused in your awareness, with nothing else added to it, can really be a powerful experience. Whenever you find yourself thinking or saying that you are something in particular, stop yourself, and bring it back to simply "I am." This will keep you centered on Being.

In *I Am That* (p. 48), Nisargadatta describes a way in which to do this most effectively:

> Just keep in mind the feeling "I am," merge with it, till your mind and feeling become one. By repeated attempts, you will stumble on the right balance of attention and affection, and your mind will be firmly established in the thought-feeling "I am." Whatever you think, say, or do, this sense of immutable and affectionate being remains as the ever-present background of the mind.

Exercise: *Shoes of the Master*

Do this exercise when you are wondering what to do about something important in your life. It involves simply asking yourself, "What would the Master do in this situation?" Or "If I were fully realized in Self, what action would I take?" In waiting for an answer, allow your mind to be still and just see what comes forward. I have found that this process can bring startlingly clear and wise answers.

Exercise: *Who Is Experiencing This?*

This is a variation on the question "Who am I?" Whatever you are doing, you can ask these questions: "Who is walking?" "Who is thinking?" "Who is speaking?" Each time, pull your awareness back to yourself—back to where your mind originates. Go to the source of all your thoughts and look. See what you find; see what you experience.

Exercise: *Listening to the Silence*

This entails listening to the true Silence that exists, even in the midst of much noise or activity. You can start by listening to the Silence that occurs in between sounds that are being uttered. You can also listen to it in between breaths you are taking, or in between thoughts you are thinking. You'll see that it is always there, waiting to be heard and experienced. Then you can begin listening to it *behind* or *under* the sounds you hear. Finally, you can actually listen to it *within* the sound itself. Silence permeates everything. By focusing on hearing it in these ways, you can begin to realize that not only is this Silence always present—it is who you actually are.

Exercise: *Follow the Yearning*

Whenever you feel a sense of desire or yearning for something in particular, realize that this feeling is just a yearning for your Self. Use it as a vehicle to take you into the experience of the Self. Dive directly into the yearning and allow it to swallow you. Allow it to burn you, devour you. See what happens.

Although I have given you here (and throughout this book) a number of techniques to help light your spiritual fire when it seems to be burning low, in the end, the whole process is really not about techniques—it's an entire approach to life—an approach infused with surrender, acceptance, letting go, and focusing on the Self. It's about the experience of the Self. Therefore, don't get caught in the techniques; just use them to give you a push into this experience.

Studying with an Enlightened Master

One very important way to keep the experience of the Self alive is to find an enlightened teacher with whom you feel a resonance and to study closely with him or her. There are people who claim that having a particular teacher is not necessary in becoming realized.

This may well be so. There are several people I know who study either with no teacher or with several teachers, and this seems to work well for them.

I have personally found, after many years of shunning spiritual teachers, that having one can be extremely helpful. This is especially so if the teacher is one whose physical presence is accessible for you to directly experience. There is definitely something to be said about the energy (or *shakti* or *darshan*) that a realized being radiates, and it can quicken and ignite the energy of someone who is earnestly seeking Freedom.

If you do find a teacher with whom to work, you may find it isn't necessary to be physically around them after awhile; you can sense them inside you, always present, keeping your "fire" lit (until it stays lit on its own). Until then, being in their presence can be an incredible way to experience your true Self. It can also be profoundly exciting.

Each teacher has his or her unique personality characteristics or methods of teaching that may or may not appeal to you. If you begin searching for a teacher who is right for you, get a feel at first for different ones; sense where you are being drawn. Actually, there is a well-known saying that the teacher finds us, when we are ready—not the other way around. But looking for a teacher may be a sign that a particular teacher is drawing you in, and you will know that teacher to be yours when you find him or her.

I believe that any self-realized teacher can be helpful. I have personally felt drawn to teachers of the direct path. Although my experience with Papaji, in particular (even before I personally met him), made it clear that he was the teacher drawing me in, I have also gotten much out of attending *satsang* and reading books by or about other enlightened teachers who also teach the direct path. For your reference, the following are some of the better-known teachers of this path that you can probably find more about on the internet—or you can look for their books in book stores:

Robert Adams	Ramana Maharshi
Adyashanti	Meera
Arjuna	Satyam Nadeen
Annamalai Swami	Neelam

Ramesh Balsekar

Paul Brunton

John DeReuter

Gangaji

Hanuman

Douglas Harding

Jean Klein

Francis Lucille

Ngeton

Nisargadatta

Arthur Osborne

Robert Powell

Ranjit

Isaac Shapiro

Eckhart Tolle

Letting Go Is an Art

Learning to truly let go in life is an art. Letting go of trying to control our life, letting go of our identification with the ego-self, letting go of our story of suffering—all demand a certain amount of inspiration, focus, and experimentation. And, as with any art, letting go can be developed over time, with practice.

Although certainly not the only way to discover spiritual freedom, learning to let go consistently and surrender in life is a powerful path to take. Yet it is not all that demanding: The only real "doing" involved is stopping the attempts to control, manipulate, and hold on to things. It does involve vigilance and awareness; yet it is ultimately effortless.

In essence, letting go is a way of simply saying *yes* to the Freedom that is already present within us. It is a way of stepping through the doorway into the vast Silence within and discovering what has been true all along—that we are the Freedom, the Love, the Joy, the Peace we have always been seeking. This is what we always have been and always will be. Truly, we can relax, let go, and simply ride the flow—for the search is finally over.

List of Exercises

Bibliography

Adams, Robert. *Silence of the Heart*. Sedona, AZ, Infinity Institute, 1997.

Adyashanti. *The Impact of Awakening*. Los Gatos, CA, Open Gate Sangha, 2000.

Ardaugh, Arjuna Nick. *Relaxing into Clear Seeing*. San Rafael, CA, Self Xpress, 1998.

Balsekar, Ramesh. *Consciousness Speaks*. Edited by Wayne Liquorman. Redondo Beach, CA, Advaita Press, 1993.

Balsekar, Ramesh. *A Duet of One*. Redondo Beach, CA, Advaita Press, 1989.

Balsekar, Ramesh. *A Net of Jewels*. Redondo Beach, CA, Advaita Press, 1996.

Bluestone, G. *Enlightening the Way of Inquiry*. Durango, CO, Avant Press, 1991.

Brunton, Paul. *Inspiration of the Overself* (Vol. 14 of the *Notebooks of Paul Brunton*). Burdett, NY, Larson Publications, 1988.

Gangaji. *You Are That!*. Boulder, CO, Satsang Press, 1995.

Godman, David. *Living by the Words of Bhagavan*. Pondicherry, India, All India Press, 1994.

Klein, Jean. *Transmission of the Flame*. Santa Barbara, CA, Third Millennium Publications, 1990.

Klein, Jean. *Who Am I?* Edited by Emma Edwards, Longmead, Shaftesbury, Dorset, England, Element Books, Limited, 1992.

Maharshi, Ramana. *Be As You Are*. Edited by David Godman. Middlesex, England, Arkana Books, 1985.

Maharshi, Ramana. *More Talks with Sri Ramana Maharshi*. Edited by A. R. Natarajan, Bangalore, India, Ramana Maharshi Centre for Learning, 1993.

Maharshi, Ramana. *Words of Grace*. Tiruvannamali, India, T.N. Venkataraman, 1969.

Mitchell, Stephen. *The Enlightened Heart*. New York, NY, Harper-Collins Publishers, 1989.

Nisargadatta Maharaj. *I Am That*. Durham, N. Carolina, The Acorn Press, 1973.

Nisargatta Maharaj. *Seeds of Consciousness.* Edited by Jean Dunn. New York, NY, Grove Press, 1982.

Osborne, Arthur. *For Those with Little Dust.* Sarasota, FL, Ramana Publications, 1990.

Poonja, H.W.L. ("Papaji"). *Nothing Ever Happened.* Edited by David Godman. Boulder, CO, Avadhuta Foundation, 1998.

Poonja, H.W.L. ("Papaji"). *The Truth Is.* Edited by Yudhishstara. Los Angeles, CA, Yudishstara, 1995.

Poonja, H.W.L. ("Papaji"). *Wake Up and Roar.* (Vols. 1 & 2). Maui, HI, Pacific Center Publishing, 1993.

Powell, Robert. *Dialogues on Reality.* San Diego, CA, Blue Dove Press, 1996.

Powell, Robert. *The Wisdom of Sri Nisargadatta Maharaj.* New York, NY, Globe Press Books, 1992.

Rumi, Jelaluddin. *The Essential Rumi.* Translations by Coleman Barks with John Mogue. New York, NY, HarperCollins Publishers, 1995.

Tolle, Eckhart. *The Power of Now.* Vancouver, British Columbia, Canada, Namaste Publishing, Inc., 1997.

Walker, Brian. *Hua Hu Ching, the Teachings of Lau Tzu.* Livingston, MT, Clark City Press, 1992.

About the Author

*I*N 1993, VIDYA FRAZIER had an extraordinary experience in which she awoke to her true nature and realized spiritual freedom. Two years later, she felt called to India to visit the spiritual master, Papaji, who validated her experience and encouraged her to use it to assist others. Upon returning to the U.S., she began developing the counseling and teaching practice she'd had for 20 years into what she calls "Consciousness Counseling," incorporating the teachings of the Direct Path of awakening as a foundation for her work. She soon began seeing the emergence of a specific pathway to freedom she was teaching, based on the simple teaching of letting go, and has since been offering classes and workshops on this subject. She currently lives in Middletown, California.

Made in the USA
Lexington, KY
22 November 2011